*History and Ideology in
the Old Testament*

History and Ideology in the Old Testament

Biblical Studies at the End of a Millennium

The Hensley Henson Lectures for
1997 delivered to the University
of Oxford

JAMES BARR

OXFORD
UNIVERSITY PRESS

OXFORD
UNIVERSITY PRESS

Great Clarendon Street, Oxford OX2 6DP

Oxford University Press is a department of the University of Oxford.
It furthers the University's objective of excellence in research, scholarship,
and education by publishing worldwide in

Oxford New York

Athens Auckland Bangkok Bogotá Buenos Aires Calcutta
Cape Town Chennai Dar es Salaam Delhi Florence Hong Kong Istanbul
Karachi Kuala Lumpur Madrid Melbourne Mexico City Mumbai
Nairobi Paris São Paulo Singapore Taipei Tokyo Toronto Warsaw

with associated companies in Berlin Ibadan

Oxford is a registered trade mark of Oxford University Press
in the UK and in certain other countries

Published in the United States
by Oxford University Press Inc., New York

British Library Cataloguing in Publication Data

Data available

Library of Congress Cataloging in Publication Data
Barr, James, 1924–
History and ideology in the Old Testament: biblical studies at the end of a millennium/
James Barr.
p. cm.
"The Hensley Henson Lectures for 1997 delivered to the University of Oxford."—Cip t.p.
Includes bibliographical references and index.
1. Bible, O.T.—Evidences, authority, etc. 2. Bible, O.T.—History of Biblical events. I.
Title.
BS1180.B27 2000
221.6′7—dc21   99-055615
ISBN 0-19-826987-0

1 3 5 7 9 10 8 6 4 2

Typeset in Bembo by
Cambrian Typesetters, Frimley, Surrey

Printed in Great Britain
on acid-free paper by
Biddles Ltd., Guildford & King's Lynn

For Dietrich Ritschl

Preface

THIS work was originally presented as a series of four lectures in May 1997. The lectures were revised and amplified for publication during 1998, in particular during a stay at the Rockefeller Study and Conference Centre in Bellagio, Italy, in November and December 1998. I have to express my gratitude to the Rockefeller Foundation for its generosity in the magnificent splendour of the Villa Serbelloni and for the kindness and helpfulness of its staff.

It was never my intention to provide in this volume a full account of the complex questions involved in the title, or to review the relevant literature in full. Nor was it possible, within the limited space available, to offer my own version of a right answer to all these questions. My plan has been rather to discuss examples that will illustrate certain contemporary discussions.

For this I had the advantage, during the year after the lectures were delivered, of literature that had recently appeared. Indeed, so much has been written on my theme in recent years that I was unable to include, except by references in footnotes, some important work that came to my notice at a late stage. I must mention, however, two books that were published in time for me to use them and which made much difference to the presentation of my arguments. I was particularly indebted to *The Cambridge Companion to Biblical Interpretation*, edited by Professor John Barton. This work furnishes excellent exemplification of many aspects of my theme, within a compass easily accessible to all readers. Readers of the present work will do well, therefore, to use several of its articles as a true Companion to my pages, and I have therefore abbreviated its title to *Companion* with this in mind. One other recent work, less often quoted here but equally significant for my argument, is Harriet Harris's *Fundamentalism and Evangelicals* (Oxford: Clarendon Press, 1998).

I am grateful for the honour of being invited to lecture in the series dedicated to the memory of Bishop Hensley Henson, and hope that my work may have done something to further the cause to which the Bequest is devoted.

J.B.

Claremont, California
1999

Contents

Abbreviations

BA	*Biblical Archaeologist*
BASOR	*Bulletin of the American Schools of Oriental Research*
CD	*Christian Dogmatics* (Barth)
DBI	R. J. Coggins and J. L. Houlden (eds.), *Dictionary of Biblical Interpretation* (London: SCM, 1990).
EKL	*Evangelisches Kirchenlexikon*
ET	English Translation
FS	Festschrift
JBL	*Journal of Biblical Literature*
JBTh	*Jahrbuch für Biblische Theologie*
JNWSL	*Journal of Northwest Semitic Languages*
JR	*Journal of Religion*
JSOT	*Journal for the Study of the Old Testament*
JSOT [Sup]	Journal for the Study of the Old Testament [Supplementary Series]
JSS	*Journal of Semitic Studies*
JTS	*Journal of Theological Studies*
KuD	*Kerygma und Dogma*
SBL	Society of Biblical Literature
SJT	*Scottish Journal of Theology*
SOTS	Society for Old Testament Study
ZTK	*Zeitschrift für Theologie und Kirche*

I

The Bible, History, and Apologetics

UNDER the terms of the Hensley Henson Bequest, the general subject of the lectures on which this book is based is defined as 'The Appeal to History as an Integral Part of Christian Apologetics'. A kindly addendum provides, however, that this requirement may be 'taken in a very wide sense' by the lecturers, and this latitude of interpretation has indeed been used by many of my predecessors. I shall begin by indicating several ways in which I too will take the subject in a very wide sense. What I propose to do is to discuss the situation of modern academic study of the Bible in relation to theology and religion, with some special attention to questions of history, to indicate some aspects of where biblical study seems to stand at the present time and in what directions its future problems and its future development may lie. To start this on the day of an important general election in Britain (this chapter was first delivered as a lecture on 1 May 1997), and within a few years of the end of a millennium, imparts to the theme a pleasing tang of the apocalyptic.

In two respects I intend to avoid stressing the term 'Christian apologetics'. First, my specialism is in the Hebrew Bible or Old Testament and my examples and arguments will be predominantly based within it. Not that the New Testament will be absent from my thoughts, but I will give less direct attention to it. This has two consequences that are worth mentioning. First, within these pages I will not be making primary reference to some of the traditional questions associated with the life, death, and resurrection of Jesus Christ. Not that I think that these are unimportant; on the contrary, they are extremely important. Nevertheless, in approaching our general attitude to biblical scholarship there is much to be said for starting with the Old Testament. It has not been without reason that the Old Testament has been held for much of this century to be the central focal point for the theological idea of history. Without its anchorage in the Hebrew Bible, it has often been alleged, New Testament Christianity could become a sort of Gnosticism unconnected with history. Whether this specific allegation is true or not, the importance of the Old Testament for the historical basis of religion has been very generally acknowledged. Thus it was, I believe, a disadvantage in a classic study such as Van A. Harvey's *The Historian and the Believer* to focus attention on the question of the historical Jesus, while scarcely looking at questions of history as they are manifested in the Hebrew Bible.[1] Anyway, rightly or not, this present work will be focused mainly on Old Testament studies and will take most of its examples from that field.

Secondly, under these circumstances, while our subject specifies Christian apologetics, it will be impossible to forget that the same arguments may be equally relevant for Jewish religion and theology, and in fact I shall often use the general term 'religion' with this in mind. The problems will not work out in the same way for both religions, but the common foundations explain how and why I shall from time to time be mentioning Judaism and Christianity together. Whether yet other religious traditions are affected is an important question, but one that cannot be taken up within the limits of space available here.

The term 'apologetics' itself will also be used only sparingly. The expression now seems to us, perhaps, to be a somewhat old-fashioned one. It was indeed about the mid-century, in fact in 1948, that Alan Richardson published a substantial volume entitled *Christian Apologetics*;[2] but few works bearing the same title or lying within the same tradition have appeared in the fifty years following.[3] On the whole, the term 'apologetics' has come to carry a negative impression. To the naïve speaker it conveys, perhaps, a suggestion of 'apologizing', of saying that one was sorry to have a religious faith and to bother reasonable people with such an odd characteristic. I remember, in my student days in the late 1940s, when the concept of apologetics was often under attack, being told by a friend that apologetics were a wrong approach 'because

---

[1]   For an important recent study, see J. McIntyre, 'Historical Criticism in a "History-Centred Value System" ', in S. E. Balentine and John Barton (eds.), *Language, Theology and the Bible* (Oxford: Clarendon, 1994), 370–84.

[2]   (London: SCM, 1948).

[3]   Cf. also J. K. S. Reid, *Christian Apologetics* (1969), which will be further mentioned below; more recently, and briefly, F. G. Downing, 'Apology, Apologetic', *DBI* 39–42.

one does not apologize for one's faith'—an argument that was a misuse of words in the typical etymological style of those days, for apologetics, of course, has nothing to do with apologizing and never had. But such arguments, wrong as they might be, did contribute something to the negative impression that the term 'apologetics' still creates—an impression that, no doubt, was completely absent from the mind of Bishop Hensley Henson as formulated when the foundation of these lectures was established.

What then was the source of that negative impression? Why did the term 'apologetics' come to be felt to have so little appeal? Why have so few books on the subject been published in the latter half of the twentieth century, and especially in the last thirty years of it?

In common use apologetics has meant the presentation of reasons that justify religious faith, arguments that may appeal to something admitted by the unbeliever and, when sufficiently elaborated, may lead to faith or at least to the admission that there is a certain reasonable basis for faith. Why then did apologetics come into such disfavour?

There are two interlinked reasons, it seems. First, it was felt that faith did not rest upon any neutral ground that was shared with unbelief. Apologetics, or at least some versions of apologetics, had tended in the past to seek some common ground on the basis of which one might argue that faith is true, or at least is reasonable. It was now increasingly felt that the reliance on this common ground was illusionary. Faith, according to this other point of view, is essentially kerygmatic: it proclaims the truth and does not argue from any shared premises. There is thus no common ground. Apologetics, therefore, does not support faith: on the contrary, it misunderstands it and undermines it. The so-called 'dialectical' theology of Barth, Brunner, and Bultmann thus encouraged people to repudiate all apologetic arguments and treat them with deep contempt: or at least apparently so, for there are certain qualifications to be made, which will be mentioned.

Second, the increasing abandonment of apologetics in wide circles had another reason, quite independent of the influence of dialectical theology: it lay in the sense that reasoned arguments for faith, whether theologically justifiable or not, simply did not work. ('Work' is here used in the sense of 'be successful in convincing the unbeliever'.) They had worked, perhaps, in an earlier age, when premisses to which apologetics might appeal were still generally accepted; but by the mid-twentieth century that acceptance had gone, and with it the grounds upon which apologetics might have some success. So Andrew Louth could argue: 'Is apologetics so successful that we cannot ignore it?'[4] And this argument is quite persuasive in itself.

Both these arguments, however, seem to build upon a common model: the model, namely, of the believer who is secure in his or her faith but needs reasons that will convince the unbeliever or the uncertain. Such may be called 'positive apologetics', for they assume the certainty of the believer: all he needs is the necessary stock of ideas, information, and arguments which can then be directed towards the unbeliever. But, putting it more negatively, apologetics may represent the inner reasonings by which the believer defends his faith *for himself* against reasonings he knows to be alleged against it by others, or reasonings the force of which he himself feels to be substantial and therefore threatening. Seen in this way, the presence or absence of unbelievers or of common ground with them ceases to be significant. The believer believes; his faith, perhaps, is unshaken and unshakeable; but there remain great areas of uncertainty which seem to demand resolution. The different churches have different doctrines; within any one given church there are different currents of thought and practice; theologians, notoriously, are in conflict with one another; the history of the church and its doctrines (and, similarly, of Judaism and its practices) are poorly known to most believers and can produce unwelcome surprises when new aspects of them come to the surface; and, of course, biblical studies and the modes of interpretation seem to keep changing. In these circumstances the task is not to take up arms against a known hostile force, but to assess and identify the degree to which novel and unfamiliar tendencies may be damaging or favourable. The believer's inward awareness of these uncertainties, and her attempt, however simple and slight, to find a path through them, is a form of apologetics—we might call it 'negative apologetics' or 'internal apologetics'—which in content closely resembles the positive apologetics described above. And for

---

4 In his article, 'Barth and the Problem of Natural Theology', *Downside Review*, 87 (1969), 269; quoted in J. Barr, *Biblical Faith and Natural Theology* (Oxford: Clarendon, 1993), 127 n.

this negative apologetic task the objections that there is no common ground and that faith is kerygmatic no longer matter very much. It is mainly with this sort of internal apologetics that this book will be concerned.

When put in this more negative sense, the importance and the theological status of apologetics become more evident, and almost the entirety of theological thought can be considered to be apologetic.

We may add another aspect: there are various kinds of apologetic argument, and they do not all suffer from the same problems. There may be, for instance, rational arguments for the existence of God. These are, perhaps, the arguments that most suffered from the criticisms that have just been mentioned. But there are also scientific apologetics: for example, in what sense can the divine creation of the universe be believed in relation to scientific knowledge of cosmology or in relation to evolution? Is it true that 'Modern physics in this respect speaks clearly in favour of the Jewish–Christian belief in creation'?[5] And, even if one is sure of belief in creation, how does that belief, thus generally stated, relate to the detailed account given in the first chapter of Genesis?

And, finally, there are historical arguments that might have apologetic importance, and it was these that particularly interested Bishop Hensley Henson. Evidences from history can be put forward as supports for religious beliefs, and equally as threats to these same beliefs, and this can be done in many different ways. Within the Bible, for example, it can be argued that one or another of the gospels is historically accurate, or indeed that all of them when combined are historically accurate. On the other hand the differences in detail, and even in larger-scale composition, between the gospels may suggest that they cannot all be exactly historical in their narration. Again, it has been argued that contemporary documents confirm the existence of social practices similar to Abraham's dealings with Sarah at Pharaoh's court (Gen. 12), and the same arguments have been rejected by other scholars as false. Historical arguments can change as new discoveries take place, and also as new criteria for historical investigation come to

---

[5] Quotation from L. Oeing-Hanhoff, *Anfang und Ende der Welt* (1981), 22; cited after C. Westermann, 'Schöpfung und Evolution', in H. Böhme (ed.), *Evolution und Gottesglaube* (Göttingen: Vandenhoeck & Ruprecht, 1988); cf. J. Barr, *The Concept of Biblical Theology* (London: SCM, 1999), 96. Original source not seen by me.

be approved. It has been argued that archaeological discoveries at Jericho fitted more or less exactly with the account of the city's capture in the book of Joshua, but, conversely, these and other discoveries have suggested to others that the ancestors of Israel came to be established in Canaan in a quite different way: not by a military invasion but by a gradual infiltration of small groups, or indeed by an internal take-over of the country from within by groups who were already there but had formerly been disadvantaged. Historically, again, but moving to another level, the characteristic action of the God of Israel in history may be seen as evidence that biblical faith is something of a quite different type and structure from the other religions of the ancient world. Do the Dead Sea Scrolls provide a good parallel to the rise of Christianity as a sect within Judaism, using its scriptures in a similar way, or do they rather suggest that Christianity deceptively copied a movement to which it did not rightly belong? Yet again, the history of the use of the Bible through the centuries can produce a distinct uneasiness in the believer, who may be disturbed by the way in which it has been used to justify a variety of evil practices.[6] Thus arguments of historical apologetic can assume many forms, and we shall come back to some of them later. We do not for the present discuss whether they are valid or invalid. For the present, these are only a few specimens of what may be included within the general category of historical apologetics. All these questions are internal to faith: they belong to the intrinsic material of religion, like the Bible, and they exist as questions for the believer, whether or not there is any argument with the unbeliever or any question of the presence or absence of common ground. Such questions of internal apologetic are integral to the life of faith and the materials upon which it exists.

But before we go further, we should look at another aspect of the theological evaluation of apologetic discussion. We have seen that the impression remains that the dialectical theology powerfully represented in different ways by Barth, Brunner, and Bultmann has encouraged the repudiation of all apologetic types of argument. It is particularly interesting, therefore, to go back to that most recent

[6] Two recent works which concentrate (excessively?) on this aspect are: R. P. Carroll, *Wolf in the Sheepfold: The Bible as a Problem for Christianity* (London: SPCK, 1991), and G. Lüdemann, *The Unholy in Holy Scripture: The Dark Side of the Bible* (London: SCM, 1997).

of the books on Christian apologetics mentioned above, the work of the Aberdeen professor J. K. S. Reid—one who was very well in touch with exactly these theological currents. That he would even write a book with such a title, in the atmosphere of that time, must indicate that the assessment commonly accepted was not the whole of the matter. And indeed, when we look into his very brief Introduction, 'What is Apologetics?', we find him stating that 'there is no absolute distinction between Apologetics and Dogmatics'. Even Karl Barth, he goes on, 'despite frequent misunderstanding by some who refer to him, can be cited in agreement with this view'. And he quotes Barth as writing: 'Dogmatics too has to speak all along the line as faith opposing unbelief, and to that extent all along the line its language must be apologetic.'[7] Reid goes on to give further details about the positions of Barth and Brunner and to express his own conclusion 'that Apologetics and Dogmatics cannot be understood in isolation from one another'.[8]

On the other hand Reid still perceived the apologetic task as one at war with a sort of *enemy*: 'Apologetics engages with confessed enemies of Christianity outside, defending it against the ignorance, misunderstanding and defamation of unbelief. It engages with the wreckers from within, defending the Gospel against heresy that would ruin or disable it.' And this may remain, in part, quite right. But it does not perceive the place of what I have called 'internal apologetics', the activity in which the believer himself confronts, for his own needs as a believer, facts and areas and sciences which can make a difference to his faith—a difference with which he has still to reckon because faith alone does not have all the necessary resources—and in which the identification of friend and foe is still far from clear. Both history itself, as specified by the Hensley Henson Trust, and biblical study in its relations with history, belong to these areas.

---

[7] Reid, *Christian Apologetics*, 13; cited from Barth, *CD* I/1. 31 (wording of the 1st English edn., *The Doctrine of the Word of God* (Edinburgh: T. & T. Clark, 1936)); corresponding passage in the later edition is on p. 30.

[8] Reid's valuable book—perhaps unfortunately for our purpose—does not address itself so much to the apologetic task for the present situation. Rather it follows a historical method, outlining 'the actual ways in which Christianity, faced with particular situations which called for defence, responded to the challenge and with what results'. He rightly believes that help will be derived from such an account for the defence of religion today; but there is no particular contact with the questions that will occupy us in the present book. See his Introduction, p. 10.

There is another sense in which an apologetic aspect is unavoidable. Some theologians, following the lead of Barth (and, if Reid is right, exaggerating Barth's actual position), excluded apologetics entirely from their theological world, thinking thereby to make the Bible more completely central to their presentation of the faith. Theology and the gospel were thus solidly based upon the Bible and not upon reasonings and arguments. Biblical exegesis was the partner of doctrinal theology. But the effect of this was sometimes that biblical exegesis itself became a kind of apologetic. It was not reasoning with those external enemies of religion, but it was performing the same sort of role in relation to any alternative theological solutions. This is not necessarily so very wrong: all it shows is that an apologetic procedure is not easily avoided.

This leads on, however, to a further point. As we have seen, apologetic arguments have become unfashionable and largely out of date, and I gave some reasons why this has been so; but now I have to go back and qualify this. They have become unfashionable and out of date, but mainly for the theologically trained élite, for those who have met and learned the counter-arguments. But there is a difference between the theologically trained on the one hand and large constituencies of religious believers on the other: for the latter the apologetic arguments are still fundamental. It is interesting that many theologians insist on 'the church' as the context in which theology is done, and that in itself is not a wrong principle; but they think of 'the church' in terms derived from their own theology, not from an input derived from the church of ordinary believers as they factually are. For large groups of these ordinary believers, the apologetic arguments remain central. And some of these may be on the more philosophical/theological level: does God exist, and is there really a God of the character suggested by the Bible? But, where the Bible is concerned, they tend to focus on history. Did Jesus really say this or that? Did he really walk on the sea, or is that narrative to be taken in a non-literal sense? Such questions define the way in which biblical materials are perceived and understood. Even if it is true that apologetic questions are not a primary concern for most biblical scholars, it would be wrong to suppose that the feelings of biblical scholars in this respect necessarily reflect the minds of the general public. To the latter, when they hear about them—which means when they are mentioned in the newspapers or on television—apologetic questions remain highly significant. Questions about the historicity of biblical stories or about the originality of biblical theologies draw marked attention.

In Nashville, Tennessee, where I have lived for much of the last nine years, a taxi ride from the airport will commonly involve one in a debate with the driver about the Mosaic authorship of the Pentateuch or some other such matter. Not that the driver will necessarily have a strong personal view about the question: I do not want to convey the impression that this is the Bible Belt, so that everyone is a committed fundamentalist. Not at all: the driver will listen with respect if you say that of course Moses wrote the entire thing, but he will be equally respectful if you say it is more probable that it was written by various other writers at a much later date. The point is not that he will have absolute convictions about such a thing; the point is that he will conceive the question as essentially one situated on an apologetic axis, or an apologetic/critical axis, where the answer can be situated towards one end or towards another, in both cases equally depending on fairly rational arguments. What will be strange to him is the idea that many modern theologians hold, namely that this is an entirely wrong way to conceive the problem, and that we should be 'proclaiming' the divine word from the passages without troubling whether Moses wrote them or not. To him that will seem a slippery, perhaps a dishonest, evasion. In other words, to a large proportion of active religious believers, and even to those hovering on the fringe of religious activity, the apologetic arguments remain very central. Contrary to common expectation, this will be the same whether we turn to the more conservative, near-fundamentalist, constituency or to the more open, uncommitted, groups: in both cases, given a biblical narrative, they will perceive it as a question requiring a *historical* appreciation. On the one side, one may say, yes, it happened exactly as described, and there are good scientific and historical reasons for accepting it as such and that is the end of the matter. On the other one may say, no, it did not take place as described: maybe some sort of event took place which has some sort of analogical relation to what the text describes, or maybe nothing of the sort took place at all but the story is a piece of religious allegory or advice, prepared by someone else altogether. In either case the evaluation is a historical and apologetic one of a kind. What people do not want to be told is what so many biblical scholars and theologians now believe, that is, that it is quite wrong to ask the question, 'What really happened?'[9] As they see it, what really happened is essential, and it is only clever élitist evasion when theologically sophisticated people tell them that they should not ask that question. I do not suggest that people will not accept an alternative mode of understanding: of course they are intelligent, and can understand and may accept it, but it has first to be explained to them, and only after the simple, obvious question, 'Did it happen or not?', has been perceived and accepted as proper. This is why, in matters of the use of the Bible, the question of history is so very central in this regard: which justifies the manner of construction of the argument of this book.

The interest in the apologetic aspect, as presented above, applies alike therefore, at least in some degree, to the more conservative understanding, sometimes approaching the fundamentalist, and to the more liberal. This may seem surprising but is deliberately meant. From both ends of the spectrum the interest in what really happened is felt to be of great importance, and from both ends arguments appealing to accepted evidences, arguments, and realities are to be heard.

That this is so at the more liberal end of the spectrum will not be surprising; but some readers may be surprised to find the same said of the conservative and especially of the fundamentalist mentality. Does not the latter rely simply on the biblical text and evangelical experience, and show deep distrust of human reason? In certain aspects this is true. Nevertheless it is easy to show that the underlying intellectual stratum of much of fundamentalism depends on a traditional apologetic procedure. Outlining the subject in her Introduction, Harriet Harris writes:

---

[9] There may be a cultural difference here, in that English-speaking people tend to ask, 'Did it really happen?', while German-speakers ask about the *ideas* being communicated by the narrative. See the discussion by J. Barton, *Reading the Old Testament* (London: Darton, Longman & Todd, 1984), 161–2. I wonder, however, if this difference may not be diminishing: cf. my quotations from Lüdemann, below, pp. 14, 20. My own interests entirely follow the 'German' line, but I think that the 'English' question remains both proper and vital. Contrast Brevard Childs, who is completely against any thought of 'what really happened'; so for example his *Biblical Theology* (London: SCM, 1992), 722: 'I have also rejected the claims [of historical criticism] . . . to filter the biblical literature according to its own criteria of "what really happened".'

The [Scottish] Common Sense philosophy has contributed to an apologetic based on the testing of evidences. The development of such an apologetic alongside deductive arguments for the truth of scripture is traced . . . through Princeton theology, turn-of-the-century traditional and radical evangelical movements, early fundamentalism, and contemporary fundamentalism and evangelicalism.[10]

We do not have to suggest that all conservative, evangelical, and fundamentalist Christianity follows this pattern: as Harris carefully argues, there are other streams of influence, among which she emphasizes currents of Dutch Calvinism. The interrelations between these different currents of conservative interpretation are well explained by her and do not need to be restated here. Suffice it for the present that apologetic modes of interpreting the Bible and of justifying the truth-claims of Christianity (and of Judaism?) are widely present within the religious communities, and may be much more influential than would be indicated by the utterances of official and professional theologians and biblical scholars.

Apologetics, therefore, continues to be with us, and we should not be ashamed of using the term just because it seems old-fashioned. For, we may say, any argument that seeks to make sense of religion, to show that it has some sort of basis, to show that it is coherent and not just a lot of nonsense, any such argument or set of arguments constitutes a sort of apologetic. Thus even those—and they are many—who reject the idea of apologetics altogether and who hold that Christianity is kerygmatic in character, that it proclaims the truth and does not admit of any neutral ground upon which one may stand to argue towards it, even they are providing a sort of (negative) apologetic by doing so.

Apologetics, therefore, is not to be defined purely through use of a neutral ground upon which arguments must be based: such is only one of the forms that it may take. Apologetics may be based on reason and philosophical argument; it may be based on history, in any one of several senses; it may be based on the Bible; it may involve a combination of several or all of these. In fact, whether we use the actual term 'apologetics' or not, all I want to convey is that there is a subject here which deserves to be talked about.

---

[10] Harriet Harris, *Fundamentalism and Evangelicals* (Oxford: Clarendon, 1998), 16; and consider the plentiful entries in her index, p. 373, under the heading Apologetics.

Moreover, we do not have to take the idea of Christian apologetics in an extremely wide sense if we are to concentrate, as I shall do, on the present position of the Bible and biblical scholarship, both in relation to history and in other relations. On the one hand, the historical elements and relationships of the Bible are a prime ingredient, perhaps the one foundational ingredient, in the conviction that history is an integral part of all argument for the truth and validity of Christianity: few would question this. When people say that 'Christianity is a historical religion', the first justification for this claim will usually be to point to the substantial content of 'history-like' narrative (I employ the useful term of Hans Frei) in a series of books of the Old Testament, which carry us from the origin of the world down to the end of the Hebrew kingdoms and somewhat beyond that, and in the gospels and Acts in the New. But the assessment of this historical content of the Bible is only one way in which its apologetic force can be indicated. Another way is by looking at the Bible as a whole and considering the modes of its internal coherence and its conceptual creativity and originality. Thus it is profitable to look not only at the more directly historical involvements of the Bible but also to consider the more general profile of biblical scholarship as a whole. The ideas that biblical scholars have about the nature of narrative, about literary criticism, about the Bible's portrayal of humanity and human life, all these are just as important for apologetics as the more direct investigation of historical reference.

To say this is not to say that the modern biblical scholar is deeply or directly interested in apologetic questions. For the most part, he or she is not, and this is not a new thing but has been the case for a century or so. For this there are several reasons. First, for the most part the modern biblical scholar has been more interested in discovering and explaining what the biblical writers thought than in proving these thoughts to be true. To prove that thoughts are true entails going outside the circle of biblical evidence and thus outside the region in which the biblical scholar feels his expertise to lie. Secondly, important theological currents of this century, as I have already hinted, have been opposed to the pursuit of apologetic questions, not so much because the validity of religion could not be proved, but because, it was argued, it was against the interest of religion that it should be proved. According to this argument, faith does not rest upon proof, and if it were proved then it would not be genuine faith. Seen from this point of view, to call an argument 'apologetic' has been something like an insult. Thirdly, the relations between Bible and belief in the twentieth century became somewhat ambiguous. In the past it had been thought, broadly speaking, that the Bible provided grounds for the truth of religion; in this century it became uncertain whether the Bible supported the truth of religion, or whether the converse was true and it was the truth of religion that gave grounds for the authority of the Bible. We do not at the moment have to work out the rights and wrongs of these various arguments: all we do is to constate that apologetics as such has not been a major and direct concern of most biblical scholarship in this century. Nevertheless it may well emerge that much that has been said and done in biblical scholarship has been significant for apologetic questions and indeed has been influenced all along by such considerations.

It can be easy to dismiss some such questions as silly, ridiculous, or unimportant. To biblical scholars and professional theologians they may be so, but to the general public they may make an important difference, not only for their faith decisions, but for their judgements on matters of science and public affairs. If they are to hear serious discussion, they turn very often not to the churches or the clergy but to the newspapers or to television, to educational media or the museum. In my first draft of this book I wrote that one might perhaps dismiss as 'lunatic fringe' people's interest in the (frequently announced) discovery of Noah's ark, but that some other phenomena have greater seriousness. Afterwards I changed my mind somewhat. Dining with members of a high-level international conference concerned with health, medical, and population problems, I talked at length with a person of leadership and importance who was greatly concerned with the matter of this same ark. Had not substantial pieces of wood been discovered on or near Mount Ararat? How could it be proved, scientifically, that the pairs of animals could not have been accommodated for a year in this sizeable vessel? And the interesting thing for me was not the direct question of the reality of the ark. It was, rather, two other things: first, the fact that this matter of the ark was, for him, the one great foremost question about the Bible, surpassing in this respect such matters as resurrection or eternal life, and secondly, the effect that such an approach would have, not upon Bible and religion at all, but upon the relation between scientific reality and the myths and legends of peoples. For this was a man working with the World Health Organization on matters where modern science and the differences of worldwide beliefs and practices interacted. And so the matter of Noah's ark, in itself only a small portion of a great reality, came to seem to me more important than I had supposed.

Take another example: what should one think about the Jesus Seminar in the United States, which solemnly votes on the historical probability that Jesus spoke this saying or that, and accords to each saying one of five grades varying from 'certainly yes' through 'probably' and 'possibly' down to 'certainly not', an activity that is plentifully reported in the popular media? Again, what if the Dead Sea Scrolls have cast doubt upon the originality of the Christian message? All questions of these types have the effect of continuing to cast basic religious questions within an apologetic mould. And, leaving the United States, what about the eight-page spread which the popular and influential German news magazine *Der Spiegel* accorded to Gerd Lüdemann for his reflections on the very limited historicity of the New Testament picture of Jesus, Paul, and in general the events associated with them? Questions of this kind remain very important in the popular mind, and the man or woman in the street is not at all inclined to accept it when scholars and theologians tell them that this is not the proper way to be thinking about such matters. This does not mean that we can answer such questions in this short book, but it does mean that we can have in mind their continued importance.

To sum up thus far: the general mode in which scholarship of our time views the Bible is of high importance for the credibility of religion. But the total profile of biblical study appears to be changing, and the effects which this may have require to be considered. If this is appropriate at any time, all the more is it so with the approaching end of the millennium. The end of a century is commonly supposed to have a certain character, best expressed in the French phrase *fin de siècle*: a certain sense of decay, degeneration, cynicism, loss of ideals perhaps. And if that takes place at the end of a century, what about the end of a millennium? It should, arithmetically, be even worse! Is that the case with biblical studies at the present time?

My purpose will be to avoid the merely technical and specialized; I will seek to emphasize the more general intellectual questions that face scholarship in our time. Thus I do not intend to report on new discoveries, results of archaeological excavations, the publication of new dictionaries or commentaries and the like. The emphasis will be rather on the more general intellectual climate of biblical study, its underlying philosophy and theology, and the tendency of its movement in the last decades of this century. Central to this book will be, perhaps, a philosophical aspect: perhaps we could crystallize it in the single word 'ideology': for one of the things that we shall be asking is: how is it that the word 'ideology', so seldom heard in the world of biblical studies two or three decades ago, is now so often to be heard, and in senses both laudatory and deprecatory?

But ideology will not be our starting-point. It will reappear soon enough. For the moment let us look at some other aspects of the way in which biblical studies are moving.

2

The New Profile of Discussion about the Bible

NOW the obvious starting-point, and one upon which almost all who know the scholarly scene would agree, is the apparent decline of traditional historical criticism. Thus John Barton writes:

The Bible in any of the forms it is encountered in the modern world gives out the strongest possible signals of unity, coherence, and closure. All the books have the same typography, the same style of translation, a consistent pagination, and a fixed order: features that arouse strong expectations that the contents will be a single 'work'. One of the first and most obvious effects of historical criticism is that it disappoints all such expectations. The disappointment is often felt quite acutely by students beginning the study of the Bible, but until recently they were usually told that the more fragmentary understanding of the Bible that resulted was truer to its contents than the illusory unity projected by our typographical conventions; and truth, even if disappointing, is always better than illusion, however attractive.

One of the most remarkable developments in biblical studies over the last twenty-five years has been a steady reversal of this tendency . . .[1]

Barton then goes on to discuss the different movements 'on the literary side' and 'on the theological side' that follow from this reversal. The extent of the reversal is indicated by another remark of his in *The Cambridge Companion to Biblical Interpretation* (1998) which he edited. In his Introduction he notes the undeniable paradigm shift, i.e. the fact that the style of biblical studies has changed radically in the last decade or so, and goes on to say, 'When this book was being planned, some advisers suggested that there should be no chapter on historical criticism at all, since it was now entirely *passé.*' In order to maintain a balance, he continues, 'Against this I have tried to show that "historical" critics raised

---

[1] J. Barton, *The Spirit and the Letter* (London: SPCK, 1997), 151.

(and raise) issues that should still be on the agenda for the student of the Bible, and will not go away.'[2] To sum up this point, the analytic, differentiating style attached to historical criticism has begun to yield to a more synthetic, holistic one, which hopes to draw support from either literary or theological considerations or both.

These changes are realized not only in books and articles but also in the practical conditions of biblical scholarship. A good example can be taken, perhaps, from the wild and inaccurate writer Walter Wink, who in the 1970s complained[3] that no one could make a career in scholarship unless he or she stuck steadfastly to the then traditional 'historical critical paradigm'.[4] In this Wink was a sort of *prophetes e contrario* or 'prophet by reversal', if there is such a thing, one who prophesied disaster because of an existing evil and then was proved right because his reason was wrong, the existing evil being the opposite of the evil upon which the disaster was predicated: for by the 1990s the opposite had come to be the case, and now anyone who professes his or her main interest to lie in the source analysis of the Pentateuch is somewhat unlikely to obtain an academic post. Jobs are for people who are interested in ideological criticism or in feminist hermeneutics or reader-response approaches. They do not go to people who are obviously or primarily interested in traditional biblical criticism.[5] In fact, without too much exaggeration, one may say that, if traditional historical criticism is to die out, it will not have died out because of intellectual arguments against it but because other motivations have assumed priority, especially on the church scene—and when I speak of 'the church scene' I do not refer to the traditional conservative/fundamentalist position, which was always, with

---

[2] Ibid. 2.

[3] W. Wink, *The Bible in Human Transformation* (Philadelphia: Fortress, 1973). I described this work as 'wild, thoughtless and journalistic' in my *Holy Scripture: Canon, Authority, Criticism* (Oxford: Clarendon, 1983), 107 n. 4.

[4] Even at that time Wink ignored some of the facts: for there were also individuals who were warned that they would 'ruin their career' if they persisted in criticisms of the then powerful biblical theology movement, exactly the opposite of the historical-critical paradigm.

[5] Note that the same point is made by J. Barton (ed.), *Cambridge Companion to Biblical Interpretation* (Cambridge: Cambridge University Press, 1998), 19, where he points out that 'adherence to "historical criticism" ' may sometimes have been 'a prerequisite for getting an academic job', and adds that 'The evil of this situation will not be purged by making it instead into an absolute bar.'

qualifications, hostile to biblical criticism, but to the modern liberal/postmodernist church scene, which is simply more interested in modern social movements than in serious biblical research—and which, as we shall see, can share some of the intolerance of the older fundamentalism.

This shift of interest, however, is not taking quite the shape that the traditional opponents of historical criticism might have expected or wished. When we look at the study of the history of ancient Israel we find something very different. One might have supposed that with the decline of historical criticism much greater certainty about the history of biblical times would have been achieved. The reverse is the case. It is true that the average older historical criticism cast doubt upon the historicity of many elements, if taken as literal fact as narrated in the Hebrew Bible; but equally the historiography of the same period built very much upon what seemed to be an assured foundation within the biblical text. History of Israel, as thus written, whether in the more conservative style of John Bright or in the somewhat more critical one of Martin Noth, was still very much tied to the Bible and its picture of historical reality. The recent trend in history, or one recent trend at any rate, has gone a quite different way. According to it, history should not depend particularly on the Bible, which is only one source and presents only one point of view; it should be the history of an area or an epoch, let us say, the history of Syria/Palestine in the first millennium BC; it should not be the history of one people, Israel, but the history of all those who lived in that area at that time; and it should no longer conceive of itself as at root a biblically based discipline, but should look for its sources primarily outside the Bible, and most of all in archaeology. Seen from this revisionist viewpoint, as it is now often called, quite radical pictures may emerge. According to one formulation, we have no truly historical confirmation that there ever was a David or a Solomon or the united kingdom of Israel and Judah over which they are said to have ruled. Much of what is told in the Bible about the earlier periods may be an expression of religious belief and ideology rather than anything approaching true historical writing. The contents of the Bible are in large measure not a true historical source but are a religious ideology expressing itself in a form purporting to be historical narrative. The move away from traditional historical criticism has carried with it—not universally, but certainly in influential force—a considerably increased degree of scepticism towards the historicity of many biblical narratives. To put it in another way: traditional historical criticism seemed to many to decrease the certainty of the Bible as a document to be read, by dividing it into different strata from different times; and the recent movement has been away from that sort of analytic approach. But that same traditional criticism was accompanied by a picture of the *history* of the central biblical period, say from 1000 to 400 BC, which stuck very closely to the Bible's own depiction; and the same recent move that has seen the biblical texts more as each being a whole has also separated them much more from the actual history, which is said not to be attainable through the Bible at all, or only in limited degree.

Thus, in particular, recent trends from various directions have been combining to suggest a late date, certainly post-exilic, for biblical materials that would formerly, even within normal historical-critical practice, have been deemed to be quite early. The J source of the Pentateuch, which in classic practice was assigned to a time around the ninth century, comes to be suddenly pulled down towards the fifth or so. In another such drastic change, the prominent Abraham traditions come to be a creation of the fifth or fourth century. Much of the picture of the Babylonian Exile, with a whole people moved away from their homeland and then, after lively religious rethinking while in Babylonia, returning to their land and restoring their commonwealth and temple, has been severely questioned. If such tendencies should be extended, the effect would be that much of the Old Testament would be seen as a product of the fifth and fourth centuries, and the depiction of much earlier times a product of the ideologies of these later eras. It has been alleged, indeed, that much of the Old Testament may be a product of the Hellenistic age.

And, just to complicate the picture, let us add another aspect. We have seen, following Barton, over the last twenty-five years a 'steady reversal' of the influence of the analytic, historical-critical perceptions of the Bible and their increasing replacement by more synthetic and holistic approaches. But it would be a mistake to suppose that traditional historical criticism is passing away. Certainly there are more people who are questioning it and doubting it. But the opposite phenomenon is also part of the modern scene. Active, highly critical, and sometimes aggressive historical criticism is if anything more to be seen than was the case fifty or a hundred years ago, when most biblical criticism was actually rather mild and theologically rather conservative, though not everyone perceived that at the time. Today a scholar such as Gerd Lüdemann can write:

> The results of historical criticism are tamed where it is said that they must not be made absolute [here he quotes a German bishop who has said just this]. Historical criticism is valid universally or not at all. To this degree it must absolutize itself and its results. However, that does not mean that it claims to be able to grasp the whole of reality.[6]

In fact it should not be supposed that the work of traditional historical criticism has somehow come to a stop and been replaced by the more novel holistic approaches. Much of the work that has in recent years begun to show us a quite different picture of (say) the Pentateuch has been in real continuity of method with the older critical tradition even where it has reversed its judgements. The movement towards a late dating for important Pentateuchal elements is common property shared by circles of revisionist historical scholarship and by circles that continue the basic values and methods of the older criticism.

This brings us to an important formulation. In the past we have commonly conceived these matters through a simple bipolar model of conservative and liberal: conservative emphasized both the unity of the text and the general historical reliability of the matter, liberal was interested in the differences between the texts and was more critical of their historical accuracy. In the newer situation, which is likely to continue into the next century, we have at least three, and in fact four or more, positions and approaches which form partial coalitions with one another, the extent of these coalitions varying as we pass from one theme to another. And this is not a passing observation but is a constant theme that will be central to this book.

The trends of which we have been speaking, one in the retirement of historical criticism into the background, the second in its vigorous reassertion, and the third in the changed perspective of revisionist historians, have in common at least one thing, a concern with history in some shape or form. A fourth major trend,

---

[6] *The Unholy in Holy Scripture* (London: SCM, 1997), 4.

on the other hand, looks in a non-historical direction, or does so in at least some of its forms. I am thinking now of the vastly increased influence of modern literary criticism. Much of this will be familiar and need not be explained at length by me: we think of structuralism on the one hand and the New Criticism on the other, and the whole development that has been finely characterized by John Barton in his deservedly successful *Reading the Old Testament*.[7] To summarize the essentials: the past history, sources, and origins of texts are not important, for the meaning—or meanings, for there is not necessarily one right meaning—lies in the text itself. Even the intent of the author is not important. Dates and historical connections are of only minor interest, or none at all.

A further development is the reader-response approach: meaning is not in the author's intention, it is not even totally controlled by the text itself, it is to a large extent the construction of the reader. Thus there has been an enormous upsurge in the production of 'literary studies', 'literary commentaries' on the Bible and the like. Alongside the traditional biblical scholar there has appeared a substantial group of interpreters whose skills, experience, and perspectives are very different. Thus far we have only barely introduced this tendency, which will come back before us in further connections later on.

Here it will be convenient to comment on a tendency which is certainly not a pure literary study, and is more of the character of historical theology linked with theological hermeneutics. I referred earlier to the expression 'history-like' and acknowledged my debt to Hans Frei for the use of this expression, which fits much of the biblical narrative very well. His famous work *The Eclipse of Biblical Narrative* has had wide appreciation and influence, especially within theology rather than within biblical studies. In large measure his book was a historical approach, tracing how the interpretation of biblical narrative, starting from the Reformation, had suffered from the growth of a historical method, which had eventually led to the eclipse of biblical narrative. In the Reformers the literal sense and the historical sense had been the same thing, but afterwards the two had been separated and the growing

---

[7] (London: Darton, Longman & Todd, 1984); the reader is advised to use the 2nd edn. (1996), which contains two additional chapters highly relevant for the matters to be discussed here.

emphasis on history had moved the meaning away from the narrative itself to an extra-textual reality, the identification of the events that had happened. This, he thought, had been fatal to the appreciation of biblical narrative. His thinking was central to what has been called the Yale school, and his influence on the Old Testament theologian Brevard Childs has been very great, as the latter acknowledged.[8] Moreover, the whole trend of his argument tended to foster the sense of hostility to the Enlightenment that has been characteristic of many movements in modern interpretation, including most postmodernism. It is therefore appropriate to mention his work here.

There are several reasons, however, why I want to dissociate myself from his line of argument, stimulating as I have found his thought to be.[9] The first is that he takes the Protestant Reformers as his starting-point. He seems, if I understand him, to assume that they had the perfect answer to the understanding of biblical narrative. I do not see any reason why we should accept this as a basis for discussion. Secondly, and in particular, he seemed to have a nostalgia for a situation where the literal sense and the historical sense were one, and a longing to return to that situation. But, it always seemed to me, once it is known that the literal sense is historically wrong or inaccurate, there is no possibility of returning to that situation. Thirdly, his total argument seems to contain confusions, in particular, his belief that this 'history-like quality' can be 'examined for the bearing it has in its own right on meaning and interpretation', without being confused 'with the quite different issue of whether or not the realistic narrative was historical'.[10] Here it will be useful to cite a serious and painstaking analysis by the Israeli literary critic Meir Sternberg, whom we shall mention again later:

---

[8] Though Childs did, uncharacteristically, state as his reaction to one of Frei's last works before his death that 'when he [Frei], in one of his last essays, spoke of "midrash" as a text-creating reality, he moved in a direction, in my opinion, which for Christian theology can only end in failure'; see Childs, *Biblical Theology of the Old and New Testaments* (London: SCM, 1992), 20. The work referred to is the essay 'The "Literal Reading" of Biblical Narrative in the Christian Tradition: Does it Stretch or will it Break?', in F. McConnell (ed.), *The Bible and the Narrative Tradition* (New York: Oxford University Press, 1986), 36–77.

[9] For a good analysis, see Lynn M. Poland, *Literary Criticism and Biblical Hermeneutics* (Chico, Calif.: Scholars Press), 120–37.

[10] Hans Frei, *The Eclipse of Biblical Narrative* (New Haven: Yale University Press, 1974), 13–16.

His [Frei's] reasonable claim that what biblical narratives 'are about and how they make sense' depend(s) on 'the rendering of the events constituting them' goes with a set of unacceptable corollaries. First, that this feature of signification distinguishes 'realistic' narrative; second, that it brings together realistic and historical narrative; and third, that this 'history-like quality' can be 'examined for the bearing it has in its own right on meaning and interpretation', without being confused 'with the quite different issue of whether or not the realistic narrative was historical' (pp. 13–16). The fatal flaw in this argument lies in its working with two concepts where no fewer than three will do: history-likeness, history telling, and historicity. In accusing his predecessors of 'logical confusion between two categories or contexts of meaning and interpretation' (p. 16), Frei himself thus falls into a triple confusion: (1) between history telling, which relates to the truth claim of the discourse, and historicity, which relates to its truth value and therefore has least to do with 'meaning and interpretation'; (2) between both and history-likeness, which turns on neither but goes as a rule with fictionality; (3) between the truth claims of history-like and historical narrative, whose variance has a large bearing on 'meaning and interpretation' since it determines the presence or absence of fictional license . . . Generally speaking, realism or history-likeness never has a bearing 'in its own right on meaning and interpretation', because it signifies one thing in a historiographical and another in a fictional context.[11]

Thus Sternberg summarizes: 'Like most "literary" approaches [to the Bible], then, Frei's is well-intentioned, even laudable, but theoretically misguided.' I do not wish to pursue this argument further; but both the introduction of Hans Frei, and the indication that a case against his views does exist, must be included here.

One other related factor may suitably be introduced at this point: I refer to the current importance of *theory*, which is particularly noticeable in the area of literary criticism. Theory takes precedence over learning or experience. I have heard of someone who was awarded a tenured position in a department of literature on the basis of a book on literary theory which contained no mention of any actual literary work or of any writer of a literary work. At examinations I hear students being asked 'What is your *theory* of literature?' The question is not, 'Have you read any literature?', or 'Do you enjoy literature?', or 'Do you think that Jane

[11] M. Sternberg, *The Poetics of Biblical Narrative* (Bloomington, Ind.: Indiana University Press, 1987), 81–2.

Austen is good literature?' No, what you have to have is the theory.[12] For readers who may not have heard about this, the correct (and politically correct) answer to the question 'What is your theory of literature?' is: 'Literature is an instrument of social control.' The function of *Winnie the Pooh*, for example, is to inculcate the values of the upper-class levels of the English social system. The theory, it is supposed on rather unclear grounds, is also the thing that will change society. A fine quotation from an academic survey is given by Frank Kermode: 'The dominant concern of literary studies during the rest of the 1980s will be literary theory. Especially important will be the use of theory informed by the work of the French philosopher Jacques Derrida to gain insights into the cultures of blacks and women.'[13] While this emphasis on theory may produce some good results, it also produces wordy expositions which may be backed by little experience of the reality.[14] And here there is a tangible contrast with traditional historical criticism, which rested little on theory and largely on a body of proposals or insights (commonly called 'results') which people found by and large convincing.[15] As we shall see, modern depictions of the 'theory' of historical criticism are generally inventions of its enemies of recent times.

Turning in another direction, we have to look at two partially competing approaches to the religion and theology of the Bible. On the one hand there is the history of religion, which is able to add to the Hebrew Bible the steadily increasing information from newly discovered inscriptions, from archaeology, from comparison with other religions of the ancient Near East, and from sociological and

---

[12] R. P. Carroll, 'Poststructuralist Approaches', in Barton (ed.), *Companion*, 50, tells us that: 'A new generation of theory-driven scholars emerged after the 1960s determined to read themselves into the text.' All too true.

[13] F. Kermode, *History and Value* (Oxford: Clarendon, 1988), 113. The quotation is from *The Chronicle of Higher Education*, 4 September 1985.

[14] In finding this emphasis on theory rather comic, we may find ourselves accused of an ethnic bias. David Jobling, of the University of Saskatchewan, discussing some work of Robert Carroll, writes: 'Carroll intends to defer "theory" and adopt an empirical approach. One is tempted to hear in this a characteristically British attitude. I do not believe that Carroll really shares the general anti-theoretical stance of British biblical scholarship . . . but he prefers to defer theoretical discussion.' So in 'Text and World: An Unbridgeable Gap?', in P. R. Davies (ed.), *Second Temple Studies*, i. *Persian Period* (Sheffield: JSOT, 1991), 175–82; quotation from 176–7.

[15] Contrast, however, Carroll, in Barton (ed.), *Companion*, 52, who tells us that 'New Historicism is essentially a turn away from theory'.

anthropological experience. The Bible, after all, has many gaps and leaves many things unsaid, and the history of religion may be able to enrich our knowledge with all sorts of information along these lines.

Biblical theology, or for my purposes the theology of the Old Testament, is more focused on the biblical text itself and seeks to identify or describe a theology, or a variety of theologies, that permeate it. Though differing from theology in the proper sense, i.e. from doctrinal theology, or from Christian theology as a whole, biblical theology, as its name may imply, has a certain analogy with doctrinal theology and may be seen—this is controversial—as a sort of intermediate stage between the exegesis of individual biblical passages and the total theological task.

Both the history of Hebrew religion and the theology of the Old Testament have seen intense activity and development in the last decades. They have also frequently come into conflict. Biblical theology has been attacked as unhistorical, as vainly seeking to achieve a concord between the diverse biblical materials, and as being tied to the apron-strings of one particular religion, namely Christianity. The approach through the history of religion has been criticized for its inability to handle, even to touch, the questions of revelation, inspiration, canonicity, authority, and the like which for many people are the only real reason why anyone reads the Bible anyway. Conflict along these lines has become more intense in recent years and will not easily be overcome. Some biblical theology has pointed to the importance of its own service to the church, as the community that uses the Bible; but recent work by the German scholar Rainer Albertz has argued that, even for the church and its task in the world, the approach through the history of religion is actually better and likely to be more fruitful. Which way this discussion will go it is as yet too early to say. What seems most likely is that some sort of combination of the interests of biblical theology and the history of religion will prove widely acceptable.

Here it will be convenient to introduce the canonical approaches to the Old Testament, which do something to bring together three things: the decline of historical criticism, the literary aspect already mentioned, and the aspect of biblical theology. Any canonical approach will emphasize on the one hand the fact of the canon of scripture: the Bible exists as a total collection, a

reality which was obscured by historical criticism with its tendency
to split books up into different sources from different times; and
on the other hand, the same thing under another aspect, the final
form of the text as the essential form for understanding, so that the
interior relations of the final form are much more important than
the relations of any part with previous forms that may have existed
at an earlier stage. These interests combine—at least in most forms
thus far known[16]—with a strong theological and churchly interest.
The canon is said to be part of the church's confession; it was the
church (and, of course, earlier on, the synagogue) that set it up and
declared its authority, and the church wants, or ought to want, to
have it interpreted as a unity. It wants and needs to hear the interpretation of the text as it now stands, rather than the history of
how it originated or came to be this way. Moreover, the canon in
these senses provides the proper guidance towards a true and valid
biblical theology (so Childs) or a valid and effective hermeneutic
(so Sanders). Canonical interpretations of these kinds remain
controversial but, even where there are powerful arguments
against some of them, it seems certain that they have a strong
appeal and are likely to remain on the scene of biblical studies for
the coming decades. Independent of new schemes for 'canonical
interpretation' and 'canonical theology', it must be said without
doubt that the canonical interest has stimulated fresh thought,
discussion, and research in a whole wide area which had been
neglected. The most striking fruit of that rethinking has again
come from Barton in his recent *The Spirit and the Letter.*[17]

All the aspects which have been mentioned belong in a general
sense to the field of biblical studies as usually understood. We go
more outside the usual realm of biblical studies when we turn to
our next aspect, namely the renewed effect of philosophy on our
subject. The typical biblical scholarship of modern times has been
rather little touched by philosophy—certainly much less than it has
been touched by theology. Going back to last century, one
remembers Vatke and his Hegelianism, and it has long been

---

[16] The qualification 'at least in most forms thus far known' is inserted here because R.
Rendtorff, whose plans suggest a more consistently 'canonical' theology than any other, but
who has not as yet published an actual full-size theology, seems to have deep interest in
remaining close to Judaism but much less interest in contact with the New Testament or
the church. On his work cf. J. Barr, *The Concept of Biblical Theology* (London: SCM, 1999),
441–7.   [17] (London: SPCK, 1997).

customary to accuse Wellhausen of the same thing though the accusation has long been proved to be an empty one. And after that we do have an influence of philosophy, but mostly on the theological use of the Bible rather than on biblical scholarship in the narrower sense: thus something of Heidegger through Bultmann in New Testament studies, and certainly quite a lot of attempts to bring Gadamer into biblical hermeneutics. James M. Robinson in his book *The New Hermeneutic*, introducing the latest trends in German discussion to the English-speaking public, showed how Gadamer had taken the lead in transmitting the heritage of Heidegger and others to the present generation; Andrew Louth likewise appealed to Gadamer in an argument that sought to question historical criticism and to support patristic methods of exegesis, including allegory; and Mark Brett thought that an injection of insights from Gadamer would help to overcome any shortcomings in the canonical approach of Brevard Childs.[18] Perhaps the most important name however is that of Paul Ricœur, who produces not only a philosophy that is relevant to biblical interpretation but also detailed biblical interpretations. His emphasis on the nature of texts and the nature of reading has a high relevance for modern discussions.

In this respect, incidentally, I should perhaps make an amendment to my remarks in *The Concept of Biblical Theology*, ch. 10, in which I pointed out how far most Old Testament scholarship was remote from philosophy. This judgement should perhaps have a temporal quantifier attached to it: it certainly applies up to my own generation. Judging from the influence of hermeneutical philosophies, and from some of what is now written in biblical studies, a kind of philosophy, especially social philosophy and what is coming to be called critical theory, is becoming more obvious and central in biblical study. But this is for the most part a new thing, an innovation as against what has been normal since about the mid-nineteenth century. It may certainly change the air of biblical study. Philosophical claims or claims of critical theory, disquisitions about poststructuralism, postmodernism, and the like may take the place of what used to be Hebrew grammar or textual

---

[18] See James M. Robinson, *The New Hermeneutic* (New York: Harper & Row, 1964); Andrew Louth, *Discerning the Mystery* (Oxford: Clarendon, 1983); M. Brett, *Biblical Criticism in Crisis?* (Cambridge: Cambridge University Press, 1991).

criticism. Derrida and Foucault will become more familiar than
the Septuagint or Brown, Driver, and Briggs. It certainly looks
that way at the moment.

From quite another direction there comes work such as the
philosophical examination of biblical criticism by Eleonore Stump
and others, mainly in the United States. A striking and often
heated debate between biblical exegesis and philosophical theology took place in a conference at Notre Dame University in 1990,
the papers of which were published by Stump and Flint under the
title of *Hermes and Athena*.[19] For the British reader it may be particularly noteworthy that much of this discussion, though not all of
it, comes from the rather unfamiliar background of American
Dutch Calvinism, and in this respect can be close to a strong biblical conservatism, philosophically justified. Thus for Stump it is a
very serious question whether, for instance, 2 Peter, if it was not
actually written by Peter himself, can have any claim to moral or
theological authority. Such a way to approach the problems would
seem antiquated in most European discussion, even from a conservative point of view. Nevertheless a thorough re-airing of the
question with full philosophical precision can only be salutary.

Particularly striking in this respect are the recent Wilde Lectures
of Nicholas Wolterstorff, *Divine Discourse*, which offer a stimulating philosophical account of the way in which the Bible can be
thought of as 'God's Book', in the sense of God's *appropriation* of
human speech, an approach which seems to me to offer—perhaps
unintentionally—a rather good avenue towards an understanding
of the *critical* approach to scripture. It is certainly important that the
conversation between biblical scholars and philosophers should
continue and increase in the coming years.

I have already mentioned the word 'ideology', and some further
consideration of it may suitably follow at this point. As I said, this
word was seldom heard two or three decades ago, and now quite
suddenly it is heard on all sides. 'Ideological criticism' has come to
take its place alongside the older source criticism, form criticism,
redaction criticism, and so on. But, where the term 'ideology' is
used, there is a great degree of variety in the senses in which it is
employed and the sort of impact that it is expected to have upon
the understanding of the Bible. At one extreme, ideology means

---

[19]   (Notre Dame, Ind.: Notre Dame University Press, 1993).

false ideas, ideas created by the social and economic system, ideas which disguise the reality of things; reality, however, can be known and can thus be opposed to ideology. At the other extreme, everything is ideology: there is no access to reality apart from ideology, for what we call 'reality' is something that we construct, and any attempt to pass to a 'real' appreciation of reality is only a more deceptive ideology than any other. As we shall see, biblical scholarship has a wide variety of uses distributed along this spectrum of difference. In a later chapter we shall try to disentangle these complications.

Another term that is becoming increasingly prominent is 'rhetoric'. Where people used to say 'your arguments', they now increasingly say 'your rhetoric'. In part this is said in tribute to the power of speech: rhetoric is an aspect, a level, of communication. 'Rhetorical criticism' is yet another of the many kinds of criticism added to the repertoire of the biblical scholar. In part, on the other hand, it is said in devaluation of reasoning. 'Your arguments' might suggest that you are appealing to some truth, that you have some reasons which you are trying to adduce. 'Your rhetoric' suggests rather that you have some skill in stringing together words that might persuade others of your opinion. Truth, evidences, and reason do not come into it.[20]

For a good example, the reader should turn to Walter Brueggemann's *Theology of the Old Testament*, which is, so far as I know, the first work on biblical theology to be centred specifically in rhetoric. Compare the following: 'Our postmodern situation, which refuses to acknowledge a settled essence behind our pluralistic claims, must make a major and intentional investment in the practice of rhetoric, for the shape of reality finally depends on the power of speech'.[21] Yet more: 'Speech constitutes reality, and who God turns out to be in Israel depends on the utterance of the Israelites or, derivatively, the utterance of the text'.[22] Again, and in sacramental language: '*I shall insist, as consistently as I can, that the God of Old Testament theology as such lives in, with and under the rhetorical enterprise of this text, and nowhere else and in no other way*'.[23] Most extremely of all, we come close to the suggestion that

---

[20] By contrast, Gilbert Murray, writing to Bernard Shaw, referred to 'the damnable vice' of preferring rhetoric to truth: quoted in *British Museum Quarterly*, 24/1–2 (1961), 17.

[21] W. Brueggemann, *Theology of the Old Testament* (Minneapolis: Fortress, 1997), 71.

[22] Ibid. 65.

[23] Ibid. 66 (author's italics).

Yahweh is created or 'generated' by Israel's rhetoric: '*The rhetorical mediation of Yahweh in the Bible is not a disembodied, ideational operation*'. 'Yahweh is generated and constituted, so far as the claims of Israel are concerned, in actual practices that mediate . . . it is a question of characteristic social practice that generates, constitutes, and mediates Yahweh in the midst of life'.[24] Yahweh is 'given to Israel in practice',[25] but this practice is a part of 'rhetorical mediation'. Rhetoric, then, in this approach is made very much into the centre of the biblical depiction and appreciation of God.

And finally we have to mention one other principal term that will pervade our entire discussion, namely 'postmodernism' or 'the postmodern'. I must confess that I do not like these terms: to me, to utter the word 'postmodern' is equivalent to saying 'I am now going to start talking nonsense'. 'Postmodern' seems to me to have that sort of contradiction built into it. When I hear people say 'That is a modern idea and is therefore out of date'[26] I feel there is some sort of conceptual misfit. But of course the term has come to be used and it is not easy to find something else that will designate the same package of phenomena.

Moreover, I was encouraged in the propriety of using it by Basil Mitchell, who tells us of how 'Bultmann and his followers have been overtaken by even more radical thinkers, generally known collectively as "post-modernists", whose views I shall consider later (chiefly in Chapter 5)'.[27] I am not sure, however, whether his postmodernists are the same people as I have in mind, for the use of these designations seems to change rapidly over a scale of time.[28] But I do agree with him when he says that 'These later thinkers, following clues in Nietzsche, go one step further and

---

[24] Brueggemann, *Theology of the Old Testament*, 574.   [25] Ibid. 575.

[26] Thus when Robert Carroll talks of 'the many modernist biblical scholars' he means 'the many biblical scholars who persist in pursuing the old-fashioned, now out-of-date, kinds of study which have been pursued over the last two centuries': Barton (ed.), *Companion*, 59. In this book, in my own writing I use the words 'modern' and 'modernity' only in the customary sense; the postmodern usage of them will be intended only when quoting other writers, or will be marked with quotation marks.

[27] Basil Mitchell, *Faith and Criticism* (Oxford: Clarendon, 1994), 8.

[28] In his ch. 5 Mitchell somewhat changes his ground and talks of 'traditionalists' and 'progressives'; what he ends the chapter by confuting is 'relativism'. The only person clearly identified as a 'progressive' is 'so moderate and thoughtful a progressive as Maurice Wiles' (p. 91); but I do not think Professor Wiles would count as a postmodernist in my usage of the terms. Cf. Mitchell's statement that 'it is true of academic theologians that "we are all liberals now" ' (p. 89).

abandon the concept of objective truth altogether' (p. 8). In general this is certainly true of the postmodernists I have in mind. There is no objective truth and all knowledge is human social construction. The central reality is 'power', a term endlessly repeated and underlined. History is essentially ideology, so is science, so are the convictions of the various religions, so is the writing of books and the reading of them and the criticism of them. And this is not a bad thing; on the contrary, it is how things are and how they ought to be. And thus—in one variant at least— it is quite proper that the contents of the Bible should be regarded as ideology, for what else could they be?

But just here—and this is my final point for this chapter—once again we have to depart from the bipolar model of 'conservative' and 'liberal'. Mitchell, in the words I quoted, used 'post-modernist' as a term for 'even more radical thinkers' than 'Bultmann and his followers'. But postmodernist thinking as I have it in mind has something of that same ambiguity of which I spoke earlier: it is commonly opposed to 'liberal' and to 'progressive', yet it is not 'conservative' either; it aspires to be, and in some ways is, a position of its own, and one that can be ambiguous in relation to the positions that were once 'radical' or 'conservative' or what-ever else. We shall later return to these relationships.

3
Biblical Criticism

IN the previous chapter I used the term 'historical criticism' a number of times, because it is the phrase commonly used, but I did not use the expression 'the historical-critical method', and that was deliberate. I think these terms require to be looked at carefully and reconsidered. I once wrote an article called 'Historical Reading and the Theological Interpretation of Scripture',[1] and a reviewer commented on my diction, saying: ' "Historical reading"—by which he means historical criticism'. In fact I used the term 'historical reading' precisely because I wanted to differentiate it from historical criticism, though I thought, and tried to make it clear, that historical criticism may very well follow from historical reading. In rejecting the term 'the historical-critical method' I can appeal to the authority of Martin Hengel,[2] who wrote that there are *methods* used by historical criticism but there is no such thing as *the* historical critical method.[3] And in more recent times I acknowledge the help received from John Barton, to whose remarks we shall return. The matter is not one of terminology only, but has serious importance for our entire subject.

What I propose to do next is to look at one illustration of the questions involving history and historical criticism. I will sketch out the way in which a postmodernist approach may perceive historical criticism, and how ideology may figure within this perception. The book which I shall take as example is the attractively written *Narrative in the Hebrew Bible* by David M. Gunn and

---

[1] In J. Barr, *Explorations in Theology*, vii. *The Scope and Authority of the Bible* (London: SCM, 1980); American title *The Scope and Authority of the Bible* (Philadelphia: Westminster, 1980), pp. 30–51.

[2] M. Hengel, 'Historische Methoden', *KuD* 19 (1973), 85–90.

[3] For a good example of the contrary approach, see Edgar Krentz, *The Historical-Critical Method* (Philadelphia: Fortress, 1975).

Danna N. Fewell.[4] That this book is 'postmodernist' is rather obvious and will be illustrated shortly; and that it emphasizes 'ideology' will also become very evident. In its first chapter it takes the story of Cain and Abel as an example in order to outline various approaches to Hebrew narrative, approaches of all kinds ranging from the ancient Targumists through John Calvin to modern African interpretations. The only one of these approaches that it treats with almost total negativity is the historical-critical, which it exemplifies from the treatment by the Jewish scholar E. Speiser in his volume on Genesis early in the Anchor Bible series. The authors say they find the historical-critical approach almost totally useless and for the most part of their book thereafter they disregard it entirely.

Historical criticism, they say, was 'the dominant method of biblical interpretation in the universities of Europe and America'. Both of them, they tell us, were 'taught that it was the only "responsible" method for biblical scholars'. All I can say, as one who studied in the relevant period, is that my experience was quite different. Historical criticism was under challenge and pressure fifty years ago, I would say from the 1920s on, and this is leaving aside fundamentalism and all sorts of totally anti-critical approaches which have always been there and will always be there. What I mean is: within central, recognized academic scholarship, 'mainstream' scholarship, to use the modern term, historical criticism in the classic sense was under pressure. None of the professors with whom I studied, unless perhaps one, thought that the historical-critical was the only responsible method; even those who taught us traditional historical-critical views did not think this nor did they say it. We were certainly given a good and clear account of such things as the source criticism of the Pentateuch, the various strata of the book of Isaiah, or likewise the document Q and the various sources of the gospels. But even those who taught us these things did not suppose that they were absolutes as depicted by Gunn and Fewell. On the contrary, anyone who said that this method 'established some kind of absolute truth' (Gunn

[4] (Oxford: Oxford University Press, 1993). For a fuller discussion see J. Barr, 'A Question of Method: The Alleged Leviathan of Historical Criticism in Speiser's Genesis Commentary', in William P. Brown (*et al.*?), *God Who Creates*, FS for W. S. Towner (Grand Rapids: Eerdmans, forthcoming).

and Fewell, p. 7) would have been laughed at. Many theologians, liberal and conservative alike, were sceptical of the assurances of critical scholarship. And, from quite another side, many Hebraists and Orientalists, as distinct from Old Testament specialists, also failed to align themselves with the critical approaches. Even among Old Testament scholars much interest and consideration went towards trends and methods that seemed to rival and— potentially—to displace the historical-critical. Such approaches included form criticism, the Scandinavian emphasis on tradition, the Noth/von Rad tradition approach, and of course the entire looming edifice of biblical theology. Take a book such as Eduard Nielsen's *Oral Tradition*, published in the 1950s—it took the story of the Flood, still today often used as a supremely convincing example for source criticism—and made fun of that particular piece of 'historical criticism', or 'literary criticism', as it was then generally, and rightly, called.[5] Emphasizing the nature of the chronological detail of the story,[6] Nielsen argued that a simple division into two sources would not work. 'Our present text is a work of art, composed of different traditions, it is true, but in such a way that a unified work has been the result.' The author responsible was not a redactor, and 'he must quite certainly have been a great artist'. This sounds like Gunn and Fewell themselves; but it was in 1952.

Anyway, returning to Gunn and Fewell, against historical criticism they direct an avalanche of criticisms. In it there are, they aver, 'three major and (usually) crippling disadvantages'. First, there is circularity of argument, 'a fundamental problem for a method that claimed to be establishing some kind of absolute truth'. Secondly, the analysis of sources was 'basically dependent on aesthetic premises which were often arbitrary and rarely acknowledged'. Underlying most source criticism has been an 'aesthetic preference for rationalistic, literal reading of literature'. Thirdly, privilege (note the word 'privilege', another key term of the postmodern) was accorded to the notion of the 'original', and this is 'devastating' to the understanding of the final, canonical

---

    [5] E. Nielsen, *Oral Tradition* (London: SCM, 1954), 95–103. The Danish original was published earlier.
    [6] My own lasting interest in biblical chronology began with my reading of this passage in Nielsen.

text, which is the text people read.[7] To these are added (p. 8) the concentration of Bible interpretation in the hands of scholars, the assumption that texts have only a single right meaning, and the conviction that historical criticism is *the* correct method by which to seek it. 'Historical criticism, indeed, was the summit of the interpretational pyramid.' 'The arrogance of this position', they conclude, 'is, of course, breathtaking, but recognizably Western.'[8]

Now many of these points have been made before and have little that is original about them. And there may be some truth about some of them: circularity of argument, maybe, but it is not so clear that circular argument is always necessarily wrong (the 'hermeneutical circle', after all, is said to have great prestige within modern hermeneutics and is actually popular with the recent opponents of historical criticism); too much emphasis on 'the original', yes, and I have said that myself, but equally it can be said that emphasis on the later stages, and especially good final form exegesis, is also a part of historical-critical exegesis, a completion of it and not something different from it. We shall not argue over every point that has been made. But there are two that deserve particular attention. One is the alleged claim of 'objectivity' on the part of historical criticism: it is 'a method that claimed to be establishing some kind of absolute truth'. Here the authors are spinning ideas out of their own heads: characteristic of postmodernism, as we have seen, is its hostility to notions of objective truth, and when it dislikes something it attributes to it claims of objectivity, whether these claims were ever made or not—there is nothing in Speiser's commentary as quoted that claims to be 'absolute truth'. We thus find a sort of reversal of the older arguments against historical criticism: opponents used to say it was 'subjective':[9] it did not rest objectively on the evidence but was only some individual's idea. Now we have the opposite: the idea, imputed to it, that it claims objectivity and 'some kind of absolute truth' is in

---

7 This is what is generally said, but no real evidence is offered for it, and it is quite contrary to my experience. Although considering some of the customary divisions of 'sources' to be correct, I never found that it constituted any difficulty for reading the texts *as they are*, whether devotionally or liturgically or in any other way.

8 Gunn and Fewell, *Narrative in the Hebrew Bible*, 8.

9 'Fundamentalists and evangelicals are deeply suspicious of the subjective', writes Harriet Harris, *Fundamentalism and Evangelicals* (Oxford: Clarendon, 1998), 180; she goes on (p. 182) to quote J.Packer as writing: 'Evangelicals are bound, as servants of God and disciples of Christ, to oppose Subjectivism wherever they find it.'

itself a good reason for condemning it. By contrast, the interpreter is 'hopelessly subjective' and cannot be otherwise, and should delight in it.[10]

Now it is interesting that, though Gunn and Fewell are very negative towards historical criticism and consider it proper to ignore it completely in the main body of their work, they say they do not want to 'denigrate' it.[11] They recognize important values that have been achieved by it: it has been 'instrumental (following the spirit of the Renaissance) in opening the Bible to scrutiny as a document of human literature, and in that sense a profoundly "literary" study'.[12] It has a future, they continue, 'in a major reconstruction of its programme in terms of social world studies, with its positivistic ("objective") notion of "history" radically reconceived'. That is to say, historical criticism was actually a step on the path to the postmodern and, if its 'objectivism' could be eliminated, its value would be clear. Thus again 'as historical criticism has taught us', '[the social world of ancient Israel] is a world spanning many centuries and so encompassing much diversity over time'.[13] In spite of these positive achievements of historical criticism, and despite its character as 'a profoundly "literary" study', which in Gunn and Fewell's language is high praise, it remains proper and right to ignore it completely in the actual work of interpreting Hebrew narrative. In effect all they do is to denigrate it.

One other major element is the representation of historical criticism as a mode for determining meaning. The idea that historical criticism was 'the correct method to seek' the one right meaning and was thus 'the summit of the interpretational pyramid' seems to me to be remote from reality. People did not think as Gunn and Fewell imagine them to have thought. No one said the sort of things that they put into the mouths and minds of the scholars of that time. In particular, I would question whether historical criticism was thought of as a mode for determining meaning. I do not remember anyone in the relevant epoch saying this. What *was* said, and frequently, and both uttered as a complaint against historical

---

[10] Cf. the quotation below, p. 38.

[11] Gunn and Fewell, *Narrative in the Hebrew Bible*, 11.

[12] It must be admitted that their connection of it with the Renaissance is a great improvement on the infinitely repeated connection of it with the Enlightenment.

[13] Gunn and Fewell, *Narrative in the Hebrew Bible*, 193.

criticism and admitted by some of its practitioners, was the very opposite: that it did not even *try* to determine meaning. It stopped short of doing that. This characterization has some reality about it.[14] Indeed, it fits to some extent what Gunn and Fewell say about Speiser himself, but it is quite the reverse of what they say in their generalizations about historical criticism.

This, then, is the first series of points that we take from this particular example of postmodern reading: it is not only completely negative towards historical criticism, with a degree of negativity far exceeding that applied by them to any other of the various readings they survey, but it includes an expression of their ideas of what historical criticism is and how it works in the minds of its practitioners. These ideas will be valuable to us as we go on later to consider postmodernism in general.

Meanwhile, one general criticism of their work: whatever one thinks of historical criticism, their discussion is seriously unfair to Speiser, whose volume on Genesis they take as their example. For the Anchor Bible, as it was in those early days, was not intended as a full-scale commentary or indeed as a commentary at all.[15] It was a translation with notes, particularly notes needed to explain any novel wording in the translation. Speiser made it quite clear how he interpreted this format. The Book of Genesis had been worked over by many interpreters and it was not his business either to repeat their discussions or to multiply them. Only at certain particular points had he some special piece of information, commonly derived from his specialized knowledge as an Assyriologist, which might affect the translation, justify it, and explain it to the reader. Otherwise, for most of the time, he made no attempt at interpretation in depth. Gunn and Fewell are grossly unfair in the way they make fun of Speiser's notes, which were never intended as thorough interpretation, and in the way they use them to make fun of historical criticism, which they do not represent anyway.

---

[14] Cf. the somewhat analogous remarks of John Barton in the concluding sections of his *Reading the Old Testament*, 2nd edn. (London: Darton, Longman & Todd, 1996), 244–5, in particular: 'Biblical "methods" are *theories* rather than methods: theories which result from the formalizing of intelligent intuitions about the meaning of biblical texts.' It is a mistake to see source criticism, or form criticism, or the like, as 'a set of procedures which, when applied to the text, elicit its "true" meaning'. This consideration, of course, confirms my refusal to talk about 'the historical-critical method'.

[15] For fuller discussion of this aspect, see Barr, 'A Question of Method'.

When we leave aside Gunn and Fewell's utterances about historical criticism and turn to their own interpretation of biblical narrative, we find that their positive approach is one based on ideology. 'The Bible, like all other writings, is a product of culture . . . We should remember, too, that very probably literature was the product of an intellectual and economic elite . . . those attuned to the injustice of racism, classism and sexism may not find the Bible's dominant ideologies—as they reconstruct them—at all agreeable.'[16] What the Bible contains and communicates, then, is ideology, some of it rather nasty. As for the readers, they contain the same thing, ideology, too. 'Inevitably, whatever they may say about being "neutral" or "objective", readers not only bring their own ideologies to bear on the interpretations of texts, but they use texts to push their ideologies on to others.' 'As hopelessly subjective readers, we can often see in biblical characters only our own values.'[17]

To see how this works out, consider some comments of Gunn and Fewell on the character of Abraham. 'For readers who are willing to read the whole story in its final form, however, Abraham can be seen as a man of frequent surprise and great contradiction. Waffling between faith and unbelief, courage and cowardice, he meanders along supposedly in search of the fulfilment of God's promise.'[18] He is much less concerned with being a blessing to other families of the earth, than 'he is with saving his own skin'.[19] We hear again that 'Abraham is a man who has shown that he has no problem about sacrificing members of his family.'[20] How much of this is 'our own values' and how much the values of the ancient Hebrews we must leave undetermined for the present.

What remains to explain is the outcome of this sort of study. How does the Bible help us at all? The answer lies in the ironies that are discreetly hidden in the biblical text. Thus

Because of its multivocal nature, the Bible, despite its biases of gender, race/ethnicity, and class, makes provision for its own critique. [This is what we shall later see to be 'deconstruction'—J.B.] It points to its own incongruity . . . The Bible shows us not merely patriarchy, élitism and nationalism; it shows us the fragility of these ideologies through irony and

---

[16] Gunn and Fewell, *Narrative in the Hebrew Bible*, 193.   [17] Ibid. 195.
[18] Ibid. 90.   [19] Ibid. 93.   [20] Ibid. 98.

counter-voices. Xenophobic Joshua and Ezra are undermined by the book of Ruth. David is countered by Hannah and Rizpah. The patriarchy of Persia is threatened by the single woman Vashti. Voices from the margins, voices from the fissures and cracks in the text, assure us that male sovereignty is contrived and precarious, that racial/ethnic chauvinism is ultimately insupportable, that social élitism is self-deluding, that religious rectitude is self-serving . . .[21]

Thus these texts

may be uncovering a world in need of redemption and healing and a world-view much in need of change. This is the kind of reading that can transform us. If we realize that the world of the Bible is a broken world, that its people are human and therefore limited, that its social system is flawed, then we might start to see more clearly our own broken world, our own human limitations, our own defective social systems. And who knows? Maybe we shall find ourselves called to be the agents of change.[22]

Basically, then, the Bible operates through the diversity of its own ideologies and through the ironic counter-voices which are heard here and there. This may seem a 'rather thin' testimony to the importance of the Bible.[23] And, funnily enough, some at least of the examples revealed through this new and sophisticated reading method, like the idea that Ruth is a counter-voice against the ethnocentric voice of Ezra, are exactly the same as were thought by historical critics a century ago, or indeed—in this case—were familiar even before historical criticism got started. Nevertheless, postmodernists of this particular trend are not lacking in a conviction of their own importance. Describing the intellectual changes in which they consider themselves to be taking part, they write grandiosely: 'we find ourselves participants in a major epistemological shift which is, in the larger picture, but a phase in a long-standing Western debate, stretching back to Aristotle and beyond'.[24] Few of us can do better than that.

Anyway, this is an example of where we may go if historical criticism is abandoned and ideology given a central place. As you

---

[21] Ibid. 204.

[22] My trouble with this is that I can see our own broken world, our human limitations, and our defective social systems very well already, thank you, with or without help from the Bible understood as a collection of ideologies.

[23] 'Rather thin' was the comment of Gunn and Fewell on Speiser's notes, as quoted below, p. 49.

[24] Gunn and Fewell, *Narrative in the Hebrew Bible*, 10.

will have seen, actual history hardly comes into Gunn and Fewell's exposition: we just have stories with their ideologies, and it really does not matter whether any of these things happened or not.

We do not pretend that all postmodern thinking or all use of the idea of ideology must lead to the same defects which have been illustrated in this particular work by Gunn and Fewell. Nevertheless they have illustrated some of the points which have been touched on already. They are quick to repudiate 'objective truth', which illustrates Basil Mitchell's remark quoted in the last chapter. They single out historical criticism for maximum negativity, associating it with claims to attain to 'absolute truth'. As for the Bible, being a product of culture, it is very probably the product of an élite and will express the ideologies of that élite. Fortunately, the ideologies of the élite did not succeed in dominating every single portion, so that some fragments of other ideologies have survived and can be heard (with some help from such élite interpreters as Gunn and Fewell). Even this small balancing element, however, does not mean that the Bible overcomes its own biases. For readers, having their own ideologies, not only use them in interpretation but use the texts to press their own ideologies onto others. The concluding, almost evangelical and missionary note, to the effect that, given some good fortune, we may also be 'agents of change' for our broken world, is therefore rather surprising. On the other hand, ideology being so omnipresent, it will not be surprising if the entire picture of historical criticism presented by the two authors is also a piece of ideology: it certainly has the advantage of not being 'objective truth'.

For the rest of this chapter I propose to return to the idea of historical criticism and present an account of how it seems to me. To begin with I would say that I prefer the term 'biblical criticism', which would reduce the emphasis on the historical aspect.[25] Within biblical criticism there are several different operations, of which only some are strictly historical and these not all historical in the same way.

  1. The identification of strata within books or texts. Contrary to the common view, according to which biblical criticism is

---

[25] Here I agree entirely with the arguments of John Barton in *The Cambridge Companion to Biblical Interpretation* (Cambridge: Cambridge University Press, 1998), 16–19.

analytic and ought to be replaced by a holistic approach, the identification of strata is, in favourable circumstances, a holistic operation. (I say 'in favourable circumstances' because small and isolated
fragments may belong to a stratum but leave insufficient evidence
for identification.) Identification of strata is essentially a literary and
theological operation, working from vocabulary, style, cohesion,
and theological commonage. The operation is essentially a holistic
one—to envisage, for example, what constituted P—though its
effect on the particular piece of the given text is an analytic one.
The given text, nevertheless, is the starting-point, as is the case in
all operations of biblical criticism. Notice that the operation as thus
seen is not necessarily a historical one: it distinguishes, for instance,
D from P, but does not tell us which came earlier, or indeed
whether they might have come from the same time. There were,
in earlier times, theories that the Pentateuch was a composite of
two editions, both prepared by Moses himself. That D and P were
contemporary, growing up in different circles over the same
period, is a possibility that the latest critical studies leave open.

2. There is the quite different operation of deciding the date
and the circumstance of origins of texts. In this, many factors may
have to be considered. Style and language are important, but
depend to a large extent on the existence of comparable texts
which have already to some extent been dated. References to
historical events are particularly important, and this is why this
operation has been so prominent in some biblical materials
(though not all: texts having no reference to historical events, like
most of the Psalms and wisdom literature, have been much less
touched by dating operations). Something may also be done
through perception of differences along a scale of thought, an
earlier version being corrected by a later:[26] hence, for example, the
presentation of Abraham's action with Sarah in a foreign country,
as in Gen. 20, might represent further thought in comparison with
the similar incident in Gen. 12.

Such a criterion is likely to suffer mockery, because it requires
taste rather than solid evidence, but is in fact a well-established
procedure: one can distinguish a later dialogue of Plato from an

---

[26] Cf. the use of this approach by David Brown, *Tradition and Imagination* (Oxford:
Clarendon, 1999), p. 216–17; J. Barr, *The Concept of Biblical Theology* (London: SCM, 1999),
ch. 35.

earlier one, a later medieval painting from an earlier one. In the
Bible it can happen where there is no question of distinguishing
strata within books: thus one can discuss whether Colossians is
earlier than Ephesians, without dividing either of them into various 'sources'. This is one of the main fashions in which biblical
criticism can fairly be considered as 'historical'.

  3. A third operation is the provision of linguistic information.
One can add here other *realia*, such as geographical facts, knowledge about animals, and so on, but the linguistic information is the
most important. Thus, to go back to one of the most fundamental of all pieces of biblical criticism, rightly brought to mind by
Barton, the existence of 'bishops and deacons' in the New
Testament does not validate a particular church order in modern
times, since the words in question did not at that time mean
'bishop' and 'deacon' in a more modern sense.[27] This is highly
relevant to those who read the Bible in translation, but the same is
true for scholars working in the original languages: serious
mistakes can be made by reading biblical Hebrew words with the
sense that the same word had some centuries later.[28] A similar sort
of information is applied when a meaning, previously unknown, is
suggested for a Hebrew word on the basis of a Ugaritic, Akkadian,
or Arabic word of known meaning.[29] Now the application of
linguistic knowledge in this sense is hardly such as to be rightly
called 'historical criticism'. It is historical in a general sense, in that
the material adduced has to be from a historical provenance that is
relevant for the biblical passage in question. Some general knowledge of historical linguistics is required. But, though the operation
surely belongs to biblical criticism, it is misleading to describe it as
'historical criticism'. Yet, in works such as commentaries
commonly described as 'historical critical', a good deal of the
information given is of just this kind: thus, to return to Speiser, a
great deal of the annotation in his Genesis volume was of exactly
this kind. Linguistic information of this sort may indeed be
combined with the identification of strata within texts (type 1

----

[27] Barton, *Companion*, 11, 16–17.

[28] Such mistakes are now beginning to reappear in the 'literary' studies of the Hebrew
Bible, authors of which are sometimes unaware of the distinctive semantics of words in
biblical Hebrew and read them with the nuances of later (or even of modern) Hebrew.

[29] On this approach see J. Barr, *Comparative Philology and the Text of the Old Testament*
(Oxford: Clarendon, 1968).

above) or with the dating of texts (type 2 above), but this is not necessarily so. Indeed, works of conservative scholarship which reject the entire 'historical-critical' enterprise will often include this kind of material, and indeed take much pleasure in doing so.

4. A fourth operation has been one that seeks to determine the degree of *historical accuracy* that attaches to the texts in their depiction of persons and events (or, secondarily, in their relation to any persons named as their writers). This seems to me to be the fundamental operation that people usually have in mind when they speak of *'historical* criticism', with a stress on the first word. It has a double basis: on the one hand, in the fact that many parts of the Bible contain narrative information of a historical type (successions of kings, chronology, rise and fall of empires, narrations of the lives, sayings, and deaths of individuals); on the other hand, in that the religions attribute transcendental theological importance to the happening of at least some of these events. Moreover, in spite of the supreme religious importance of these events, they are narrated or mentioned in various biblical (often parallel) sources in a way that makes the absolute historical accuracy of them all difficult to maintain. Thus the comparison of the four gospels is a fundamental case for 'historical criticism' of this kind. If two or more biblical sources give a different account of what appears to be the same event, then it is a *critical* historical operation to take a decision between them. Moreover, if the two differ, it may mean that the event was different from *both* the biblical accounts of it. And, going one step further, if this is so, then an event may have been different from the biblical account of it even if only one such account of it exists. Critical historical exegesis attempts to deal with these problems.

Once again, historical criticism of type 4 is in principle separate from the other types. One can practise it without being involved in the distinguishing of strata within existing books (e.g. within any one of the existing gospels, as just mentioned). One can distinguish different strata within books without necessarily producing historical problems such as those met with in type 4. Again, the origins and dates of texts are in principle separable from historical criticism of type 4: a late text may have historically accurate information about an early event. The linguistic information, again, is certainly separable from historical criticism of this type.

Nevertheless an interpenetration of these various types is a very common occurrence. A distinguishing of strata within a book (type 1) or a dating of sources (type 2) finds itself often associated with a historical criticism of type 4: people often think, or have argued, that an early source is likely to be more accurate than one composed some centuries afterwards. Mixtures of these types are common: but we have already shown cause why the entire mixture should not be *simply* called 'historical criticism'.

Particularly is this the case in type 1, the discrimination of strata, when it applies to non-narrative material. Of a text which appears in the Bible as one Psalm (such as Ps. 19) there may be a question whether one poem is involved, or two. Decisions of this kind are hardly historical decisions: even if they result in a judgement that one part was there before the other, that is hardly a historical decision: no one can tell when things were put together or separated, no one knows the dates or times within a century or more. There is no historical evidence: it is a matter rather of the style, content, and cohesion of the text.

These thoughts are confirmed if one goes on to the various forms of biblical criticism that are often listed. Form criticism is a striking example.[30] It looks primarily not for the date or the origin of a text or for sources from which it may have been composed; it looks rather for the *function* of the text, the way in which it may have been used. That is not to say that it may not also have *effects* that come close to historical criticism; sometimes it certainly has done so. Thus, in the New Testament, if a saying appeared to have a function that would be natural in the life of the church but not in the ministry of Jesus himself, that has sometimes been taken to imply that the saying did not come from Jesus. A historical effect of form criticism on Deuteronomy is illustrated by John Barton.[31] Nevertheless in the Psalms, for instance, the overwhelming effect of form criticism was to *remove* historical-critical explanations from the interests of most scholars. In the Psalms this has been the case since the 1920s. The same has been the case in much of the literature that does not have historical content, such as Job and Proverbs. The presence of form criticism disproves the commonly repeated claim that historical criticism dominated the scene

---

[30] See already M. G. Brett, *Biblical Criticism in Crisis?* (Cambridge: Cambridge University Press, 1991), 77; and my review in *JTS* 43 (1992), 138.

[31] Barton, *Reading the Old Testament*, 40–3.

throughout much of the twentieth century. And form criticism was one of the most powerful forces; moreover, many of the other, more recent developments, have built more upon form criticism than upon the more historical types named above.

I do not wish to multiply types of biblical criticism excessively, and so I add only, in general, that there has been a great deal of genuine biblical criticism that did none of the things I have been describing, or only one of them: work that neither distinguished strata, nor decided dates and origins, nor determined the historicity of events; work that is critical in the sense that it provides a serious critique of possible or proposed interpretations, on the basis of the text itself. Of the 'types' that I have listed, the only one that would seem to be necessary for this function is type 3. I quote Barton again:

So-called 'historical criticism' has the task of telling the reader what biblical texts can or cannot mean, not merely what they did or did not mean; to say of this or that interpretation, 'No, the text cannot possibly mean that, because the words it uses will not bear that meaning.' This is potentially an iconoclastic movement, because it refuses to allow people to mean anything they like by their sacred texts. So far from this movement having had its day in the churches, it has scarcely even arrived there.[32]

We are not, then, arguing that historical criticism has been right: rather, we are arguing that the tradition of critical biblical studies has been a mixture, only part of which has been really historical. The assertions often made, as that the scholar regards the dating of the text as the first action to be taken, are only sometimes true: good examples to the contrary are given by Barton.[33] The basic critical analysis was more literary in character:

It is in the sophistication of their literary analysis that most so-called 'historical' critics excelled. When they turned to write history in the normal sense of the term their efforts were usually far less sophisticated, being often guided by theological assumptions or even by a tendency to paraphrase the biblical text (very obvious in Bright, *History of Israel*).[34]

---

[32] Barton (ed.), *Companion*, 17–18.   [33] Ibid. 14–16.

[34] Ibid. 14. Note also how Barton goes on (p. 15) to point out how 'Genetic concerns have been comparatively uncommon in the study of Paul's epistles, which the majority of commentators interpret as self-contained theological works, despite the fact that correlations between them and Paul's career as it can be established from the epistles and Acts together have also been made (see classically Knox, *Chapters in a Life of Paul*). Most interpretation of Paul has until recently been more open to the criticism that it studies him in a historical vacuum than that it is excessively historical in its interests (cf. Sanders, *Paul and Palestinian Judaism* and *Paul, the Law, and the Jewish People*).'

When such opponents of the traditional source criticism as Ivan Engnell described it, they called it 'literary criticism', and rightly.[35] This was the usual term earlier in the twentieth century.

The tradition of biblical criticism, then, was not primarily historical criticism, and, more important, it was not 'the historical-critical method'. Here again we turn to important thoughts established in the 'Conclusion' to the second edition of Barton's *Reading the Old Testament*, which cannot be too much emphasized, for, though present in essentials in his 1984 original, they have not received adequate attention in the subsequent discussion:

A method—source analysis, or form criticism, or redaction criticism, or the new canon criticism—is supposed to be a set of procedures which, when applied to the text, elicit its 'true' meaning; though, as we have seen, what kind of meaning is the true one is variously defined. But there is little doubt in the minds of many scholars, and still less in those of their students, that biblical criticism is about discovering the meaning of texts: indeed, the suggestion probably sounds so obvious as to be trivial. The main conclusion towards which my argument has been leading is that this understanding of critical method is mistaken. Biblical 'methods' are *theories* rather than methods: theories which result from the formalizing of intelligent intuitions about the meaning of biblical texts . . .

and later:

The theory—which, when codified, will become source analysis or redaction criticism or whatever—is logically subsequent to the intuition about meaning. It may lead to useful insights about other texts . . . but it can never be a technique which can always be used with the assurance that it will yield correct results.[36]

Thus scholars have 'become disillusioned with each of the methods they have committed themselves to', because 'they have asked too much of them' and have converted 'startlingly original insights' into 'pedestrian "methods" which are supposed to provide a key to everything in the Old Testament'. The disappointment in turn leads to the fury with which 'each new method tries to abolish its predecessors', notably so canon criticism and structuralism in recent times.

---

[35] Cf. I. Engnell, 'The Traditio-Historical Method in Old Testament Research', in his *Critical Essays on the Old Testament* (London: SPCK, 1970), 3–11. Engnell's thinking on this matter went back to a much earlier time than the publication of this article in this form.

[36] Barton, *Reading the Old Testament*, 2nd edn., 244.

This is entirely convincing, but in the context of the present work it suggests a further extension.[37] There is no 'historical-critical method'. Biblical criticism is not a method. When related to discussions of postmodernism, this (very correct) observation takes on a new importance. For the hermeneutical philosopher Gadamer, with his book *Truth and Method* (*Wahrheit und Methode*), widely quoted in works on biblical studies,[38] has made this a central criterion:

It follows from this intermediate position in which hermeneutics operates that its work is not to develop a procedure of understanding, but to clarify the conditions in which understanding takes place. But those conditions are not of the nature of a 'procedure' or a method, which the interpreter must of himself bring to bear on the text, but rather they must be given.

One of the basic thoughts is that it is the villainous Enlightenment that ordained that knowledge should be subjected to criteria of method. Biblical studies being understood as 'the historical-critical method', they fall under this judgement. Since, however, as we have seen, biblical criticism is *not* a method but a group of theories that formalize valuable intuitions, the Gadamerian criticism, whether valid or not in other respects, ceases to be relevant to this aspect of biblical study.[39]

It may be asked, 'If biblical criticism is not a procedure or method for discovering the meaning, from where then does the meaning come?' What biblical criticism furnishes is not a meaning where there formerly was none, but a means of criticism of those with which the reader approaches the text. Meanings, more exactly alleged meanings, are there already, having been provided (most commonly) by the churches or synagogue and the theological traditions, sometimes, but less commonly, by other educational instances, by current world-views and so on. What happens in biblical criticism is that these previously given understandings

---

[37] I should say that I have not discussed this extension with John Barton, who is therefore not to be blamed for any misuse I may have made of his ideas.

[38] See e.g. A. Thiselton's article, 'Biblical Studies and Theoretical Hermeneutics', in Barton, *Companion*, esp. 100–4.

[39] H.-G. Gadamer, *Truth and Method* (London: Sheed & Ward, 1975), 263. Cf. the place taken by this quotation in the discussion of Z. Bauman, *Intimations of Postmodernity* (London: Routledge, 1992), 129. For the suggested influence of Gadamer on biblical theology, see Barr, *Concept of Biblical Theology*, ch. 28.

are placed in hypothetical status, and the constraints of the verbal form, the literary genre, the possible historical relationships, are pointed out. From such a process, carried out many times and at many levels, potential boundaries for interpretations are worked out. This applies in the same way for historical and for theological questions.

This brings us back to the postmodern positions as alleged by Gunn and Fewell, and by many others. Central to the objections against traditional biblical criticism is its supposed claim to be 'objective' or to attain 'absolute truth'. Or, as others put it, it claims to be 'value-neutral' or 'value-free'.[40] But where are these claims to be value-neutral and value-free? Take the case of Wellhausen, commonly used as the prime example of a historical critic. According to widely agreed opinion, he looked with favour on the early, 'natural', religion of Israel, and had a dislike for the late, priestly, developments. Having thus the advantage of being thoroughly 'prejudiced' (a term given some favour by Gadamer, and, following him, by hermeneutically minded evangelicals),[41] he ought to be praised for this. He was doing the right thing. One cannot blame him both for value-neutrality and for preferring one set of values over another. And Wellhausen is only one among many. We have already seen other examples, as quoted above from Barton. We can usefully add the following: 'E. P. Sanders's trenchant criticisms of most scholars who have written on Jesus and Paul show that their reconstructions have normally been heavily influenced by their religious beliefs: by the need to show the uniqueness of Jesus, or the essentially Lutheran character of Paul's teaching.'[42] And to this we can easily add the opinion of many Jewish scholars, who perceive Christian historical criticism as heavily value-loaded with traditional Christology and

[40] So, e.g., among many others, E. Schüssler Fiorenza, *Bread not Stone* (Boston: Beacon, 1984), 106–8; thus, 'traditional historical critical biblical scholarship that prides itself on being impartial, objective, and value-neutral' (p. 107). Carroll, in Barton, *Companion*, 54, appears to say that not only the critical scholar and his product was supposed to be 'value-free' but the Bible itself was supposed to be 'value-free': 'No longer inscribed as a value-free work, the Bible is now seen as the construction of a writing elite in the Persian or Greek period . . .' But Carroll surely cannot mean this: *nobody* thought of the Bible as 'value-free'. I suppose he must mean: the Bible was formerly thought of as a perfect and exact registration of history and thus not affected by anyone's 'values'. Note his use of the verb 'inscribe', a true symptom of postmodernism.
[41] Harris, *Fundamentalism and Evangelicals*, 279.
[42] Barton, *Companion*, 15.

Trinitarianism, plus traditional disparagement of Judaism (while many conservative Christians see the same phenomenon as loaded with the values of secularism, scepticism, deism, and the rest).[43]

What has been mistakenly represented as a claim by biblical criticism to 'objectivity' or to 'absolute truth' might be more correctly represented as something else: the truth behind it was the ability to turn to the Bible in itself as distinct from the interpretations of it by the churches. This was not absolute objectivity but it was a limited sort of objectivity in that particular direction. And of course it can be argued that there were other influences which could impinge upon interpretation just as church traditions of meaning had done. But it is unrealistic to place these other influences on the same level. Until the mid-twentieth century (at least), the churches were overwhelmingly greater in their power to influence and control the understanding of the Bible than any other instance. There were other ideological influences, but no other ideological influence that focused directly, deliberately, and constantly on this task, namely that of saying what the Bible meant. And, though the churches were clear that the Bible was the authority, in their practice what they imparted was not the Bible in itself but the particular church's, the particular theology's, the particular tradition's understanding of its meaning. On the other hand, in turning to the Bible in itself, critical scholarship was still following what the churches had *professed*, namely that the interpretation was subject to the biblical text.

Now it is of course possible that, though biblical criticism was often by no means value-free, scholars thought and claimed that it was. This is the fairly standard postmodern allegation. But then it has to be *shown* that this was thought by critical scholars. Just to say that they thought it is not enough. And I very much doubt if they thought it much of the time or in many regards, though they may have said something of the sort from time to time. When Gunn and Fewell say that historical critics thought that their 'method' led to 'absolute truth', I think that is purely ridiculous. That Speiser considered his information (which they cite) about words for dogs in Akkadian to be 'absolute truth' only shows their own carelessness about truth, even non-absolute truth, concerning the people they are writing about. If one had seriously asked most of the traditional

[43] For the primary recent Jewish source see J. D. Levenson, *The Hebrew Bible, The Old Testament, and Historical Criticism* (Louisville, Ky.: Westminster, 1993).

historical critics what they considered to be the way to absolute truth, they would mostly have answered 'by faith in Christ'; some might have added to this some philosophical principle, as has been the case in all or almost all theologies. But that they would have said, or that they thought, that the historical-critical method was the unique path to absolute truth is too much to believe. In other words, with the assertion that historical criticism was thought to be the path to absolute truth we are face to face with *ideology*. And the authors concerned can hardly object to this result, because ideology is just what they like and prize and admit.

A helpful step at this point may be to turn once again to Barton's account of reading:

Texts are perceived as having certain sorts of meaning—or, just as interestingly, as failing to convey meaning—by reading them with certain vague expectations about genre, coherence and consistency, which are either confirmed and clarified, or disappointed and frustrated. Then reading begins again, this time with a sharper focus; and at the end of the process there emerges a distinct impression of what the text means, together with an explanatory theory as to how it comes to mean it.[44]

The importance of this, as I see it, is that it points towards an acceptance that explanations and decisions are partial and tentative. The accounts of things given by Gunn and Fewell are distinctly totalitarian: what people thought to be relevant or to contribute towards an explanation or to be confirmatory data or parallels—as is the case in Speiser's examples as cited above—is transformed in their language into a claim to 'absolute truth'.

The same applies to the familiar disagreement about objectivity. Objectivity is bitterly opposed in postmodernism, and the reluctance to grant any measure of validity to it at all leaves the door open to unlimited deception and propaganda. Would it not be better to grant that some degree of objectivity is better than none at all? A similar argument occurs to me in reading the passage from Schüssler Fiorenza quoted above. She by no means rejects historical criticism entirely, and affirms that 'we need to use the methods and means of historical-critical scholarship while at the same time scrutinizing and contesting its androcentric philosophical-theological presuppositions, perspectives, and goals'.[45] (She does

---

44 Barton, *Reading the Old Testament*, 244.
45 Schüssler Fiorenza, *Bread not Stone*, 106.

not here give evidence for the existence of these perspectives and goals: these are, perhaps, to be assumed.) But she goes on to object to historical criticism because (according to her) it claims to be 'impartial, objective, and value-free'. It is clear, however, that her real interest is in a particular aspect, i.e. that it is androcentric, '*biased* to the extent that its intellectual discourse and scholarly frameworks are determined only by male perspectives primarily of the dominant class'.[46] But, we may ask, what evidence is there that this has affected *all* historical-critical decisions? Does she mean, for instance, that it was male perspectives that distinguished J from P or identified the Q document in the gospels? If so, how? If not, then does it not mean that historical criticism was only *partially* biased: maybe it obscured the role of women, but identifications like those of J, P, and Q were not specifically directed to that object. In fact, though she does not say this, the obscuration of the role of women was probably the same in androcentric biblical interpretation whether it was historical-critical or not (and this I think to be in fact the case). Why then does she turn on historical criticism specifically? Presumably, because she thinks that it claims objectivity. Androcentric scholarship, it is implied, would be quite all right if it made it clear that it was biased from the beginning. But what bias specifically *against women* is involved in distinguishing between J and P? In fact she goes on to say that 'a feminist reading of biblical texts and the reconstruction of their historical-social worlds therefore need to utilize *all available historical-critical methods and means of inquiry*, in order to reconstruct the historical-theological tendencies and rhetorical aims of the redactional process of the history of the tradition'.[47] So in fact 'historical-critical methods', and not only some of them but 'all available' ones, are all right after all. And no wonder, for another factor enters: according to Schüssler Fiorenza, the bias against women is not particularly a product of historical criticism or indeed of any other interpretative approach, for it is factually there in the New Testament texts themselves:

The formation of early Christian traditions and their redactional processes followed certain androcentric interests and theological perspectives. This androcentric selection and transmission of early Christian traditions seems to have engendered the historical marginality of women. New Testament

---

[46] Ibid. 107.   [47] Ibid. 112 (my italics).

texts are not an accurate reflection of the historical reality of women's leadership and participation in the early Christian movement.[48]

If this is so, the bias of past historical-critical scholarship has not distorted the New Testament, but has continued in the tradition of the documents themselves. The future feminist investigation will have to be truly historical-critical in the traditional sense, penetrating behind the existing documents and *reconstructing* things as they really were, 'the historical reality of women's leadership and participation'. 'In order to break the hold of androcentric biblical texts over us, it is necessary to *uncover* the mechanisms and *incoherencies* of such texts, to see the *inconsistencies of our sources*' and so on.[49] But will the results of this 'feminist model of historical reconstruction'[50] not be 'what really happened' in the ancient church? If not, what use are they? She is back in the 'Rankean paradigm' from which she seeks to escape (p. 114).[51]

We spoke earlier of the importance of theory in postmodern argument. Nowhere is this clearer than in talk about historical criticism. ' "Historical criticism" ', Barton writes, 'is thus defined [in the postmodern response to it] in order to invite this response.'[52] Undoubtedly so. Most descriptions of historical criticism published today are creations of its enemies. And, Barton rightly adds, 'The usual perception today is that historical criticism derives from the Enlightenment'.[53] But why does that matter?

For most of those who argue in this way, it matters because they think: a thing can be explained by explaining the origins from which it arose. Historical criticism had its origins in the Enlightenment: therefore it has the characteristics of the Enlightenment.[54] This is the true historicist approach: ironically

---

[48] Schüssler Fiorenza, *Bread not Stone*, 111.   [49] Ibid. 113 (my italics).
[50] Ibid. 112.
[51] Ibid. 114. Ranke, of course, did not himself conform to the 'Rankean paradigm', which is a product of distinctively American ideology. I pointed this out in my *Old and New in Interpretation* (London: SCM, 1966), 177, where I wrote: 'The "positivist" image based on Ranke was in large degree an American creation; long disputed in German scholarship, it has nevertheless been permitted to provide theological thinking with its paradigm of nineteenth-century historiography.' I quoted G. G. Iggers, 'The Image of Ranke in American and German Historical Thought', *History and Theory*, 2 (1962), 17–40. The reuse of the same image in the 1980s by so scholarly a writer as Schüssler Fiorenza only shows its tenacity.   [52] Barton (ed.), *Companion*, 14.   [53] Ibid. 16.
[54] A good example is F. Watson's article 'Enlightenment', *DBI* 191–4, a selective depiction clearly planned not in order to describe the Enlightenment as a whole but to enable readers 'to understand the superficially obvious and self-evident principles of the discipline' and 'the foundations upon which modern biblical studies still rest' (p. 194). Cf. my article 'Allegory and Historicism', *JSOT* 69 (1996), 105–20.

so, because 'historicism' is just one of the main faults blamed upon
historical criticism, and is an approach rightly repudiated by any
right-thinking postmodernist. Whatever the case in the past of the
subject, when one looks at the scholars who have used historical
criticism in their work in this century it is obvious that the
Enlightenment heritage has been a very small element in their
thought, if it existed there at all. Who would be so lunatic as to
classify Gerhard von Rad, for instance, with the rationalist and
scientific spirit of the Enlightenment? And, if one must trace a
movement back to previous stages, what about Romanticism,
which came between the Enlightenment and modern times?
Romanticism, in a general sense, would be a much more appropriate setting, with Herder as a start and the much publicized
influence of Hegel on Vatke, leading on appropriately to
Wellhausen and certainly to von Rad in recent times.[55]

But the whole attempt at historicist explanation is based on a
biased selection from within the past and should be ignored. More
serious would be a biographical study of typical critical scholars of
the past, to see what they had actually thought, as distinct from the
fictions imposed upon them as a generality by postmodern writers.
We would find, as is obvious, that the guiding principles to which
most of them adhered were principles of Reformational
Christianity—as has been obvious to Jewish commentators
throughout. We could take a hallowed principle such as *sola scriptura*, which means that the Bible can and should be consulted on
its own: apart on the one hand from any official church *magis-
terium*, and apart on the other hand from any overriding authority
of the later interpretation of the biblical documents. (The
Reformers had, of course, in fact been very substantially guided by
the patristic interpretation of the Bible; but that is not what came
out in the post-Reformational confessions, in which the Bible
itself, and the confession itself, were primary, and the patristic

---

[55] Eichrodt, a major figure in the theology of the Old Testament, took it in this way.
He took the product of the older dogmatic tradition together with Enlightenment 'ratio-
nalism' as one unit, which ended up with a 'meaningless confusion of *disiecta membra*'. The
historical approach—which he by no means glorified, since it was his aim to react against
it—was in its time a correct reaction against this 'rationalist' domination. It began with
Herder and de Wette and reached its high-water mark with Wellhausen and his school. It
'dismissed once for all the "intellectualist" approach, which looked only for doctrine, and
sought by an all-inclusive survey to grasp the totality of religious life in all its richness of
expression'. See W. Eichrodt, *Theology of the Old Testament* (London: SCM, 1961), i. 28–9.

interpretation secondary, if mentioned at all.) The historical-
critical emphasis on 'the original' comes straight out of this: the
original writers were what mattered, and how they were interpreted in later ages might be interesting but had no kind of authority. Authorial intention of the original writers was paramount.[56]
Add to *sola scriptura* the equally hallowed principle of 'comparing
scripture with scripture', and you end up—not necessarily, but
very fairly—with what people like Wellhausen had done. Add to
this the affirmation of the 'plain sense' as intended by the writers,
and the rejection of allegorical interpretation, and one has the lines
which lead naturally to biblical criticism, whether or not the
Enlightenment had any influence.[57] The controversial critical
scholar W. Robertson Smith, for example, was entirely convinced
of the rightness of evangelical Protestantism.

One or two other remarks remain to be added on the above
themes. First, the attempt to explain historical criticism on the
grounds of its inheritance from the Enlightenment is a clear
instance of intrusion of a general historical ideology or world-view
and the use of it as a criterion in matters of biblical interpretation
and theology. For it depends not only on the pseudo-historical
explanation of biblical criticism as arising from the Enlightenment,
but also on the assumption that the Enlightenment was an evil and
a total disaster in every aspect. For, once one admits that the
Enlightenment did some sort of good in some ways, then it opens
the question of whether biblical criticism (if it did derive from this
source) might not have been a part of the good that came out of
it. And one cannot on theological grounds simply condemn the
Enlightenment as an attack on all religion, for one has to consider
the positions of modern theologians who maintain that the
Enlightenment put into effect aspects of the total Christian
programme which earlier stages, including the Reformation, had
failed to carry out. Add to this the fact that the Reformation was,
in important ways, a major contributory *cause* of the
Enlightenment and support to it. The idea that mere association
with the Enlightenment is enough to condemn any movement of
thought or interpretation is pure (mistaken) ideology.

---

[56] B. S. Childs, *Biblical Theology of the Old and New Testaments* (London: SCM, 1992),
47, writes that 'Calvin identified the literal sense with the author's intention, which
accounted for his stress on the need for careful literary, historical and philological analysis
of each biblical writer.'   [57] Cf. Barton, *Companion*, 16–18.

It is interesting, however, to note that the anti-Enlightenment arguments now take two forms. In Old Testament theology they are well represented by the contrary positions of Childs and Brueggemann. The first form, represented by Childs, seems basically to long for a return to a pre-Enlightenment mentality. The Reformation is the ideal, though we have occasional later eruptions of the same ideal, notably in the German theological debates of the 1930s. Very occasionally Childs will use a postmodern argument, looking forward with pleasure to a postmodern, postcritical world in which all vestiges of thoughts going back to the Enlightenment will be destroyed.[58] But his ventures into hope from the postmodern world have not brought much success, as we see in his support for the more 'literary' approach to the Bible, which, as he soon found out, came to disaster even faster than the historical-critical pattern which he had hoped it might replace.[59] This basically pre-Enlightenment stance is one possibility.

The other is a more fully postmodern position: among Old Testament theologians it is represented by Brueggemann. He also disdains historical-critical approaches, hardly bothering even to mention them or to attack them as Childs does. On the other hand he sees that the Reformation in itself provides no refuge: its position about the Bible is unstable, it was (he maintains) anti-Jewish, and it is too tangled up with the Enlightenment to be relied on. So Brueggemann's attack on the Enlightenment comes entirely from the postmodern side.[60]

I remarked earlier that, in spite of the reduction of attention given to traditional biblical criticism, there was also a resurgence of the same in a very absolute mode. In addition, I pointed out, much of the change in attitude to such matters as the origins of the Pentateuch or the date of the various historical books has actually come from a *continuation* of the traditional approaches, though with different results. In some respects, therefore, what has happened is not so much an abandonment of traditional criticism and its replacement by newer approaches, but a convergence (in certain respects) between the two. Since in the next chapter we shall be concentrating on the 'revisionist' approaches to the history of Israel, it will be useful at this point to say something more about

---

[58] See *JSOT* 46 (1990), 7.   [59] See Childs, *Biblical Theology*, 204–6.
[60] On this see Barr, *Concept of Biblical Theology*, ch. 31.

changes of opinion which have come about through renewed application of the traditional approaches. These can be illustrated from studies of the Pentateuch.[61]

It is often said that the traditional analysis of the Pentateuch was in terms of the four sources J, E, D, and P. But if one was to think of four coexisting strands running through the entire material, this would be a mistaken impression. From an early time E was considered to exist only at limited points, or not to be clearly distinguishable. Moreover, from the mid-century on many followed the view that D was separate from the other sources: it existed in Deuteronomy and was connected with Joshua and the later books, which came to be called the Deuteronomistic History, but scarcely existed in Genesis–Numbers, while the other sources existed only marginally in Deuteronomy (primarily, at the very end). This meant that for many purposes one could work with a very simple division in Genesis–Numbers, between 'old material' and 'late material', roughly speaking, between JE and P. P was, at all stages, the easiest to identify, the most difficult to regard as dubious.

J was thought to be the earliest source. What happened in the later twentieth century was, for one thing, that the date of J, which had been connected by von Rad with the Solomonic Enlightenment and thus placed in the tenth–ninth centuries, came to be moved to a later time, by various scholars but especially by the Swiss scholar H. H. Schmid, who brought the composition of J into contact with the Deuteronomic History, placed by him in the exilic period.[62] Moreover, signs of Deuteronomic influence came to be detected in passages that had formerly been regarded as J. In addition, the influence of Deuteronomic redaction in the historical books came to be seen as divided into various strands and currents, the effect of which might be to bring more of the content of these books down to a later period.

One very influential redeployment, as we might call it, of the Pentateuchal material has come from E. Blum, who, following guidance from R. Rendtorff, ends up by assembling the material under two great compositions, KD and KP, a D-composition and a P-composition.[63] KD 'was composed subsequent to the

---

[61] For fuller information see E. W. Nicholson, *The Pentateuch in the Twentieth Century* (Oxford: Clarendon, 1999).   [62] See ibid. 97.

[63] See ibid. 124, 202–4.

Deuteronomistic history'.[64] What was formerly regarded as the independent source P is actually not a source nor a redaction but a 'layer', a reworking of KD.[65]

It is not my purpose to discuss or evaluate these proposals; I simply report them, as proposals that have been widely influential. What I want to stress is the other side: namely, that these proposals, whether right or wrong, are a result of the basic continuance of the *kind* of perceptions, evaluations, and comparisons that have been basic to Pentateuchal research for most of two centuries. Thus, to take the example of Rendtorff himself, he is much less interested in origins, often supposed to be the obsession of historical critics, and he actually prefers to find a late date, which fits with his emphasis on the closeness of the text to later Judaism.[66] His values may be said to be different, but in actual procedure he is very close to traditional historical-critical approaches. He perceives numerous stages of working-over to which the story complexes have been subjected—and the comparative shortness of the time factor makes these more conspicuous (and more difficult to accept). Editorial additions, glosses, and combinations are found very frequently. Nicholson writes of him that he 'finds evidence of several stages of development in the promise of land, of an earlier and a later formulation of the promise of blessing for others through the descendants of the patriarchs, and of two mutually independent groups of formulations of the promise of numerous progeny'.[67] This production of numerous stages of development leading to the present text is characteristic of historical criticism as most people conceive of it.

Thus things like the adoption of a late date for biblical sources in recent scholarship arise from the convergence of two quite different traditions: on the one hand the continuance of Pentateuchal criticism and other analogous operations, with basically the same methods as before but with a different vision and values, an alteration of course in which one can see little if any influence from postmodern values, and on the other hand the influence of literary reading practices, revisionist historical approaches, and ideological critical aims, all of which may be associated with

---

[64] Ibid. 124.   [65] Ibid. 202.
[66] Cf. Barr, *Concept of Biblical Theology*, 442–7.
[67] Nicholson, *Pentateuch*, 107, cf. 113, 116.

postmodernism, though in varying degrees. It is therefore important, when we study revisionist historiography in the next chapter,
to bear in mind that it is not the sole influence in the recent
changes of the scholarly mind. In many individuals, in fact, there
may well be a mixture of the two.

The striking thing about biblical criticism is that it is not really a
theological problem any more. The majority of central theologians
find no difficulty in it. Emil Brunner, back in the 1940s, agreed
that it was entirely wholesome; the central Dutch Calvinist
Hendrikus Berkhof, in the late 1960s, accepted it fully; David
Brown, in the end of the century, though (rightly) doubting some
of its manifestations, sees it as imparting a view into the historically
conditioned character of the Bible which is positively important.
They recognize, rightly, that, whatever biblical scholars do, people
as a whole have a historical sense and are interested in the historical quality, high or low as it may be, of many things they read in
the Bible. Contrary to what is often said, the symbiosis of biblical
criticism with mainstream theology has been remarkably successful. Among theologians, only certain individuals have really challenged it. Strikingly, it is not principally from doctrinal
theologians, who have generally accepted it in a general sense and
appreciated that, whatever the details, it has made clear the histor-
ical-conditionedness of the Bible, but from biblical scholars themselves, with their strife over methods, that the recent opposition to
historical criticism has come.

The basis for that opposition is, in many respects, ideological
rather than either practical or theological. But before we concentrate on ideology we must look at the history of Israel.

4

The History of Israel

AMONG the various operations commonly classed together as
'historical criticism' I classified as type 4 the assessment of the
historical accuracy of the depiction of events, persons, and sayings
in the Bible, and suggested that this might be, for most people, the
fundamental one among the operations that they have in mind
when they talk of 'historical criticism'. It may also, we may add,
be the most important from the angle of religious apologetics.
People ask, 'Can we be sure that the walls of Jericho really fell
down when the Israelites marched around them seven times?'
'How do we know that there was such a person as Joseph, who
became "chief ruler" in Egypt?' 'Is it a fact that the army of
Sennacherib was destroyed overnight by some divine action?'
'Which of the sayings of Jesus have "the critics" left for us to
believe that they were actually spoken by him?' Though this
group of questions is important, I have left them aside in the previous chapter. They are well illustrated in the current controversies
about the history of Israel, to which we now turn.

As already indicated in Ch. 1, there is at the present time some
considerable controversy about the historical character of the
Hebrew Bible, and especially about its portrayal of the earlier periods: and by 'earlier' we mean not only the primeval tales such as
the first part of the book of Genesis but essentially the more central
materials such as the books of Samuel/Kings. Revisionist historians have argued that, of the narrative material right down to the
end of the Judaean kingdom, very little depends on actual historical knowledge, while the major part is generated out of theological or ideological concerns from a later period. One main reason
for this judgement is that confirmation from extra-biblical sources
is said to be lacking. The result is that the main body of Hebrew
text had its origins in a late period, say in the Persian empire or
even, more extremely, in the Hellenistic period. If we want to
know something about the history of the earlier times we should

turn not to the Bible but to extra-biblical sources and especially to archaeology.

This position clearly has an effect on our idea of the historicity of the narrative material. First, although (as we have seen, and as has generally been admitted) a late source may contain an accurate version where an earlier source is faulty, the probability of this becomes smaller with scale: if large bodies of material are separated by seven or eight hundred years from the events recorded in them, the chances that they are accurate may seem to be less than if the separation was of only one hundred years. Second, the argument in revisionist work has been based less on sceptical assessment of this or that detail, and more on the *general* assertion that the material is ideological in character. To this general assertion, indeed, many arguments on points of detail are added. Nevertheless the overarching force of the general assertion is obvious. This makes a difference, perhaps, in comparison with much of the older critical scholarship. The position is in this sense more a definitional one: the texts *by their own nature* reflect the ideology of a much later time rather than direct memories or archival sources close to the events. It is not a matter of going through the text and regretfully eliminating this or that event when we come to it: rather, we are told we should start with the awareness that the texts are ideological material from which we may learn what the authors of their time may have thought, and that there is no reason to expect that they will truly represent the situations and events of early times.

Thus sometimes ideology is given priority over the possibility of other explanations. One interesting instance is the handling of the case of Omri, king of Israel, by Robert Carroll, one of his three main examples in one particular article.[1] The biblical depiction of Omri is a brief and stereotyped account (1 Kings 16: 16–28), and this is peculiar because he was mentioned in foreign sources and is known to have been a very important monarch. Carroll writes: 'The failure to treat Omri adequately is a good indicator of the ideological nature of the biblical text and a serious mark against the historical reliability of the biblical writings.' The ideology implied is Deuteronomistic and southern/Judaean, anti-Israelite. Carroll's complaint is not that the biblical passage

---

contains historical falsehoods, but that it is too short. 'A text which can dismiss him [Omri] so briefly is itself fatally flawed as an ideological document untrustworthy on the subject of history.' The importance of this passage is that it illustrates the alacrity with which hostile ideology is adopted as the obvious explanation. There are many possible reasons one could suggest why the passage about Omri should be brief, but no others are even considered.[2] The approach through ideology is here the preferred approach.

There are other factors which were only just touched on and have to be mentioned here again. Revisionist history urges that history should not be done so close to the Bible as was the case in earlier *Histories of Israel*. The Bible should be only one source among others. Inscriptions and archaeology are of great importance, especially in that, unlike many biblical texts, they can be dated (not without disagreements, however, as we shall see). Even more far-reaching is the principle that we should not be writing the history *of Israel* at all: it should be the history of all the peoples of Syria/Palestine, or however we denominate the area. By even *trying* to write a history of Israel we are 'privileging' (again the postmodernist word) one people and neglecting ('marginalizing' is the correct word) the others, just as we are privileging the Jewish Bible and ignoring other evidence. The case in this form is argued particularly by K. W. Whitelam. He sets the historiographical process, as it has been, in parallel with the establishment of the modern state of Israel and the concomitant 'silencing' of the Palestinians. His thought derives quite a lot from the work of the anti-orientalist Edward Said.[3]

And we should emphasize that the revisionists are by no means

---

[2] Jeroboam and Ahab also, for example, were presumably disapproved by the same ideology, but plenty is written about them. As for Omri's building of Samaria, which Carroll says to be 'a metonym of viciousness and representative of anti-YHWHist culture' in biblical symbolic terms, I do not see why this should be the case for *all* mentions of Samaria: more likely, the writer here mentioned it as a rather noble and memorable event, which it surely was.

[3] For readers who may be unfamiliar with these terms, I should explain that part of Said's argument is that Western orientalists have done their work in such a way as to fit oriental society into a Western framework and thus to obscure the reality, or, in postmodern terms, to 'silence the voice' of the people being talked about. For Whitelam, similarly, the writing of the history of Palestine and Syria in ancient times as if it was the history *of Israel* is fully analogous to ways in which the state of Israel has obscured and denied the reality of Palestinian identity.

to be classed as one homogeneous group: there are probably substantial differences between one and another, as we shall see. But, just to name the persons commonly mentioned, we should think of Philip Davies of Sheffield, of N. P. Lemche of Copenhagen, of Thomas L. Thompson, an American teaching, at the time of writing, in Copenhagen, and of K. W. Whitelam, already mentioned, teaching in the University of Stirling. Others who have some affinities and have been brought into the discussion are the late Gösta Ahlström of Sweden and Chicago, and the Italian scholar Giovanni Garbini. Some differences between them will be mentioned below.

We find, then, the surprising position that—to oversimplify it somewhat—some theologians want to be sure that the Bible relates history because they think that this is important for theology, while some historians argue that, because it is theology, it cannot be history. This seems to be a puzzle that requires investigation.

The position should not be entirely surprising, since some sort of development of this kind has been going on for a long time. By older tradition (up to the eighteenth century or so) the Bible was—among other things—an exact historical manual going right back to Methuselah, to Adam, and to the seven days of creation.[4] It is not much over a century ago that authoritative voices in the churches began to modify this, saying that later sources such as the gospels were entirely reliable historically but that the earlier chapters of Genesis, say down to Abraham, were not meant to be taken literally.[5]

From the mid-twentieth century on, the sequence from Abraham down through the descent into Egypt, Moses and the Exodus, the entry into Canaan, and the time of the Judges had to some extent gone the same way (Martin Noth's *History of Israel* was originally published in 1950 and forms a good marker). All that material belonged to 'the Traditions of the Twelve-Tribe

---

4 On the Bible as a manual of universal history in early modernity see K. Scholder, *The Birth of Modern Critical Theology* (London: SCM, 1990), esp. ch. 4, pp. 65–87; note e.g. his statement, 'If the Bible was already no textbook of mathematics and physics, it was certainly a historical textbook. It was a textbook of incomparable status and unique quality' (p. 68).

5 This position was taken e.g. in the historic volume, E. Gore (ed.), *Lux Mundi* (London: John Murray, 1889).

Confederation' but, though it contained real historical material, it was in essence not 'history of Israel'. It was rather the body of sacral traditions around which the later Israel organized itself, plus some individual tribal memories of contacts, usually conflicts, with the Canaanites.

Thus it came to be widely accepted that the starting-point for the knowable history was when the union of twelve tribes with the name 'Israel' was already established in Palestine. From that position Noth could reach back and discuss the traditions of the tribal confederacy, amphictyony as he called it, traditions that went back to the Exodus, to the patriarchs before that time, to Mount Sinai. But effective narration of history began around 1200, and actually there is not much detail until we come to Saul, David, and the beginnings of the kingdom, starting with the Philistine invasion about 1,000 BC. Only with the reigns of David and Solomon do we seem to be in real history, and Noth then narrates it in terms that often stand very close to the text of Samuel and Kings themselves. According to him,[6] the earliest event in the history of Israel that can be exactly dated is the death of Solomon. This was 'in the course of the year that ran from autumn 926 to autumn 925'.[7]

With David, Noth writes, we have a quite new stage in the process by which Israel passed to political power development, and correspondingly we have a new kind of historical writing. Up till then, even into the time of Saul, we had in essence only popular

---

[6] Here Noth followed an earlier scholar, J. Begrich, *Die Chronologie der Könige von Israel und Juda* (Tübingen: Mohr, 1929). This exactitude in dating was optimistic, since biblical chronology may contain a substantial element that is theoretical or schematic rather than accurate: see J. Barr, 'Why the World was created in 4004 BC: Archbishop Ussher and Biblical Chronology', in *Bulletin of the John Rylands University Library*, 67 (1985), 575–608; 'Biblical Chronology: Legend or Science?', Ethel M. Wood Lecture, University of London, 1987; 'Luther and Biblical Chronology', in *Bulletin of the John Rylands University Library*, 72 (1990), 51–67; J. R. M. Hughes, *Secrets of the Times* (Sheffield: JSOT, 1990). The schematic character of biblical chronology does, indeed, constitute a factor, and not a negligible one, that may support the ideological view of the biblical narrative. The figures of forty years each for David and Solomon are very likely to be schematic, and in this sense stand in contrast with the years given for all other kings of Judah and Israel. Cf. in the New Testament the schematic character of the genealogy of Jesus in Matt. 1. But P. R. Davies, *In Search of 'Ancient Israel'*, JSOTSup 148 (Sheffield: JSOT, 1992; 2nd edn. 1995), exaggerates in saying that in the Bible 'chronology is almost an indication of *non*-historicity' (p. 27); there is no plausible ideological explanation for many of the numbers of years given for the kings after Solomon.

[7] M. Noth, *History of Israel* (New York: Harper, 1958), 225.

narratives and cultic traditions, while the David tradition is for the most part real historical writing. Thus in the reigns of David and Solomon Noth's account, as already observed, follows quite closely the detail of the biblical text.

Seen this way, then, we had a generally good historical narrative from about 1,000 BC on. What revisionist historians do is to move this starting-point a few centuries later, or, going rather further, to say that there was no starting-point at all. The source that covered the kingdoms after Solomon is the one contained in Samuel/Kings and now commonly called the Deuteronomistic History: that is, it had a framework roughly corresponding to the ideas and laws of the book of Deuteronomy, a framework into which older materials had been fitted. But, by other, closely related, critical theories, Deuteronomy itself was a latish source and connected with the finding of a law-book by King Josiah as late as 622. It was thus related to an important religious reform carried out by him, not long before the end of the Judaean kingdom. But if this great narrative came as it stands from a circle related to Deuteronomy, then perhaps the stories it encloses are stories designed to inculcate exactly the viewpoint, the ideology, of that circle?

And even that circle may perhaps be moved to a time later than King Josiah. Quite long ago some scholars placed Deuteronomy *after* the beginning of the Babylonian exile. Moreover, the older critical position, though questioning in regard to so many things, was rather accepting towards the reality of Josiah's religious reform as described in 2 Kings. The historicity of the narrative about the reform was basic to the dating of Deuteronomy, pivotal for the entire criticism of the Pentateuch. But what if some aspects of that narrative were also ideological? What if the actual Josiah carried out only a small part of the reform attributed to him, while the rest represented the *aspirations* of a reform group in later times, just as (it might be) other traditions had tried to push back the idea of some of the same reforms to the yet earlier 'reforming' King Hezekiah? So one can see how the idea of a historically valid total narrative of almost the entire kingdom within the Bible could tend to evaporate. It is a process similar in kind to what had already happened to other parts of the Bible.[8]

---

[8] This last argument is important, because it is used by revisionists to support their case: thus Davies, *In Search of 'Ancient Israel'*, 26–7, writes: 'One obvious case is the so-called

Let us take an example of the sort of argument that has been used. Here is a statement by the Danish scholar Lemche: 'The traditional materials about David cannot be regarded as an attempt to write *history*, as such. Rather, they represent an ideological programmatic composition which defends the assumption of power by the Davidic dynasty.'[9] Extending this somewhat further, we may find that we have no truly historical confirmation that there ever was a David or a Solomon or the united kingdom of Israel and Judah over which they are said to have ruled. Still less did the united kingdom of Israel and Judah control a substantial empire extending far to the north and east. Much of what is told in the Bible about the earlier periods may be an expression of religious belief and ideology rather than anything approaching true historical writing.

To appreciate the importance of the argument as presented, especially, by Davies, one has to see how radical it is. It is not just, as one might at first imagine, an argument that the people of Israel existed over all this time but that its 'historical' narratives were inaccurate. It is an argument that there was *no people 'Israel'* there at all, not a people whose lineaments can be discerned, whether by critical or by non-critical means, from the biblical texts. 'Ancient Israel' is thus properly enclosed in quotation marks, for it is a *literary construct*, something that exists in the Bible but is the product of the imagination of scribal writers from long afterwards, who

---

"patriarchal period", which has certainly been treated, even fairly recently, as if it were a historical era . . . but is nowadays accepted by the great majority of biblical scholars to be non-existent, to be, as I have put it, a literary construct . . . The "patriarchal age" is an epoch in the literary, biblical story but not in the history of the ancient world.' Davies goes on to extrapolate from this: the same is widely, but not quite so widely, acknowledged for the 'Exodus' and 'wilderness' periods, and again, somewhat less widely, for the 'period of the judges'. How then can one suppose that the following narratives, from Saul and David onwards, are historical in a way that the preceding material was not?

9 N. P. Lemche, *Ancient Israel: A New History of Israelite Society* (Sheffield: JSOT, 1988), 53, cited by Provan, *JBL* 114 (1995), 586 and n. 4. It is curious that D. M. Gunn's work, *The Story of King David* (Sheffield: JSOT, 1978), is frequently cited as a turning-point towards the revisionist views: e.g. K. W. Whitelam, 'The Social World of the Bible', in J. Barton, *Cambridge Companion to Biblical Interpretation* (Cambridge: Cambridge University Press, 1998), 38; Davies, *In Search of 'Ancient Israel'*, 29 n. 9. Whitelam is here right in saying that Gunn argued for understanding of the story as 'skilful and serious literature rather than primary sources for the monarchy of Saul and David'. But on the other hand the insistence of Lemche that the same represents 'an ideological programmatic composition which defends the assumption of power by the Davidic dynasty' is expressly ruled out, or at least made marginal, by Gunn, *The Story of King David*, e.g. 26.

were seeking to construct an 'ancient' history in order to provide legitimation for their own view of, and plans for, their own quite different society. Not all revisionists necessarily take this view, but this view, exemplified by Davies, well illustrates the questions that are raised.

In fact, however, there is at present no agreed move, in Old Testament scholarship as a whole, in the direction just described. What has emerged is rather a somewhat extreme programme strongly supported by a rather small revisionist group, and some equally strong contradiction from others. A good illustration of this, offering several conflicting viewpoints, is to be found in the *Journal of Biblical Literature* of 1995.[10] Another is in *The Cambridge Companion to Biblical Interpretation*, where we have articles from quite different viewpoints by both Whitelam and Provan. Let us look first, however, at the *JBL*.

I will mention first, in passing, an article by Marvin Sweeney entitled 'The Critique of Solomon in the Josianic Edition of the Deuteronomistic History',[11] because the historicity of the portrayal of Solomon is one of the questions hotly debated under the impact of revisionist historical work. Sweeney, however, in this article stays outside the debate which we shall be reviewing, although his discussion is indirectly highly relevant.

It is otherwise with the first article in the number, by the young Scottish scholar Iain W. Provan, which is entitled 'Ideologies, Literary and Critical: Reflections on Recent Writing on the History of Israel'. Provan notes the increased emphasis on 'the Bible as literature' along with the tendency to a late dating of the texts.[12] Why then, he asks, 'assume that the narrative world thus portrayed has anything to do with the "real" world of the past? Why not regard it as a "fictive world", an ideological construct created by its authors for their own purposes?'.[13] Ancient history should then be found not in the biblical texts but 'in the artefacts, buildings and inscriptions the people themselves left behind'. It is this perspective, Provan continues, 'that dominates much of the recent writing on the history of Israel'.[14] And here he begins to quote from Lemche, from the late Gösta Ahlström,[15] from Philip

---

[10]   *JBL* 114/4 (1995).   [11]   M. Sweeney, ibid. 607–22.
[12]   Provan, ibid. 585.   [13]   Ibid. 586.   [14]   Ibid.
[15]   Thompson in his reply to Provan rightly indicates that Ahlström should hardly be counted within the same group. On this see below, pp. 90–1.

Davies, and from Thomas Thompson.[16] Analysing various utterances of this 'school', as he calls them, Provan identifies a 'faith' that comes to expression in their work, and designates it as 'positivist' (or, he would add, 'materialist', but 'positivist' will do for the moment).[17] And here he argues, 'that positivism is intellectually incoherent—incoherent, among other reasons, because if its level of scepticism with regard to some favourite things were applied consistently to everything, there could be no knowledge of anything'. And here at least we have got a philosophical position of some importance.[18]

Provan goes on: 'The "favourite thing" of the positivist historians of Israel in this respect, of course, is the biblical text, which is treated with a scepticism quite out of proportion to that which is evident when any of the other data relating to Israel's history are being considered.' And in conclusion, Provan writes, he does not dispute that biblical historiography is, in at least a very general sense, ideological literature, or that ideology has partially shaped the literature of the last century or two on the history of Israel[19] (I take it that he here means the more traditional modern histories of ancient Israel, before the recent revisionist trends that have disturbed him). So, he sums up, 'confessionalism of a religious sort

---

[16] A little extra background about Thompson's work may be helpful for the non-specialist. He has long been known for his book *The Historicity of the Patriarchal Narratives* (Berlin: de Gruyter, 1974). This book was in essence a reaction against the movement which, from the late 1930s on, sought to show that there was good evidence for the historicity of Abraham and the other patriarchs on the basis of personal names, epigraphic evidence, and knowledge of social customs from Mesopotamia. A leading part in this movement was played by the great American scholar W. F. Albright and his pupils. This is why Thompson's article, objecting to criticisms from Iain Provan, is called 'A Neo-Albrightean School in History and Biblical Scholarship?'. In his book (p. 9) Thompson argued that 'Not only has the historicity of Abraham not been proven, but it does not seem to be implied in the biblical narratives themselves.'

[17] *JBL* 114/4 (1995), 601. The use of the term 'materialist' is given some justification by W. G. Dever, 'The Contribution of Archaeology', in P. D. Miller, Jr., P. D. Hanson, and S. D. McBride (eds.), *Ancient Israelite Religion* (Philadelphia: Fortress, 1981), 221–2: 'Almost no historian of Israelite religion seems to have realized that archaeology's most useful contribution to biblical studies in the future may lie in another direction, in its *increasing capacity for writing social and economic history* [author's italics] and thus providing a setting in which events described in biblical accounts may become credible. *The new agenda is unabashedly materialistic* [my italics], in the sense that the study of material culture is one of our best clues to culture.' On the other hand, as we shall see, Dever, ironically, is opposed to the revisionists in general. Perhaps however there is a point in common here?

[18] Provan, ibid. 602. For a significant and concise summary of criticisms of Provan see Grabbe (ed.), *Can a 'History of Israel' be Written?*, 29 n. 25.

[19] Provan, ibid. 605.

is attacked in the name of critical enquiry and objectivity; but the noisy ejection of religious commitment through the *front* door of the scholarly house is only a cover for the quieter smuggling in (whether conscious or unconscious) of a quite different form of commitment through the *rear*)'. Provan concludes with an expression of preference for 'an intellectually liberal, pluralistic, broad world, where differing beliefs and philosophies are recognized as just that' and 'where differing approaches to the subject, deriving from these beliefs and philosophies, are accepted as valid'. To this end he pleads for greater 'awareness of one's own presuppositions and predispositions'. He wants to debate these latter rather than to 'anathematize one's opponent'.

Anathematization, however, is just what resulted. The same number contains replies from Thompson and Davies,[20] and these contain some strong language. Provan is guilty of 'deliberate distortion', 'ubiquitous distortion', 'ignoring the context', 'fundamentalism as defined by J. Barr', 'outright falsification' and 'blatant falsification'.[21] Davies's title, 'Method and Madness: Some Remarks on doing History with the Bible', well expresses his opinion, with the word 'Method' standing for his own allegiance and with 'Madness' representing the path along which Provan is going.

Now there is no possibility that I could disentangle, now or at any time, all the accusations and counter-accusations made in this debate. I can make only a few comments. I must say that, on the basis of the *JBL* articles alone, my first sympathies lie for the most part with Provan, though I think that he has used a number of old-fashioned theological arguments that would have been better rethought. For example, he follows much traditional theology in inveighing against the 'neutral, uninvolved observer', in other words in putting himself against objectivity and playing into the hands of his opponents. Again, I think he made a mistake in calling his opponents 'positivist', and Davies is quick to pick up this weakness.[22] It is indeed traditional in theology and biblical studies

[20] *JBL* 114/4 (1995), 683–98, 699–705.

[21] Ibid. 685, 691, 694, 704.

[22] Ibid. 601 ff., 700. Davies rightly argues: 'Positivism, strictly speaking, uses natural science as its epistemological model: I know no historian who takes such a line'. He goes on to discuss a 'weaker sense' for the term 'positivist', and also the sense in which 'materialist' may be meaningful.

to use 'positivist' as a pejorative term, and it has usually been used, as Provan uses it here, as against the more critical or radical side. But as I see it (this point is not raised in the discussion we are following) the real analogy to positivism in theology and biblical studies lies on the conservative side: it belongs to the idea that there is a body of limited and defined data which is 'given', is available in physical form or in black and white: the Bible is a primary example. I do not think 'materialist' would really help either.[23] Nor am I sure that Provan was right, from his own point of view, to admit that biblical historiography is ideological;[24] it looks as if he does this reluctantly, rightly saying 'in at least a very general sense', and Davies turns it against him.[25] Nor am I convinced by Provan's desire that we should all go along revealing our presuppositions and that that would help to solve our problems; this presuppositionalism is too much a fashion of a limited theological current.[26] Nevertheless with these and some other qualifications Provan seems to have argued a good and well-informed case, and the bitter resentment with which his arguments have been met only goes to show how serious they are. Nevertheless there remains this observation, that in some ways Provan sounds as if he is against the postmodern positions, and in part this is true: he stands for the older fashions; but in his rejection of objectivity (which, however, he seems elsewhere to retract somewhat) he stands rather more *with* the postmodern trends; so also with his 'pluralism'. And one must add that Provan's later additions to his argument, as in the article in *The Cambridge Companion to Biblical Interpretation*, seem to have weakened his case rather than strengthened it, and introduced contradictions that were not there before. We shall return to these shortly.

In the counter-arguments of Davies one aspect should be stressed, namely his extreme insistence on *method*. 'The historian's task is not "scientific" or concerned with objectivity. There are no

---

[23] But cf. Carroll, in Barton (ed.), *Companion*, 52, who talks of 'a set of cultural materialist readings of the Bible'. [24] *JBL* 114/4 (1995), 605.
[25] Ibid. 702.
[26] Incidentally—and this, though brought to mind by Provan's words, does not refer to him in particular, but is relevant for the whole discussion of ideology and postmodernism—there is, running through much of these concepts, a sort of Freudian, psychoanalytic, atmosphere, a desire to reach into the unconscious, to reveal what is in there, with the idea that much good will be achieved by so doing. This is found in some very traditional theology, and equally in *avant-garde* thoughts about ideology.

"hard facts". All historical research involves subjectivity. A historical account is a story: meaning in history lies in the human mind, not "out there".'[27] 'It is precisely because I am no more free from subjectivity than any human being that I insist on working to a methodology that will enable me and my fellow historians to agree on what counts as historical knowledge and how we aim to secure it.'[28] Again,

His [Provan's] next criticism is that I am attacking other scholars for their ideology. The charge is partly true, but misleading. My own position (which no other reviewer has so far misunderstood) is that in the case of 'ancient Israel' a *certain set* of ideological notions is interfering with the application of a method which most scholars fundamentally accept. My target, then, is (a) a *particular* ideology and applies (b) *only when* that ideology interferes with method.[29]

Thus he quarrels with Provan on this ground: 'Provan is blind to the distinction between bias and method. He represents my method as a bias because he does not want to talk about method.' Again, 'He [Provan] apparently fails to recognize the vital principle that method, when it declares its presumptions and procedures openly and insists on consistent application, is our best defence *against* ideology, bias, and presupposition!'[30]

So method is the decisive thing. But is this right, and is there a historiographical method that is common to all competent historians and produces decisive agreement among them? If Davies is 'using the same method as the majority of biblical scholars',[31] why did so many of them write histories of a quite different kind from his own? And is not Davies, who looks so postmodern in his detailed positions, rather reverting to old-fashioned 'modernity' with his insistence on method as the answer—just as he, though distinctly anti-theological in his general position, joins his opponent in the theological air of some of his own arguments?

For here again we have one of the differences between the members of the revisionist group: Davies's production, thus far at any rate, seems to me to be more theory of history or philosophy of history than actual historical writing. In comparison with a real historian such as Ahlström, he has many historical ideas and proposals, many of them highly stimulating, but what comes out of it in the end is hardly a history; at times it seems more like a negation of history (hence the term 'nihilistic', which has occurred to many commentators).[32] Or, one could say, he seems like an anti-theological theologian of history. Not all the revisionists, however, are necessarily the same in this respect.

Or put it in this way: *if* there is a perfect method, if there is a method which can uniquely eliminate all ideology, bias, and presupposition, how does that method differ from objectivity? In fact it is the very same thing. It carries us back to those same principles of the Enlightenment which postmodernism so strongly opposes. Or, again, what is the belief that one has the perfect method other than an excellent example of ideology itself? On either of these grounds, Davies's reliance on method seems to self-destruct.

Which is just the point. Let us pass to another spokesman, the American archaeologist William Dever. Dever is no outmoded religious believer and is well established in the postmodern world, holding as he does that 'the biblical text we have is indeed a "literary construct", the product not of any historical conscious-ness in the modern sense, but rather of the literary imagination of late, elitist, nationalist religious parties who finally edited various materials into our Hebrew Bible'.[33] He 'readily acknowledges that many of the biblical "stories" are just that, i.e. myth and legend interwoven with some factual material, or "historicized fiction" '.[34] One might have expected Dever to agree with Thompson and Davies, just as a revisionist archaeologist should agree with a revisionist historian. In fact this is not the case. And Dever too has a command of strong language. Revisionist histo-

---

[32] Thus W. G. Dever, of whom more shortly, comments that Davies's *In Search of 'Ancient Israel'* is 'the antithesis of a history, its basic tenet being that no history of Israel is possible': 'Will the Real Early Israel Please Stand Up', *BASOR* 297 (1995), 67.

[33] W. G. Dever, 'What Did the Biblical Writers Know, and When Did they Know It?', in J. Magness and S. Gitin (eds.), *Hesed ve-Emet*, FS for E. S. Frerichs (Atlanta: Scholars Press, 1998), 241–53. This is a recent article, but exchanges of mutual criticism go back to an earlier time. For a reply by Thompson to earlier work by Dever see Thomas L. Thompson, 'William Dever and the not so New Biblical Archeology', in V. Fritz and P. R. Davies (eds.), *Origins of the Ancient Israelite States* (Sheffield: JSOT, 1996), 26–43. For 'élitism' cf. Dever, 'The Contribution of Archaeology', 220, 237 n. 4: '*Many* of the biblical texts are both late and elitist.'

[34] Dever, 'What Did the Biblical Writers Know?', 252.

rians, according to him, produce 'constant caricatures of "biblical archaeology" '.[35] Their work consists, he tells us, of 'misinformed, ill-tempered and increasingly ideological monologues'. He writes,

No Syro-Palestinian archaeologist today wishes to 'prove the Bible', as several of the revisionists charge —not even those of conservative church background.[36] We do insist, however, that to ignore the biblical texts when dealing with the Iron Age of ancient Palestine, or to deny correlations of texts and artefacts when they do occur, is not only methodologically unsound but reckless and ultimately defeatist. If positivism is *passé* today, so is nihilism. As for the fad of deconstruction, belatedly discovered by the revisionists, it has already run its course in many other disciplines.[37]

There are, according to Dever, substantial bodies of artefacts which, even if one has no desire to prove the Bible right, do in fact show significant correlations with the biblical texts.

Thus in late biblical times no one knew anything about Philistines and what they might have been like: the 'only possible setting' for the biblical texts that mention them lies in the twelfth–tenth century BC.[38] The weight known as *pim* or *payim*

---

[35] For the non-specialist reader it may be helpful to have an explanation of the background of the terms here used. The older 'biblical archaeology' commonly worked with a correlation of biblical text and archaeological discovery: a good example is G.E. Wright, *Biblical Archaeology* (Philadelphia: Westminster, 1974). Much criticism later argued that archaeological finds had been much too easily and swiftly identified with biblical references, and the tendency moved strongly towards a quite autonomous archaeology of Palestine, working independently of biblical evidences. This movement has been, obviously, one of the wellsprings of the revisionist approach to biblical history. Hence Dever, though critical of 'biblical archaeology', is critical also of what he calls the 'nonbiblical archaeology' of the revisionists, who, as he sees it, refuse to recognize plain evidences of correlation between Bible and archaeology when these evidences are present.

[36] To explain this last remark, Dever alludes to the fact that some archaeological work has been undertaken in the conservative hope of proving the Bible to be historically true or, if not undertaken in this hope, has at least resulted in beliefs and claims that this is so. Revisionist historians, tending to keep biblical interpretation strictly separate from historical reality, have therefore at times identified archaeologists who do see such a correlation as being influenced by conservative or fundamentalist attitudes. Dever is arguing that this is not valid, for archaeologists whose church background is conservative in this sense. On the whole matter of relations between fundamentalism and archaeological work see the important article of Edward Noort, 'Fundamentalismus in Exegese und Archäologie', *JBTh* 6 (1991), 311–31, which incidentally has significant references to the present writer's work.

[37] Dever, 'What Did the Biblical Writers Know?', 243. For an elucidation of 'deconstruction', see below, Ch. 6.   [38] Dever, ibid. 244–5.

and mentioned in 1 Sam 13.21[39] had disappeared at latest by the end of the monarchy and almost certainly was a real entity of early times, not something that a late ideologist could have thought up. Substantial fortifications found by archaeology show remarkable agreement with the patterns ascribed to Solomon in the biblical text: if they were not built by Solomon, says Dever, 'then we would have to posit a similar king by another name, with or without the witness of the biblical texts'.[40] Similar arguments apply to the style of the Solomonic temple and to the area in Jerusalem known as the *millo'*.[41]

And what about the inscriptions in palaeo-Hebrew script, often explicable in relation to the biblical text in terms of historical linguistics? What, for instance, about the Siloam Tunnel inscription attributed to Hezekiah? This was usually taken to fit with the historical existence and circumstances of Hezekiah's times, as described in the Bible, and also to display linguistic features close to those of biblical texts associated with the same monarch. Philip Davies, however, along with John Rogerson had sought to show that the tunnel was of Hasmonean date and the inscription also,[42]

---

[39] Ibid. 245. For the non-specialist: the reference is to a verse about the sharpening of metal tools. It was long known to be obscure: AV had 'Yet they had a file for the mattocks.' The discovery of weights inscribed with the letters p-y-m led to the identification of a Hebrew word *payim* or *pim*, previously unknown, which was the name of this weight, and was used, like *shekel*, 'weight', as a kind of currency. Thus NEB: 'The charge was two-thirds of a shekel for ploughshares and mattocks . . .'; RSV: 'and the charge was a pim for the ploughshares and for the mattocks'.

[40] Dever, 'What Did the Biblical Writers Know?', 246.

[41] Ibid. 246–7. Presumably derived from the Hebrew root meaning 'fill', the Millo is usually taken to have been a landfill, earthwork, or rampart; see notably the building of it under Solomon, 1 Kings 9: 15–24.

[42] See J. Rogerson and P. R. Davies, 'Was the Siloam Tunnel Built by Hezekiah?', *BA* 59 (1996), 138–49. An essential part of the argument is palaeographical and technical. Rogerson and Davies argued that 'it is frequently not possible to prove *on palaeographic evidence alone whether a text in palaeo-Hebrew dates from, say, the eighth–seventh centuries or is Hasmonean or later*' (p. 146; italics in original). For the non-specialist: *palaeo-Hebrew* is the term used for the older Hebrew script which was used in ancient inscriptions and is still in use in some of the Dead Sea Scrolls, but was eventually replaced by the 'square' script now familiar for Hebrew. I personally would not venture an opinion about the complicated matter of the tunnel, but their article seems to me to be learned and well-stated, apart from the argument from the script. But, as R. S. Hendel says in reply ('The Date of the Siloam Inscription', *BA* 59/4 (1996), 233–7), 'the inconclusiveness of the palaeography is crucial to their larger argument that the Siloam Tunnel dates to the Hasmonean era'. After a detailed analysis of scripts Hendel concludes that 'The script of the Siloam Inscription fits without problem into the eighth–seventh century sequence and does not fit into the sequence of palaeo-Hebrew scripts [of] the Hasmonean era and later . . . The palaeography

but, wrote Dever, 'this is so manifestly absurd on archaeological, palaeographical and historical grounds that one cannot help but question the agenda, competence and integrity of some scholars who refuse to confront any external data that would undermine their "minimalist" conclusions (or presuppositions)'.[43] And thus Dever concludes, in general, 'The archaeological data now in our possession rule out the possibility that in the Hebrew Bible as it now stands we are dealing merely with a "literary construct" of the Persian, much less the Hellenistic, era, projected back upon an "imaginary past".'[44] 'We in the mainstream are the real "revisionists", driven not by postmodernism, New Critical theory, or any other passing fad, but by the steady accumulation of empirical data (there are some).'[45]

This shows us that we have once again a region of rather violent disagreement, which we cannot seek to disentangle within this chapter. But certainly Dever's position deeply damages the assurance of Philip Davies that basic historical methodology must support his position. Historical method seems, on the contrary, to give support to opposing sets of results.

I started by taking as an example the set of articles in the *JBL* of 1995, but there is plenty of other literature to draw on. *The Cambridge Companion to Biblical Interpretation* once again provides good material, with an article by K. W. Whitelam on 'The Social World of the Bible' and one by I. Provan on 'The Historical Books of the Old Testament'. From Provan we have also a review article of Whitelam's book, *The Invention of Ancient Israel: The Silencing of Palestinian History*[46] and, forthcoming, a paper delivered at the Oslo Congress on the Old Testament in 1998. I want to say here that I found his review article of Whitelam to be absolutely excellent—measured, reasoned, well expressed, and entirely in accord with my own experience, so much so that I shall not devote more space to that particular aspect.

When discussing Provan's *JBL* paper above, I expressed the sense that he was getting the better of that debate. Even if there were weaknesses in some of his arguments, there were many

of the Siloam Inscription belongs to the eighth–seventh century BCE sequence, right around the time of Hezekiah, and excludes a Hasmonean date.'

[43] Dever, 'What Did the Biblical Writers Know?', 249.
[44] Ibid. 243.   [45] Ibid. 251–2.
[46] In *JSS* 42 (1997), 283–300.

strong points. I certainly did not agree, on the basis of that article, that this was 'fundamentalism as defined by J. Barr'. The trouble is that some elements in his other articles in the present debate seem to me to weaken his case rather than to strengthen it. He seemed, to begin with, to be reacting against the revisionist movement in its moving the texts down to a very late period and interpreting them as the ideology of that late period, having thus little historical content. He reacted also against the centrality of 'ideology' when taken as the standard explanation of texts, and against what he saw (rightly in my view) as a more extensive use of this explanation in the case of the Bible than in that of other cultural products. In his *Cambridge Companion* article, however, he brings in other arguments that cut across these lines.

For instance, he begins his *Companion* article with an attack on past scholarship for 'not interpreting the narratives as narratives'.[47] 'The text in itself has not commonly been regarded as historical. It has been viewed simply as the narrative mine out of which the skilled interpreter may dig nuggets of history.' So it ought to be regarded as narrative, and 'narrative books' would be a better name for them than 'historical books'. But this seems to go in just the opposite direction from his *JBL* article. That article began by complaining about the treatment of narratives as 'story', which led to the handling of them as if they did not reflect historical reality. He now appears to blame scholars for not treating them as 'narrative': but treating them as narrative is exactly what led to the situation he complained of.

He also gives, most of the time, the impression that 'during the historical-critical period', very little of the narrative was treated as historically accurate or near to it. Extracting history was 'a more or less arduous quarrying operation'. One might at most 'dig nuggets of history' out of the text. We hear of 'remnants of texts that could be salvaged from the narrative through historical-critical means'.[48] This looks like a very familiar conservative assessment: critical approaches are blamed for finding only a small amount of historical reality in the Bible. But it is immediately contradicted by his own declaration[49] that most of these books 'would have been fairly highly rated in terms of their ability to

[47] Provan, in Barton (ed.), *Companion*, 199.   [48] Ibid. 201.
[49] Ibid. 199.

divulge historical information'. It is also contradicted by the fact that, in the period referred to, the weakness of works on the history of Israel was not that they dug out nuggets in an arduous operation, but that they far too easily and simply followed the biblical text, sometimes doing little more than transcribing it.[50] So his account of what happened in the period of historical-critical domination is both self-contradictory and in itself wrong.

Basically Provan seems to want the historical books to 'refer' to the real world of the past;[51] he objects to Davies who thinks that many things told in them have 'virtually nothing to do with anything that might have happened'.[52] He quite rightly objects, if the Bible has been treated with more scepticism than other documents; but it is not clear to me that the revisionist historians have actually done this, and he needs to demonstrate that they have. In any case, if it is a matter of reference to a real world of the past (he mentions this again and again), there are only two ways to go: either the straight fundamentalist way, i.e. that everything is historically true because it is in the Bible, or a historical-critical way, which will assess the historicity of reports point by point. If there is a third way, he does not tell us what it is. In his first section[53] Provan seems to get these things mixed up because he attacks both historical criticism and the revisionist viewpoint of Davies together, when the relevant characteristics are quite different.

A bad impression is created also by his section 'The Freedom of the Reader',[54] which takes as prime example the matter of the goddess Asherah and the argument that 'Asherah was the female consort of Yahweh' or had been so at some stage. We should take a moment to explain this to any readers who may not be familiar with this question.

'Asherah is a Hebrew word which was traditionally taken to

---

[50] Cf. Barton, ibid. 14, who points out that much work on actual history by 'historical' critics was often unsophisticated, being either 'guided by theological assumptions or even by a tendency to paraphrase the biblical text' (fuller quotation above, p. 45); likewise Carroll, ibid. 53: 'such constructions have often stayed far too close to the biblical text to be genuinely historiographical studies'. Among other recent works, I have myself called attention to the citation by R. Albertz of Gideon's defeating the Midianite army by means of lights and noise, which he seems to take as a straightforward historical fact: see J. Barr, *The Concept of Biblical Theology* (London: SCM, 1999), 121, and R. Albertz, *A History of Israelite Religion*, i. 82.

[51] Provan, in Barton (ed.), *Companion*, 198.
[52] Ibid. 201.   [53] Ibid. 198–203.   [54] Ibid. 204–6.

mean a sacred tree or pole, an object strictly and consistently
forbidden in the Hebrew Bible. Older English versions such as
KJV rendered it as 'grove' or 'groves', e.g. Deut. 16: 21, Judg. 6:
25, 1 Kings 18: 19, which follows the understanding of the
Septuagint. Modern translations often render with *Asherah*. The
difference was made when the Ugaritic texts (*c.*14th century BC)
were discovered, and they had a female deity *Athirat Yam*, which
would correspond to '(Lady) Asherah of the Sea'. Hence it has
been thought that the Hebrew Asherah took its name from some
sort of representation of such a goddess. In more recent times
inscriptions were found, notably at a place called Kuntillet 'Ajrud,
which *might* mean 'Yahweh and his Asherah', and this fact has
enlivened discussion about a possible female consort for the God
of Israel.

Against this Provan appeals to what 'might be considered in the
conventional way as evidence'. Even if data have been found
suggesting 'that some Israelites in certain places and at certain times
regarded Asherah as Yahweh's consort', this would not prove that
the religion of Israel was syncretistic[55] in origin and in essence. He
goes on to insist on evidence, quite reasonably. But of course at
this point, unlike some others, he has suddenly become the careful historical critic, calling for evidence 'in the conventional way'
(which could scarcely be a distinctively 'confessional' way) and
rightly repudiating the interpreters who would like to have a
female goddess because she would represent a world of religious
pluralism congenial to their own modern world-view (and, I
imagine, its feminism, though he does not explicitly say so). And
I entirely agree in rejecting any influence of modern desire for a
goddess upon the question in the history of religion. But it seems

---

[55] It seems to me that Provan is misstating his own position and misleading his readers when he uses the term 'syncretistic' in this way. The term 'syncretism' is properly used
when two different religions come to be combined. The position that Provan is combating
is the opposite of this, i.e. the view that Yahweh-religion *included* a female consort from the
start ('in origin and essence', as he himself puts it), so that the traditional monotheistic
Yahwism was produced by the *subtraction* of the consort-element. In Miller, McBride, and
Hanson, *Ancient Israelite Religion*, we note that both Coogan and McCarter, accepting the
identification of a consort, expressly deny that this view is 'syncretistic' in its consequences.
Thus Coogan, ibid. 119: 'It is methodologically questionable to label the 'Ajrud cult as
syncretistic', and McCarter, ibid. 149: 'The cult reflected at 'Ajrud is not syncretistic in the
strictest sense. It is a form of Yahwism that derived its essential features from internal developments, but it is not the Yahwism of the prophets and reformers, and not the Yahwism
we know from the Bible.'

to me quite slanderous to attribute this as a motive to the serious scholars who have investigated this problem and considered the possible hypotheses.[56] At this point Provan seems to stand for a combination of a liberal/rational criticism, depending on 'what might be considered in the conventional way as evidence', with a roughly fundamentalistic view, the latter applied however not to historical events but to the purity of Israelite religion.[57]

Provan points out that there is no evidence for an Asherah in the Jerusalem temple before Manasseh, and its mention there (2 Kings 21: 7) is said by him to show that it was an innovation. But even if it was an innovation *in the Jerusalem temple*, there is plenty of biblical reference to the previous existence of the object: Gideon's father had one (Judg. 6: 25), and there is a host of prohibitions which suggest that the Asherah was familiar enough. Even if Manasseh did something new in putting it in the Jerusalem temple, the innovation lay in installing there an object that was already well known in Israel. This depends, of course, on the dating of the various relevant sources. At best, Provan is here signalling a difference of opinion in the historical-critical evaluation of evidence. In general, the matter of the Asherah was not a good example for Provan's argument at this point.

[56] Cf. e.g. Coogan, ibid. 119: 'The simplest explanation is to take the two standing figures as representations of the two deities mentioned in the inscription . . . the larger male figure is Yahweh, and the appropriately smaller female figure slightly behind him is his consort Asherah'; similarly McCarter, ibid. 149: 'The religious milieu at 'Ajrud is that of the Israelite court at the beginning of the eighth century. It is the court religion from which Hosea and the other eighth-century prophets dissented. Yahweh is worshipped alongside a goddess.' A contrary view comes from Tigay, ibid. 180: 'the essentially non-polytheistic onomastic picture given by the Bible all the way back to the beginning of the divided monarchy is realistic . . . After the united monarchy, perhaps even earlier, the evidence currently available makes it very difficult to suppose that many Israelites worshipped gods other than YHWH'. We note that Tigay's argument, built basically on personal names, does not carry us back before the end of the united monarchy or 'perhaps even earlier', so that it does not even attempt to deal with the question of how it was a century or two before that time; and it denies that 'many' Israelites so worshipped, not that any Israelites at all did so.

[57] This seems to be a position rather akin to that taken by J. D. Fowler in her *Theophoric Personal Names in Ancient Hebrew* (Sheffield: JSOT, 1988), on which see my review in *JTS* 41 (1990), 137–9. The religion of Israel was, historically and factually, exactly as it is described in the Hebrew Bible. But of course the Hebrew Bible itself complains a lot about the people worshipping other gods, notably Baal and probably Asherah. Provan (Barton (ed.), *Companion*, 205) puts a lot of weight on the argument that Asherah did not find a place in the Jerusalem temple before Manasseh, and then it was regarded as an innovation.

It was faulty in another way, for this section is meant to address 'the Freedom of the Reader', that is, as he summarizes it at the end of the section,[58] the problem created by 'reader-response' theory, where interpreters can 'absorb the biblical narrative texts (or any others) into their world, reading their own dreams and visions into it'. Provan is right to address this problem: but the Asherah question, which occupies the whole centre of the section, is not a good example: or, if it is, he has not shown how it is.

Provan has a concern for 'truth and rationality',[59] and, as we saw, he wants to avoid 'anathematization'. But, if so, he has to begin by himself abandoning the anathemas such as 'positivism' and 'materialism' which he utters, similarly the repeatedly used depiction of other people's ideas as 'unexamined assumptions'. He takes up a presuppositionalist position, which is one now widely spreading in the more intellectual strata of evangelicalism, and would like us all to exchange information about our presuppositions. But his own 'presuppositions' seem to have exactly the same status as the 'unexamined assumptions' that he finds other people to have. While his concern for 'truth and rationality' is definitely welcome as an answer to many postmodernists, there may be doubts whether all his arguments are equally based on that same concern.

On the other hand, Provan's argument that the revisionist view displays a degree of scepticism towards the biblical narrative that is not shown towards other comparable sources seems to me to be very likely valid. There may well be no extra-biblical information to confirm this or that event referred to in the narrative. This in itself, however, does not seem to me to be in itself adequate ground for doubting the reality of the event. I would have thought that there are thousands of incidents related in ancient historical documents for which no definite external confirmation exists. Provan is very likely right in holding that it is precisely the fact that the Bible is a religious document of living religions that induces the swift recourse to a total denial of substantial elements.

In his *JBL* article, again, Provan wrote of how 'confessionalism of a religious sort is attacked';[60] we have already noted this (pp. 67, 77), but something more should be said about it. It leaves a

---

[58] Provan, in Barton (ed.), *Companion*, 206. [59] Ibid. 202.
[60] *JBL* 114/4 (1995), 605.

number of problems unanswered. What Provan here writes can well be true of some people: most obviously of Davies, who might well accept it of himself. But what Provan does not show is that there is an intrinsic connection between the revisionist historiography and the rejection of religious confessionalism. The sentence from which I have quoted does not seem to fit in its place, where the paragraph is mostly about the place of ideology. Though no lover of ideology, I do not see why either revisionist historiography or an interpretation of texts as ideological *must* be incompatible with serious religious appreciation (I refuse to use the word 'confessionalism' myself, except in quoting others).

And, putting it the other way, what we do not gain from Provan is any clear statement of what a proper confessionalist answer to the historical questions would be. Obviously this might not be needed in the *JBL* article, but when we turn to the *Companion*, where he is writing an article exactly on 'The Historical Books of the Old Testament', we do not gain a picture of what his positive view of the books, in relation to their *historical* value or accuracy, is. He seems to be dubious about historical criticism, at least to a considerable extent; he is considerably against interpretation as ideology; he is against interpretation that might suggest that Hebrew religion was different from the pattern that the text presents (at least, unless we can present something 'that might be considered in the conventional way as evidence');[61] in addition—as we have seen above—he is against a sort of reader-response approach, where 'the distinction between text and interpreter has become blurred', where interpreters can 'absorb the biblical narrative texts (or any others) into their world, reading their own dreams and visions into it'.[62] When one reads such interpretations, one discovers that one is 'finding out considerably more about the interpreter than about the Old Testament'. Quite so. But what is left? At the end of his article he turns to Childs and the canonical approach,[63] and he seems to feel a sympathy here, but he emphasizes (surely excessively?) Childs's starting out from historical criticism, and his failure to give attention to 'the massive amount of work carried out in the last two decades which has gone some way towards undermining the very historical-critical approach which he presupposes'.[64] But a very large proportion of this 'massive work' belongs to those same categories that he himself has just opposed as erroneous.

Again, we saw that Provan spoke warmly of 'an intellectually liberal, pluralistic, broad world, where differing beliefs and philosophies are recognized as just that' and 'where differing approaches to the subject, deriving from these beliefs and philosophies, are accepted as valid'. But, if this is his basic view, why is he so annoyed at the revisionist historians? They have 'differing beliefs and philosophies', i.e. different from his own, which he has recognized as 'just that', and he wants 'differing approaches' to be accepted as valid. Why then not leave the revisionists alone, and allow them to develop their 'valid' views without interruption? They would lie alongside his own different view and the whole would constitute a 'liberal, pluralistic, broad world'. At present it looks as if we shall have to wait some time for that world to emerge.

Thus, all these being said, what view of the historical character of the 'historical' books does he offer? Is it a canonical approach that has nothing to do with historical criticism? Or a narrative one that has nothing to do with history at all (he seems to query the validity of the label 'historical' for the books)?[65] But, if the latter, why is he so troubled when revisionists cast doubt on their historical character?

And finally—I apologize for raising so many difficulties in Provan's position, when I started by expressing support for it, but the points he raises are important and need to be worked out in their full implications—we need to know from him how he would stand in relation to a moderate critical position like that of Noth, where the material up to the Judges is the sacral traditions of the tribes but more serious history—not infallible or without all ideology, but still serious historical material—begins around the time of David (or the time of whoever wrote the story of David). Is his position, which rejects the revisionist one, one that could be content with a more moderate stance such as Noth's?

The trouble, I feel, is that some of his arguments, though directed against the revisionists, would in fact have the same effect on the moderate critical position: and if that is the case, then he

[64] Ibid. 209.   [65] Ibid. 203.

has been misleading us somewhat, for his argument would then be a more completely anti-critical one, for which the irritation of the revisionists would be only a catalyst. It is to be hoped that he will express himself on this matter.

Summing up this question, I find the revisionist views to be unconvincing. The main reason for this lies in the excessive weight placed upon the concept of ideology. Not that ideology is absent from the Bible or should be excluded from our thoughts in interpretation, but I think that the whole programme of the revisionists is excessively dependent on ideology, and in more than one way. First, they appear to take it that once ideology can be detected in a text, then that text is to be explained *totally and exclusively* through ideology. It no longer has any historical value. I see no reason to believe this. Just as historical texts will commonly be ideologically slanted, ideological texts will commonly contain historical material. One could say that this is true of every newspaper every day. Of course the news is slanted: but it would be excessive to suppose that on that account none of the reports have any factual reality at all behind them. If one asks how one identifies the difference between historical realities and reports as they stand, the answer is that this is exactly what the despised historical criticism (of any book or report; type 4 in my classification) tries to do.

We may here adduce the sensible remarks of H. M. Barstad:

'Bias', 'preconceived opinions', 'underlying motifs', or whatever one chooses to call it, has formed a 'natural' part of historiography at all times and the current distinction between 'history' and 'ideology' must be judged as rather artificial . . . Even if the historiographers of the Hebrew Bible have as their prime aim the production of 'ideology' and the reuse of the ancient traditions in order to demonstrate something for contemporary society, rather than attempting to find out 'what happened' in the past, this does not imply that these texts do not yield a lot of historical information . . . Despite the scepticism of some recent scholarship, somewhere in the cognitive 'force field' between 'what happened' and the 'ideology' of the sources, and the 'ideology' of the modern scholars, there are some 'facts' to be learned.[66]

Secondly, many of the readings of texts in revisionist works seem to be biased in order to produce results that point towards

---

[66] *The Myth of the Empty Land* (Oslo: Scandinavian University Press, 1996), 36 n. 18. For further quotation from this important note, see below, p. 108.

ideology. Thus I simply do not believe Lemche's assertion (see quotation above, p. 65) that the story of David in Samuel/Kings is told in order to provide ideological support to the Davidic dynasty: here we can quote support from David Gunn who, though not treating the story as a proper historical source, equally denies that it is pro-Davidic propaganda.[67] To me the story points rather the other way, and suggests a tragic and empathetic, but critical as well as accepting, view of David. I see it much more as a story told by someone who knew a lot of factual detail about David, even if it was embellished with fancy. And even the embellishments do not seem to me to point univocally towards any ideology of the Davidic house or such matters. I cannot see how much of the detail provided can have been simply *invented* out of the imagination of a later ideologist. This does not deny that the story may have been altered and reinterpreted and that portions of the material very likely come from a different time and provenance. But what we know of later ideologists in the Hebrew tradition does not confirm the impression that invention of a detailed novelistic story of this kind was part of their repertoire.

Moreover, especially in respect of the stories of Saul and David, one has to note the extent to which the revisionist historians are influenced by literary readings such as those of Alter and especially of D. M. Gunn.[68] But since these books were written precisely with the *purpose* of emphasizing a literary approach and de-emphasizing a historical one, this is not a strong support. A work that can

---

[67] 'The simple problem confronting the definition of the story's genre as political propaganda, viz. that the direction of the propaganda is unclear, remains a problem': so Gunn, *The Story of King David*, 26 n. and cf. 21–6 in general.

[68] See e.g. Whitelam, in Barton (ed.), *Companion*, 38, who tells us that these books have 'had a profound effect on the way in which biblical narratives were read as artful constructions. Thus the books of Samuel . . . were increasingly understood as skilful and serious literature rather than primary sources for the monarchy of Saul and David. Many biblical books which had previously been considered to be historical, in the sense that they preserved a reasonably accurate picture of the history of ancient Israel or later communities, became the subject of detailed literary treatments.' But Gunn's whole approach is one that does not deny, but certainly bypasses, the matter of the historicity of the story. As he says (*The Story of King David*, 16), he does 'not propose to make an assessment of its historicity, which is a complex matter deserving full treatment in its own right'; his approach 'does not amount to a denial that we might nevertheless have also historical information of value, though it does make it more difficult to be sure of precisely what that information might be'. As I see it, the fact that one can make a perfectly good commentary on a narrative taken as a literary piece does not touch on the question of whether it is useful as a historical document.

be read as excellent literature can also be an important historical source: Thucydides is an obvious example.

Thirdly, the heavily *theoretical* character of the argumentation simply removes it from historical significance. Look at Gottwald's 'search for the social world of the Bible':[69] Gottwald's whole approach is governed by his Marxist ideology. Why should we believe this? Not that Marxism has nothing from which we can learn; but, at a time when, after a long period of tyrannical cruel oppression, it has proved a total political and economic failure in the countries where it has been dominant, it is not evident why we should be impressed by its ability to interpret the Bible. Whitelam's whole article in *Companion* is rich in generalities but thin in factual substantiation:

We know, for instance, that the pastoral-nomadic element has been a constant in the social continuum of the region. Yet this element of society does not form part of the self-perception of those responsible for the development of the traditions. While nomads may have been a constant in the history of the region, their part in the past, and so the present, has been silenced by the literate elite of the Second Temple period, or whoever is responsible for this construction of this past.[70]

This is typical of Whitelam's arguments. Nomads are not mentioned: therefore they have been 'silenced' by the 'literary elite'. Conspiracy by the 'elite' to 'silence' the voices of the populace is a commonplace of his thinking. Moreover, he himself does not know if it was 'the literary elite of the Second Temple' or someone else, 'whoever is responsible'.[71]

Some of the theories about ideology that have begun to circulate are obviously absurd. It is commonly argued, for example, that 'history is written by the victors', the implication being that the true account of the facts lies not with the victors but with the

---

[69] Whitelam's wording, in Barton (ed.), *Companion*, 39.

[70] Ibid. 42–3.

[71] Whitelam's depiction of the modern scholarly tradition may well be questioned in other regards also. Thus he emphasizes (ibid. 45) 'the evolutionary development of society' as an assumption that has informed scholarship from the 19th century onwards and talks of 'the tremendous hold that evolutionary theory' has 'imposed upon biblical studies in general'. This might be true up to the 1930s or so, but thereafter the reverse was very emphatically the case, and evolution was generally thought to have been discredited: see Barr, *The Concept of Biblical Theology*, ch. 7. Similarly T. L. Thompson, *Early History of the Israelite People* (Leiden: Brill, 1992), 189, who writes: 'The paradigms of development and evolution . . . have been used all too long as interpretative models.'

defeated or 'marginalized'. This principle, if true, will mean that the true history of the twentieth century should be written by the surviving fascists, who were thoroughly defeated and marginalized. Such a conclusion would, of course, be most unwelcome to those who utter the principle. It is surely asinine stupidity to assert a principle that must contradict one's own most dearly held convictions. Actually, a good case could be made to the opposite effect, that some good histories are written by the defeated. Thus central to Thucydides' work is the disaster of the Athenian expedition to Sicily and, though the work as a whole ends before the final ending of the war, Athens hardly seemed to be heading for a glorious victory when the history came to its conclusion. In the Bible itself the so-called Deuteronomistic History, taken as a whole, looks more like a history leading to disaster than anything else.

Others of the theories, one suspects, are worked out by sociologists on the basis of experience in the modern world, the only place, of course, where ample sociological material can be gathered. Whitelam writes,

This has been followed by an appeal to and application of social-scientific theories of small group formation and development, sectarianism, conversion and deviance. In all cases contemporary models have been used to understand how and why Christianity spread throughout the Mediterranean world, its diversity and inner tensions, and the social world embedded within the biblical texts.[72]

Whitelam's article contains practically no factual evidence, only a listing and outlining of *methods* which will allegedly produce progress (sometime).[73]

More powerful still is the argument that revisionist history attempts to explain the uncertain by pushing it into the unknown.

[72] 'The Social World of the Bible', in Barton (ed.), *Companion*, 44. Must we always follow the guidance of models because they are 'contemporary'? In the case e.g. of Carroll's application of 'dissonance theory' from psychology to explain 'the development and applicability of prophetic texts', how do we know that this theory, built upon observations made within the *modern* world, is not distorting when applied to ancient Israel?

[73] Cf. the words of the revisionist Thompson, *Early History*, 405: 'What is amazing about the "models" of Mendenhall and Gottwald (and one could easily add Coote and Whitelam here) is not that their theories were unsupported by evidence, but that these theories, lacking evidence, were ever proposed. Logic, discipline and method were never entertained. . . . A sound sociological approach must allow evidence to precede theory.' Passages such as this seem to place Thompson closer to Provan's ideals than either of them have perceived.

Because (allegedly) the historicity of David and Solomon cannot
be positively proved, the traditions about them are to be moved
down to the Second Temple period. But what is known about *it*?
'It is ironic', Whitelam writes, 'that as the focal point of the social
world of the Bible has shifted from the Iron Age to [the] Persian,
it has become evident that *very little is known about the social and
historical background of the Second Temple period*' (my italics). Indeed
so. The traditions created by the 'literary elite' 'tell us little or
nothing of how these societies . . . were linked to the wider econ-
omy . . . nor are they informative of demography, settlement
patterns or economic trends, the best indicators of the deep-seated
movements of history which provide the wider perspective'.[74] But
when we hear about demography and settlement patterns, what do
we receive but scraps of information plus further outbursts of
theory and outlines of methods which will, it is hoped, produce
more in the future?

On the other hand, the Second Temple period is not so
completely unknown. It was indeed a period when biblical and
para-biblical traditions were formed, so that we know the sort of
thing they were writing. We have examples in Ezra, Nehemiah,
Chronicles, Esther, *Jubilees*, *Enoch*, and other works. I was about
to say: what we do not have from that time is something comparable to Samuel/Kings. In the past I would have been inclined to
say that Chronicles was not a real parallel. Here, however, I was
brought to a stop by A. Graeme Auld, for he makes a strong case,
from a detailed critical investigation, to the effect that both
Samuel/Kings and Chronicles are revisions of an earlier text,
which he calls 'the Shared Text'. Moreover, not only did they
both revise an earlier text, but at various points Chronicles retains
the older text, or stays nearer to it, than does Samuel/Kings.[75] I
will not go into the details of this, but for our purposes it means

---

74 Whitelam, in Barton (ed.), *Companion*, 43. Cf. Carroll, 'Textual Strategies', ibid.
109: 'So little is known about the social and historical background of the early Second
Temple period that many scholars have recourse to ideologically constructed social structures often drawn from the classical world.'
75 A. Graeme Auld, *Kings Without Privilege* (Edinburgh: T. & T. Clark, 1994). The
very useful and thoughtful work of M. Z. Brettler, *The Creation of History in Ancient Israel*
(London: Routledge, 1995), starts out with a chapter on 'Chronicles as a Model for Biblical
History', but it unfortunately overlapped with the publication of Auld's book and assumes,
if I understand it rightly, that Samuel/Kings were complete before Chronicles was
composed; this affects its argument considerably.

that Chronicles and Samuel/Kings can be closer to one another—
in type, in procedure, and possibly in date—than previous assessments would have suggested. This leaves open the date when the
Shared Text was composed, of course; but it certainly damages
the impression that Samuel/Kings comes directly from some
near-contemporary source. Or, in other words, if Chronicles is
still thought of as 'a late book', it provides a kind of parallel in
general genre for the idea that Samuel/Kings was 'a late book'
too, at least in some degree.[76] On the other hand it confirms the
major point that I want to make, namely, that the dominant literary activity in narrative was revision and interpretation. What I
cannot see a parallel for is something like 'historical fiction
inspired by ideology'. I cannot see anything closer than Tobit,
and it is not very close. The Dead Sea Scrolls had plenty of new
writing, plenty of interpretation and revision, but original writing
of historical narrative over a long space like the David story I
cannot see. I just cannot see that anyone in the Second Temple
period, inspired by ideology, would just *invent* all the material
about Abner and Asahel and Ittai the Gittite and Paltiel the son of
Laish. Elements of invention, yes, one can see in any story, but
the invention of material on such a scale seems entirely unconvincing as a theory. As for Ezra and Nehemiah, even if they were
inventions or propaganda or the like, I would not consider them
to be parallels in genre, and in any case I do not believe the
suppositions of their generally fictional character. They may
contain genuine letters and pieces of memoirs, around which,
quite possibly, politically and/or religiously aimed works have
been constructed in the course of revision. But, if we have no
definite evidence about the date of the text of Samuel/Kings as it
was before revision, I would be inclined to place it earlier rather
than later: at a time when information about names, persons,
places, incidents, still circulated in society. If we go on to consider
the Greek period, given preference by Carroll over even the
Persian,[77] we have considerable knowledge of how Jews were
writing at that time, information from the 'apocryphal' texts, the
Dead Sea Scrolls, papyri, and so on. What we do not have is

---

[76] See also Auld, 'Re-Reading Samuel', in V. Fritz and P. R. Davies, *The Origin of the Ancient Israelite States* (Sheffield: Sheffield Academic Press, 1996), 160–9.

[77] In Barton (ed.), *Companion*, 43; also by Davies, *In Search of 'Ancient Israel'*, 24 etc.

anything comparable with the origination of a major independent historical text covering the earlier monarchy.

Basically, it seems to me, it has been a mistake to suppose that ideology can or could initiate historical narrative. Ideology is a set of ideas. It can affect historical narrative and bias it, but it does not originate it. Ideology has characteristically *non-story* character. The story has to come from somewhere else—from memories, from traditions, from older books—and then ideology may build upon it, revise it, embellish it. Ideology is characteristically described as a system, and scholars have often emphasized that system is very different from narrative, and this is quite right in its way. Excessive reliance on the concept of ideology in modern times has caused quite improbable credulity towards notions of what it can accomplish. The idea that ideology could be transformed into complex narratives like the David story—at any time—seems absurd. But we are anticipating here, and we shall return to this theme in the next chapter.

Returning for a moment to talk of knowledge of the Persian period, it is noticeable, in view of the emphasis laid on this period in recent scholarship, how extremely little attempt has been made to learn Old Persian or encourage the study of this language among students. The majority of students of the Hebrew Bible may have some knowledge of the Greek of the Bible (though the Septuagint is sadly neglected in most centres), but very few will have the knowledge to read such historians as Herodotus (much appealed to by Van Seters) or Ptolemaic papyri. Fewer still will know a word of Old Persian: Hebrew studies have had their extension almost solely into the Semitic language family (hence Ugaritic, Aramaic, Phoenician, etc.), but Iranian languages, being from a quite different family, have been almost entirely untouched. For the present purpose this means that students who are learning that the essence of the Old Testament belongs to the Persian and Greek periods are at the same time being left very ill-equipped to judge for themselves what these periods were like, and are not much helped by the fact that their teachers, to judge from the literature produced so far, mostly know little or nothing of Old or Middle Persian and are themselves dependent on secondary sources. This leaves them all the more vulnerable to the largely ideological pictures, lacking in specific detail, that are being fed to them.

Again, one's doubts about revisionist positions are only increased by the hectic and hazardous character of some arguments that are used. One example already discussed (above, p. 73) is the matter of the Siloam tunnel inscription. However reasonable it may have been to question the commonly accepted date for the building of the tunnel, the launching of an argument on palaeographical grounds against the dating of the inscription in Hezekiah's time presents an impression of desperation, of seeking at all costs to discover something, however unsubstantial, that might undermine an early dating and confirm a Hellenistic dating for evidence relating to the Bible. Similarly, Thompson, among various arguments for a Hellenistic date, claims that 'sound methodology requires that we must look to the mid-second century as the earliest possible date for the extant form of the Pentateuch, and such a late date is confirmed by the variant chronologies of the LXX and the Samaritan Pentateuch'.[78] Certainly it is reasonable to attribute these chronological variations to that time. I fully agree with it. But all that the argument proves is that the 'extant form' is not a relevant criterion. For it proves too much. If one is strict about the 'extant form', we will end up proving that the Hebrew Bible 'as we have it' originates in the early Middle Ages. The existence of chronological differences in the third or second century does nothing to prove, or even to suggest, that all the narratives of the monarchy, even of the early monarchy, were products of a post-monarchical time. The use of such extremely marginal arguments only increases the impression that revisionist historiography is desperate for evidence.[79]

The most incredibly naïve of all such arguments, however, is Whitelam's explanation of the origin of kingship ideology, a subject to which he devotes an entire article.[80] Royal ideology was (of course) intended 'to overcome opposition and thus maintain

---

[78] Thompson, *Early History*, 356 n. 10.

[79] I now see from a recent review (*The Financial Times*, 20–1 Feb. 1999, p. v) that Thompson, in a new book, *The Bible in History: How Writers Create a Past* (London: Jonathan Cape, 1999), maintains of the Mesha inscription from Moab that 'research shows that the inscription, once interpreted in the light of the Bible rather than vice versa, is far later than its biblical interpretation says it is'. This would seem to be the same type of argument. But I have not seen the work itself.

[80] K. W. Whitelam, 'Israelite Kingship: The Royal Ideology and its Opponents', in R. E. Clements (ed.), *The World of Ancient Israel* (Cambridge: Cambridge University Press, 1989), 119–39; ref. to 121.

royal power'. But why depend on ideology? Because 'the use of force was too costly and on the whole inefficient . . . reliance upon coercion and force would destroy the very relationships upon which the ruling elite depended for their wealth and power'. All the elaborate structures of kingship ideology, built into a variety of religions, came into existence because *it would cost too much* to force people to obey! I have teased my friends Brevard Childs and Walter Brueggemann for their overuse of the term 'reductionism', but here I have to use it myself. As an explanation, this comes close to the definition of the true, prototypical reductionist: the man who, asked to define a violin sonata, said that it was 'a noise made by dragging the intestines of a cat across a piece of wire'. For childish absurdity, as a piece of explanation of religion, this is hard to beat.

We should also go back to our original mention of the revisionist historians and add the important point that they are by no means identical in their views. People do not like to be classified together, and not surprisingly Thompson objects to Provan's describing them as a 'school'[81]—though Provan put the term in inverted commas, showing that he did not mean it too seriously. For there are considerable differences between them.[82]

Thus take Gösta Ahlström, whom Provan quoted three times at the beginning of his article.[83] The quotations are quite accurate, and Ahlström did write such things as that 'the biblical narrators were not really concerned about historical truth' and that their product 'reflected the narrator's outlook and ideology rather than known facts'. He certainly could 'play off' ideology against history, to use Provan's terms. And thus his thinking does provide some of the elements which are characteristic of the revisionist movement. He, for example, undertook the writing of a history of Palestine and not one of Israel, and thus in principle, if unequally in fact, represented all the peoples of the region. He also, obviously, underlined the centrality of archaeology for his work. He was also

[81] *JBL* 114/4 (1995), 693–4, 601.
[82] For one example among many: Thompson, *Early History*, 151 n. 81, writes that 'Coote and Whitelam's interpretation of my understanding of nomadism is blatant nonsense. What they assert as my understanding is at times a caricature of my published views, and at times a total misrepresentation.' There is, then, a certain amount of disagreement within the revisionist group.
[83] *JBL* 114/4 (1995), 586–7, cf. again 594.

strongly negative towards anything like biblical theology or the intrusion of theological considerations into his historical work. In other ways, however, he was a bad choice for Provan to use as an example. In respect of the quotations Provan cites, Ahlström was somewhat like the man in the gospels who said he would not go but nevertheless went. For in spite of his many expressions of doubt about the historicity of the biblical narrative ('The presentation of David's life as a courtier in Saul's service reads more like an artistic novella than critical historiography'[84]), many pages of his writing in the period of the early kingdom follow very closely the biblical text, in a style similar to that which earlier historians had used, but more critical. Thompson is right to comment that while his group 'do date biblical texts relatively late', 'this cannot be said of Gösta Ahlström, who is rather very much in line with his generation'.[85] Much of the detailed material, e.g. about Absalom's rebellion, is restated, apparently as history, in Ahlström's work. David's 'empire', though perhaps reduced in size, is still there. Moreover, very tellingly, 'A certain kind of "historiography" may have been written in Jerusalem during the period of the united monarchy'.[86] The writings about David and Solomon do not really constitute history in the modern sense of the term. But, 'even if there are no [external] corroborations, the historicity of the Davidic-Solomonic kingdom should not be doubted . . . The period of the united monarchy was something exceptional within the history of Canaan, something that had never happened before nor happened since'.[87]

Thus, contrary to Provan's use of him as an example, Ahlström seems to me to be a considerable witness *against* the revisionist point of view. He belonged to an older-fashioned, fact-based outlook and was not close to the postmodern views which we shall be discussing. His severely critical spirit and his rejection of the impact of theological considerations only makes more striking his implied affirmation that the biblical story of the early kingdom *did* reflect the 'real world of the past'. Though he could use the word 'ideology', he did not belong to the postmodern world.

Nor does Garbini, of whom Davies rightly says that he 'seems

---

[84] G. W. Ahlström, *The History of Ancient Palestine* (Sheffield: JSOT, 1993), 458.
[85] *JBL* 114/4 (1995), 686 and n. 8.
[86] Ahlström, *History of Ancient Palestine*, 540. [87] Ibid. 541.

to combine a rigorous scepticism with the oddest flights of fancy'.[88] A fine expert in language and epigraphy, he seems to belong to that tradition, familiar on the frontiers between Semitic linguistics and biblical studies, of epigraphic expertise combined with a strong scepticism towards the text and traditional interpretations and an excessive credulity towards very remote counterproposals.[89] For one good example of the latter, one might be able to swallow the non-existence of Ezra as a historical person, but the precise alternative, that it all comes from Alcimus and his religious reform of 159 BC,[90] is too much to take seriously. David's 'empire' was only a small state; Solomon did not marry Pharaoh's daughter and did not enrich himself with international trade. 'All the rest is part of the story of Hebrew ideology.'[91] But at least there was a David and a Solomon, and they did something that is reflected in the biblical narrative. Garbini does not belong to postmodernism either. He does, however, in a later article, come down more clearly on the side of the Persian period as the 'two centuries that saw the writing and, most importantly, the reworking of a large part of Hebrew literature', while such writings as the Nehemiah memoirs come from the Greek period.[92] The book of Joshua 'reflects a historical situation markedly later than the exile and an ideology which it is difficult to date before the third century BC'.[93]

Again, John Van Seters has produced arguments that could appear to relate to the revisionist position. His book on Abraham argues steadfastly that the Abraham traditions date from about the time of the exile. His *In Search of History* argues that the Deuteronomist was Israel's first historian, while the Yahwist wrote

---

[88] Davies, *In Search of 'Ancient Israel'*, 15 n. 3.

[89] The statement on the back cover of the English translation of his book, to the effect that he 'might be said to be Italy's James Barr', is of doubtful canonicity.

[90] G. Garbini, *History and Ideology in Ancient Israel* (London: SCM, 1988), 151–69, ch. 13, is entirely about this suggestion for Ezra.   [91] Ibid. 32.

[92] Garbini, 'Hebrew Literature in the Persian Period', in T. C. Eskenazi and K. H. Richards, *Second Temple Studies*, ii. JSOTSup 175 (Sheffield: JSOT, 1994), 180–8; quotation from 180.

[93] Garbini, *History and Ideology in Ancient Israel*, 132. Garbini's arguments which lead to this conclusion take up an entire chapter (ch. 11, pp. 127–32) and form a good example of his reasoning. His final sentence is: 'The lack of a head, of a king, while improbable for social groups in Palestine at the beginning of the Iron Age, is, however, conceivable for a small group with a hierocratic government like that of Jerusalem after the exile—a "Hebrew people" without a "king" in Palestine existed only before the Hasmonaeans.'

still later.[94] This agrees with the late dating of sources, which is however only one of the features of the revisionist historiography. Van Seters also considers the 'documentary hypothesis' of the Pentateuch to be 'obsolete'.[95] But in general his approach through a comparative historiography seems, even if its results are different, to be more akin to traditional biblical criticism, and in fact many of its results are compatible with those reached in Pentateuchal researches of recent times. The term 'ideology' seems (mercifully) to occur seldom, if at all, and is absent from the index.

This chapter has concentrated mainly on the general history of Israel and has not particularly entered into the question of the history of religion and its relations with the theology of the Old Testament, a subject which was briefly mentioned in Ch. 2. We should, however, take up this question again, for it is of great importance in relation to the ideas of 'history' that have circulated in scholarship. For this purpose we go further back in scholarly history than the recent developments discussed above, for the problems are best exemplified by the work of Gerhard von Rad, doubtless the most renowned of Old Testament theologians in the past century. In his work the place of 'history' was central; but it also contained an ambiguity. On the one hand von Rad accepted and affirmed the basic results of biblical criticism in the Old Testament, and especially the form of 'tradition criticism' which had been developed by Alt, Noth, and himself. These remained fundamental to his scholarly vision. But to him, 'history' was more importantly a theological entity: it was the medium in which the God of Israel revealed himself. Thus the structure of his two volumes seemed on the one side to satisfy the historical–critical requirement of a sequential presentation, and on the other hand it seemed to show forth the stages of divine revelation. It was important to him that the Old Testament 'was a history book'. God had acted in history, something that, he implied, placed ancient Hebrew faith in a special revelatory category. But he was a critical scholar and did not suppose that actual history had been exactly the same as the narrations in the Bible suggested. He himself thought, perhaps, that the difference would not matter, but critics

---

[94] Cf. E. W. Nicholson, *The Pentateuch in the Twentieth Century* (Oxford: Clarendon, 1999), 149.

[95] John Van Seters, *In Search of History* (New Haven: Yale University Press, 1983), 16.

pressed the point. Were there two histories of ancient Israel, one the history as the texts depicted it, the other the history in which God had acted? What about those periods and episodes in Israel's history which were simply not reported in the Bible? And was it not impossible to envisage a history of salvation which stopped and started according as people responded to it or failed to respond to it? Or, as critics like Hesse insisted, if we affirm that God acted in history, does this not have to mean that he acted in the entire history of Israel as it really took place, so that the biblical depiction would be basically ancillary, a subordinate adumbration of the reality?

Von Rad, I think, never solved this problem: it vexed him but he could not overcome it. He tried two paths: one was to say that it was 'positivism' to identify a history more real than that which the biblical texts delineated, to try to know what had really happened, and the name of positivism, he thought, was enough to scare people away from that. But of course it was not positivism at all: it was a perfectly proper historical question. The other path he tried was to say that the difference was not so very great in the long run: the gap between the biblical narration and the actual history existed, but was quite slight. (In this respect it was he who came closer to positivism!) He was unable to overcome this difficulty and in the end, I think, gave up.

There is one way in which it could, perhaps, be overcome, and here the postmodern suggestions may help us. There was much that was *history* although it was not inscribed as such in the Bible (the use of the word 'inscribed' shows that I am becoming something of a postmodernist myself!). The point is not so much that there are inaccuracies, that events are described in the Bible differently from how they really were. Critics of von Rad perhaps concentrated too much on this aspect, and it is in itself perfectly valid. Nevertheless the main point is, rather, that there was much that was history that did not find its way into the Bible. Von Rad, of course, knew this perfectly well; but the focus of his mind was on salvation history as it was represented in the Bible, and how that might be reactualized today. If we continue to think of 'God in history'—and this question lies beyond our discussion at this point—we do best to modify von Rad's thinking and think of a history that included much that never found its way into the Bible. It would have to include such things as the history of women and of non-Israelites, and the history of times lying outside the biblical canon. The Hebrew Bible would thus function as a canonical sign that pointed towards this totality. In this respect I think of H. Berkhof, who, at the point of his *Christian Faith* where it would be normal to place a chapter on the Old Testament, placed rather a chapter on the 'Way of Israel'. The Bible consists of the memories which Israel retained out of all this history, as a guide to the theological interpretation of it. To say today that God 'acted in history' would be to go back into the world of the Bible but to see beyond it that wider world much of which the Bible leaves unmentioned.

When we go beyond this to ask why some things were selected and retained, other things left out and forgotten, this brings us to one of the central objections against the concept of ideology as it is currently used. The idea that things unmentioned in the Bible were 'silenced' by the 'literary élite' seems to me a baseless modern myth. I am not convinced that there was any 'literary élite', and would wish to see a lot of evidence about its character before judging what it did. As for its 'silencing' other voices, this reminds me of a student I once knew, a Communist, who wrote a letter to the newspaper about some matter and, when the paper did not print it, complained that his letter had been 'suppressed'. Of course the paper did not suppress it; they just did not print it. I do not doubt that aspects of Israelite life and history may at times have been wrongfully passed over: the modern scholar Albertz argues that Chronicles wrongly failed to express the needs of the poor.[96] But that the 'silencing' of the poor, of women, of non-Jews, and of substantial portions of history was *always* or *normally* the effect of such a process, in other words that the essential shape of the Bible was created by such action, I just do not believe.

And ultimately this goes back to the idea of ideology. In much postmodernism ideology is conceived of in a purely selfish way. According to it, no one thinks anything or does anything except for their own, or their own group's, status and prosperity, all of which is ultimately reducible to power and wealth.[97] But when

---

[96] Albertz, *History of Israelite Religion*, ii. 556; cf. Barr, *The Concept of Biblical Theology*, ch. 8.

[97] Here, I realize, I come closer than I expected to Provan's suspicion that revisionist historiography was 'materialist', though I do not think he explained this very well, or indeed at all. The 'material' in question at this point is not physical matter, but power and

religion is involved in ideology, we have to consider that people think things, and do things, for their religion itself. Religion is of course socially linked but it is not so directly socially linked that nothing happens in religion except for social advantage. Obviously religious motivation does not make all actions good—*tantum religio potuit suadere malorum*—but it presents a different facet of the picture from the one that much postmodernism has offered.

On the other side, the postmodern material that we have surveyed is unquestionably prejudiced against the supposed élite. This is not new, and has been noticed before: Sundermeier called attention to it in Albertz's work, arguing that his 'anti-élitism causes a distortion'.[98] But the prejudice has grown greatly in recent times.[99] Why should leadership not have seen, at times, more clearly than other people? Why should not right decisions have been suppressed by the pressure of popular hostility? It certainly happens in the modern world. Perhaps postmodernists could admit these as possibilities, but they certainly do not allow them to figure much in the material we have surveyed.

And the reason is obvious: the ideology of postmodernism, at least in this aspect, very much reflects the modern, Western world. It reflects a world of freedom, in the sense that all persons have a vote and have opportunity; they have equality—not, of course, in the matter of wealth, but they have (theoretically) the chance to become wealthy. There is a constitutional government of some kind and some organized sort of access to justice. Élites are wrong because they have some sort of advantage (privilege is the correct word). In other words, all this reflects the culture of the modern world under its American leadership.

What it does not reflect or understand is a society where many of these conditions do not exist, where élites may be necessary for the functioning of the society—as is still the case in many societies today, notably religiously dominated societies, and also in fact, even if not in theory, in such fully modern societies as the United

wealth. In Dever's use of 'materialist', referred to above, n. 17, he is referring to physical remains, detected and explained by archaeology, from which knowledge of culture can be derived; that is something different.

98   Th. Sundermeier in *JBTh* 10 (1995), 204; Barr, *The Concept of Biblical Theology*, 126.

99   Thus W. Brueggemann in his *Theology of the Old Testament* (Minneapolis: Fortress, 1997), the first such work to take a clearly postmodernist approach, tells us several times that Plato was an 'elitist' and that the Sophists are much to be preferred on these grounds; see Barr, *The Concept of Biblical Theology*, 556–7.

States. Why did peoples have kings and emperors, right up into the twentieth century? Why did soldiers give their lives for them?

I pointed out earlier in this chapter that it was no new thing for biblical sources to be assigned to periods considerably later than the events related in them, and that this had been fairly widely accepted, stage by stage, as it happened. Even if Moses himself wrote the Pentateuch, he was a 'late' source in relation to the events of Abraham's life (over six hundred years earlier by the chronology of the Masoretic Text). That the traditions of the time of the Judges were somewhat vaguely related to history could probably be accepted by many. Why then should we be disturbed if the traditions of David and Solomon are judged to be largely unhistorical and the sources begin only around the sixth century or later, or indeed in the Persian period? And if in the Persian period, why not in the Greek period? What difference does it make? If the first step was theologically acceptable, why not the others also? Is there any fundamental issue for theology in the matter?

I think there is, because it is not a matter only of the date of sources or the accuracy of this story or that. Especially if we take Philip Davies's position into account, it is primarily and ultimately a question of the existence of the people of Israel altogether. As I have argued above, much revisionist history seeks to explain the uncertain by pushing it into the unknown. In spite of the emphasis of historians on archaeology, their writings are full of complaints about the lack of information to be gained from that source. Push the biblical sources down to the exile, and here again we have complaints about the lack of information. By all means let us admit that in these bad times there were people who would have wished to construct their people's past in a way that fitted with their ideology, but what evidence is there that they would have written such material as the story of David and Solomon and the earlier kings? Moreover, the reader may object, once we get into the Persian period we have definite examples of historical writing in Ezra and Nehemiah. Not necessarily so. For, admittedly, even on older traditional assumptions, the books with these names are full of detailed difficulties; notoriously, it was difficult to be sure which of the two came first, and how their activities overlapped. From this it is a small step to considering that they too were perhaps largely products of ideology, and if so were still later.

In fact it is in its picture of the exile and the later periods generally that revisionist historiography creates the most serious problems, more serious than the historical accuracy of the stories of David, Solomon, and the early kingdom. According to some currents of it, the picture of the exile and the return from exile is ideological too, and does not correspond to any historical reality.[100] Davies writes:

> The biblical literature presents us with an 'exile' of most of the population to Babylonia, followed by an emptying of the land, an emptiness also evaluated as a 'sabbath rest' for the land. The result is that the 'exiles' who then return constitute all of 'Israel' and have a land to themselves (apart, perhaps from alien settlers?) . . . *This* is the 'exile' and as such it is an ideological and not a historical one, though an ideologically contradictory one.[101]

Again, with an additional note of sarcasm:

> The biblical literature also presents 'Israel' two or three generations later as the descendants of these 'exiles', having become those who alone preserved the religion, and who, on their 'return', proceed to isolate themselves from the 'people of the land'. Biblical historians, it was noted, fondly imagine the deportees hugging their copies of Deuteronomy or transcripts of the oracles of Jeremiah to their chests, and spending evenings in Tel Abib ruminating on their plight and preserving the faith, developing their literature into long histories and bodies of law and huge collections of oracles, all the while longing to return to 'Zion' (i.e. Jerusalem).[102]

A similar view is quite heavily emphasized by Thompson:

> Isaiah 40–48 understand Cyrus as 'restoring' the traditional people of the land—of course now misunderstood by the Persian administration and Isaiah as 'Israel'—the people destroyed by the Assyrians some two centuries earlier—in *Jerusalem* and as 'restoring' their ancestral faith in the one true God. It is, of course, clear that we are not dealing with the restoration of exiles to their homeland any more than we are dealing with the restoration of an ancient forgotten cult or the rebuilding of a temple. The texts reflect the transportation and creation of a new people with a new cult, expressing an understanding of the divine that is central to the

---

[100] 'The biblical literature's sparse data on life in Babylonia (mostly in Ezekiel) are of dubious reliability: it is biblical scholarship which has painted a fanciful portrait of religious fervour and furious literary creativity among Judaeans in Babylonia'—so Davies, *In Search of 'Ancient Israel'*, 80.   [101] Ibid. 42.   [102] Ibid. 57.

imperial administration and identified with a divine name common to the larger region's traditional past. This can be described as the creation of a new society centered on a new temple and administered by the Persian administrator, who himself identifies with these people.[103]

There had been, then, if I understand this correctly, no exile of a whole people and no return of one. What happened was initiated, it seems, by Persian government policy. But, since so little is known of the Persian period, we come to rest in the Greek period. Garbini, as mentioned above, thought that no Ezra had existed in the Persian period and the book named after him came from 159 BC, in the Maccabean period.

Moreover, this is not all. For one might say, however late the writings, there is a continuity in the community, along with the transmission of traditions, all of which perhaps coalesced in the Greek period. Theologically one could live with that. But this is what Davies particularly wants to deny:

To explain the existence of the biblical literature, we must conclude that the creation of what was in truth a *new* society, marking a definitive break with what had preceded, was accompanied by—or at least soon generated—an ideological superstructure which denied its more recent origins, its imperial basis, and instead indigenized itself. Its literate class . . . created an identity continuous with kingdoms that had previously occupied that area, of whom no doubt some concrete memory remained within Palestine, and very probably some archival material too, and wrote into the history of their region an 'Israel' which explained their own post-'exilic' society and the rights and privileges of the immigrant élite within that society.[104]

And, as Davies says elsewhere,

The one major argument which binds the biblical history together is that of continuity: 'Israel' (the true 'Israel') has been in 'Canaan' a long time: the Temple has stood in its site for centuries: the predecessors of the high priests are the kings of Judah (likewise anointed). The ideological triumph of the biblical story is to convince that what is new is actually old.[105]

Thus the biblical literature did not come from 'Israel' or an actual life of a people: it was, essentially a creation of the scribe at

103 Thompson, *Early History*, 418.
104 Davies, *In Search of 'Ancient Israel'*, 87. 105 Ibid. 120.

the writing desk: 'the literature created the identity "Israel" to which a Jew could relate'.[106] 'Biblical Hebrew' was not an actual language used in ancient times: it is 'another scholarly construct; indeed we might say that it is no more than the imputed language of the scholarly "ancient Israel", and thus part of a larger fabrication'.[107]

And this is the essential thing: there was no 'Ancient Israel', no actual community delineated as it is delineated in the Bible. The cutting of the link of continuity and community is central to Davies's argument. It is central to his anti-theology. (On the other hand one cannot necessarily say that this is the case for all revisionist historians.)

It seems to me that the cutting of the link of continuity presents a threat to religion of a kind and magnitude quite different from what happened when various books or strata came to be dated 'late'. If it should be proved to be historically correct, then theology would have to consider how it should be met. For the present, I suggest that it is sufficient to deny its historical seriousness. Unquestionably the biblical picture of the exile and return has to be rated *critically*: its information may be partial and its emphases exaggerated. Relations between the exiles in Babylonia and those who remained in their land (the idea that the land was emptied, and that this was standard scholarly opinion, was new to me) are unclear (as is the case with the fate of northern Israel as described in 2 Kings 17: 24–41), and the material of Ezra/Nehemiah is difficult to reconcile and make into a clear picture or series of pictures. But, granted all these obscurities and inadequacies, it remains that the 'revisionist' picture, according to which bands of unknown people, of whom the only thing certain is that they were not Jews or 'Israel', were formed into a new society by the initiative of the Persian government (!) and provided with a newly created ideology, still under construction in the Greek period, which then identified them with a past people of Israel and made them into 'Jews' with the traditions of Abraham, Moses, and David, cult and temple—such a reconstruction, far from being well evidenced

---

[106] Davies, *In Search of 'Ancient Israel'*, 154.

[107] Ibid. 104–5. This argument, though there are some other scholars to whom Davies can appeal, seems to me to be another of the 'arguments of desperation' some of which were listed above. I think that the linguistic evidence is a very strong obstacle to the revisionist case; but details of it cannot be presented here.

historically, is—at least at present—too absurd to be taken seriously. It rests very little upon evidence, very largely on the conceptions and methods of those who have constructed it. It forms rather a *reductio ad absurdum* of the way in which the narrative traditions referring to earlier times have been handled. Central to this is the emphatic, but unequal, insistence of revisionist historiography on *proof*. Proof for the Davidic and Solomonic empire is not available, and that means that the reports of it are likely to be explicable as ideology from a much later time. But for the highly conjectural suggestions made by the same historians about the exile, the return, the supposed part of the Persian government, and the activity of the literary élite during the Hellenistic period, commonly no such demand for proof is made. Many of these proposals rest not at all upon positive proof. They tend to depend rather on a sort of residual logic: other explanations being without proof, nothing is left except to suppose an explanation through late ideology, fabrications of the literary élite, and other hypotheses. Inequality in the application of the demand for proof is a serious fault.

It should be added that there is much discussion of these topics in recent scholarship, much more than the limited amount that I have surveyed here. That Israel in some sense 'constructed' its history has come to be taken seriously, over a wider spectrum of scholarship than I have depicted in these pages. Important studies that reached me too late to be fully discussed include M. Z. Brettler's *The Creation of History in Ancient Israel* and *Israël construit son histoire* edited by A. de Pury and others.[108]

We have said enough for the present to indicate that the obnoxious term 'ideology' requires further investigation, and our next chapter will turn to that task in particular.

---

[108] A. de Pury, T. Römer, and J.-D. Macchi (eds.), *Israël construit son histoire* (Geneva: Labor et Fides, 1996).

5

Ideology

WE have seen that the term 'ideology' has come to be heard much more frequently on the modern theological scene and is quite common in relation to biblical study. 'In my opinion', wrote David Clines, ' "ideology" is going to be the catchword of the 1990s in biblical criticism.'[1] This may well have been correct. The term is used, however, in a bewildering variety of ways, so that it is far from easy to know exactly what is meant; as a first step therefore we have to try to sort out the various usages and see if they have any point of common meaning with one another.

Rather than start from the often fearsome explanations given by experts on the subject,[2] perhaps we may begin with some usages of common speech, which are not particularly related to biblical study, but might give us a hint of what speakers commonly have in mind when they use the term.

One way to go is to contrast 'ideological' with 'pragmatic': we hear this quite a lot when we talk about politics. An ideological person will have principles and convictions that will override any factual evidence or any indication of the practical possibilities; a pragmatic person may share these same principles and convictions—thus, may belong to the same political party—but will want to look at the facts, determine what is practically possible, and may even adjust the principles and convictions so as to meet these realities. That is one way to define 'ideological'. Ideology is a world-view or set of ideas that is so intensely held that factual realities and practical considerations have no power to alter or affect it. Interestingly, this usage implies, or at least might suggest, that there are degrees of involvement in ideology and

---

[1] D. J. A. Clines, 'Possibilities and Priorities of Biblical Interpretation in an International Perspective', *Biblical Interpretation*, 1 (1993), 67–87, 86.

[2] e.g. J. Plamenatz, *Ideology* (New York: Praeger, 1970); T. Eagleton, *Ideology* (London: Verso, 1991).

that one has some sort of choice in the extent to which one is involved in it.

Incidentally, the example thus illustrated from political life may have a deeper significance. People's increasing perception of things in terms of 'ideology' may well be connected with the mounting cynicism about politics (and, probably, also about law) in the great democracies in the last third of the twentieth century. The speech of politicians is perceived only rarely as rational or truthful, or as aimed at the public good and right: much more often it is perceived as ideological and hypocritical, heavily influenced by money and partisanship. What is said is more often perceived as coming out of ideology and not out of intentions about what will practically be done. The impeachment process of President Clinton constitutes in this respect a fitting culmination to the millennium.[3] But we must return to our basic theme.

Another approach might be through the quality and originality of ideas. An original thinker or academic might investigate a problem and produce an answer—say, a historical work, a scientific solution, or a volume of philosophy. Such a work would not be ideology, it would be science, history, or philosophy. Ideology would appear when some few elements or rough outlines from such work come to be picked up at second hand and become part of the world-view of people who had never followed out the original investigation and would never have understood it if they had done so. The original work is serious thought, the half-unthinking use of it is ideology. Darwin was a major scientist, but social Darwinism is, perhaps, an ideology. 'Classical economics has been the major ideology of capitalism as a system of power,' wrote C. Wright Mills.[4] The classical economists—Adam Smith, for example—may have been serious thinkers, but the application of their ideas has, according to this usage, been ideology. In theology, I have suggested elsewhere,[5] Karl Barth was a great and foremost thinker, while Barthianism might be considered an ideology. According to this definition, the character of ideology is its

---

[3] On the idea of hypocrisy, the importance of which for religion and society I consider to be often underestimated, I have written in my article 'The Hebrew/Aramaic Background of "Hypocrisy" in the Gospels', in *A Tribute to Geza Vermes* (Sheffield: JSOT, 1990), 307–26.

[4] *The Sociological Imagination* (New York: Oxford University Press, 1959), 82.

[5] J. Barr, *The Concept of Biblical Theology* (London: SCM, 1999), 437.

second-hand, half-baked, quality. We follow this line when we say of someone, 'He's just repeating the usual party ideology,' that is to say, he has not thought out anything afresh, he is just saying again what we could have predicted, because it is always said.[6]

A third way in which the term 'ideology' is used seems to stress its unconscious character, its existence as a determinate of one's species, status, or background. One does not know one's own ideology. If you are a white male born in Glasgow in 1924 you will have a certain ideology, or a high probability of having it; you may not be aware of your own ideology, but that is normal. Other people will kindly identify it for you. If you say you do not share that ideology, people will not believe you, for your denial is clear evidence of its power over you. This way of using the term 'ideology' is particularly common in relation to questions of race and gender.

A fourth aspect is that an ideology should be in some way comprehensive. In that sense a mere idea is not an ideology. Thus the term 'system' is often used in the description of ideology. One might have the *idea* that the military life is good for one and builds up character; but this becomes the *ideology* of militarism only when it is linked in a system with all sorts of other thoughts about society, nationality, and ethics (and, very likely, religion).

To this we may add the observation that ideologies normally have the form of generalizations. That Donald MacDougal, a citizen of Aberdeen, is stingy would not be an ideology; but the widely held belief that all Aberdonians are stingy would be more like an ideology. As was mentioned in the last chapter, an ideology does not create a story; but it may form a generalization which recurs in one. Thus it is reasonable to maintain that it was an ideology to suppose that all the kings of Israel and almost all those of Judah did evil, failed to remove the high places, and so on: this, whether historically accurate or not, is a generalization. But a story element, such as that Zimri killed Elah the son of Baasha while drinking in the house of Arza in Tirzah (1 Kings 16: 9) can scarcely be generated by ideology, though it may fit in with one or be affected by one. The common belief that world peace has always been secured by the balance of power (most of the time) is surely

---

[6] In biblical study, Robert Carroll's frequent distinction between the prophet Jeremiah and 'Deuteronomic ideology' may well fit into this category. See further below, p. 121–4.

an ideological generalization, and is something entirely different from the task of assembling detailed information for a history or a political study which would cover the same periods or areas.

Common ground, again, is the idea that an ideology is social property; an individual may have an idea, an opinion, but it is an ideology only when he has it because it is shared by a whole section of society. He has it because he is a lawyer, or a businessman, or a miner, or a policeman, or a member of the Rotary Club; or because he is an Irishman or a foreigner in general. Or she is a married woman or a schoolteacher.

In the previous chapters I mentioned a few times the idea of the objective, of objective truth or objectivity. Whatever the objective may be, we may be sure that ideology is the opposite of it. Ideology consists of ideas and views that have their basis not in some external reality but in the social needs and interests of those who hold these ideas and views. It is common, in fact, to deride ideas of objectivity on the grounds that they themselves are excellent examples of ideology: we have already had hints of this in the last chapter, and other good examples will be considered shortly.

One thing common to all these uses, or most of them, is that *ideology* is a pejorative term. Ideology is a bad thing. Or is it? That is the next question. Historically, it appears that the connotation of the term has changed. In earlier times it was definitely used pejoratively, and dictionaries and encyclopaedias usually begin by explaining it so. The article by Roy Bhaskar in the excellent *Encyclopedic Dictionary of Psychology* edited by Rom Harré and Roger Lamb begins this way: 'Ideology. Any false, and especially categorically mistaken, ensemble of ideas, whose falsity is explicable, wholly or in part, in terms of the social role or function they, normally unwittingly, serve.'[7] Ideologies are sets of *mistaken* ideas.

This appears to be the original Marxian sense. According to Kolakowski,

'Ideology' is a false consciousness or an obfuscated mental process in which men do not understand the forces that actually guide their thinking, but imagine it to be wholly governed by logical and intellectual influences. When thus deluded, the thinker is unaware that all thought, and particularly his own, is subject in its course and outcome

---

[7] R. Bhaskar, 'Ideology', in R. Harré and R. Lamb, *Encyclopedic Dictionary of Psychology* (Oxford: Blackwell, 1983), 292.

to extra-intellectual social conditions, which it expresses in a form distorted by the interests and preferences of some collectivity or other . . . The fact that human thought is determined by the conflicts of material life is not consciously reflected in ideological constructions, or they would not truly deserve the name of ideology . . . All philosophers are ideologists in this sense; so are religious thinkers and reformers, jurists, the creators of political programmes etc.[8]

Marx, apparently, did not specifically include postmodern biblical scholars in this list, but it would surely be unfair to leave them out.

Within Marxism itself, however, the term came later to be used differently. According to the same authority,

It was not until much later, in Stalin's time, that Marxists came to use 'ideology' to denote all forms of social consciousness, including those that were supposed to present a scientific account of the world, free from mystification and distortion. In this sense it was possible to speak of 'scientific' or of 'Marxist' ideology, which Marx and Engels, given their use of the term, could never have done.[9]

Or, following the other article which I quoted, subsequent traditions, both Marxian and non-Marxian, 'played down the "negative" connotation of false consciousness and emphasized the "positive" notion of ideology as expressing the values or worldview of a particular social group or milieu. More recently there has been a tendency, e.g. within modern structuralism, for ideology to become effectively identified with the entire cultural sphere.'[10]

And the same picture appears in such a modern biblical study as John Elliott's *Social-Scientific Criticism of the New Testament*, which defines ideology as 'an integrated system of beliefs, assumptions and values, *not necessarily true or false*, which reflects the needs and interests of a group or class at a particular time in history'.[11] According to this viewpoint, ideology is a neutral term: it may be true or false, but it is ideology in either case. Its reflection of class interests, on the other hand, is taken to be essential.

And this may be, technically speaking, quite justified. It appears also that there is a difference between different modern languages in this respect. Martin Rose points out that the standard German dictionary *Duden* indicates a dominantly pejorative sense: a theory

    [8] L. Kolakowski, *Main Currents of Marxism* (Oxford: Oxford University Press, 1981), i. 154.   [9] Ibid.   [10] Bhaskar, 'Ideology', 292.
    [11] (London: SPCK, 1995), 52 (my italics).

'remote from the world' (*weltfremd*), an 'inauthentic' (*unecht*) world-view.[12] In French, the *Petit Robert* gives no indication that the pejorative sense is dominant: 'An ensemble of the ideas, beliefs and doctrines belonging to a period, a society or a class' ('Ensemble des idées, des croyances et des doctrines propres à une époque, à une société ou à une classe'). If this is correct, it seems to me that English usage distinctly follows the German rather than the French.

Thus for most English speakers 'ideology' continues to have a strong negative connotation; this is confirmed by most of the usage by biblical scholars as quoted below, and I propose to take that as normal in what follows. No one expresses this with greater authority than the noted anthropologist Clifford Geertz: 'Almost universally now the familiar parodic paradigm applies: "I have a social philosophy; you have political opinions; he has an ideology"'.[13] Geertz, however, was not entirely happy with this situation. As he expressed it: 'It is one of the minor ironies of modern intellectual history that the term "ideology" has itself become thoroughly ideologized,'[14] and he goes on to point out that its employment tends to be distinctly polemical. We shall see that there is a strong current of exactly this usage within theology and biblical studies. Geertz himself, however, thought that this pejorative or polemical usage was a sign of a failure in sociology, which has 'not yet developed a genuinely nonevaluative conception of ideology'.[15] In theology, of course, this is not surprising, since important trends in theology would deplore the idea that a 'nonevaluative' conception was desirable at all.[16]

People do not like to hear their opinions described as 'ideology'; theologians mostly do not think that their theology is ideology; biblical scholars, some of them at least, are not happy when the contents of the Bible are classified as ideology. There may be exceptions, but this we will take as the normal position (the default position, in modern computer terminology), to which exceptions will be mentioned as they come to our notice. It remains of great

[12] M. Rose, 'Idéologie deutéronomiste et théologie de l'Ancien Testament', in A. de Pury, Th. Römer, and J.-D. Macchi (eds.), *Israël construit son histoire*, 445–6. With special reference to ancient Israel see particularly A. D. H. Mayes, 'De l'Idéologie deutéronomiste à la théologie de l'Ancien Testament', ibid. 478–87.
[13] Geertz, *The Interpretation of Cultures* (New York: Basic Books, 1973), 194.
[14] Ibid. 193.   [15] Ibid. 196.
[16] On this see Barr, *The Concept of Biblical Theology*, ch. 12.

importance, however, that although the common perception of the term 'ideology' is a perception of it as pejorative, perceptions of it as neutral or even as positively admirable do occur. One suspects that some clever writers take advantage of the possible ambiguity that lies in this.

Moreover, it is not surprising that these ambiguities exist. It remains a serious question whether the word 'ideology' is a suitable one for use in the problems we are discussing. Many have used the word but most of them have adopted it without discussion of its appropriateness. A point of great importance is made by Hans Barstad, who, while mentioning that 'all "history writing" contains elements of "ideology" ', goes on to add in a note the following (I omit the bibliographical references included by him):

> The very word 'ideology', also a creation of the intellectuals of the modern, western, European world, is equally [as] problematic as the word 'history'. It is, therefore, only with the greatest impreciseness that we can use such anachronistic conceptual apparatus on biblical narratives at all. The distinction made between 'history' on the one side and 'ideology' on the other is equally problematic.[17]

When we look back at the quotations in the last chapter and see how very often 'history' and 'ideology' have been contrasted, we realize how necessary this comment is. Equally, the sense of 'history' in reference to the Bible is felt to be unclear, and attempts have been made to replace it with another word; why, if so, should 'ideology' be treated as if it was a clear and wholly satisfactory term? It may be worthwhile to add that 'history', though not a biblical word, was certainly integrated early into religious usage in Christianity; 'ideology', on the other hand, came into use at the earliest in the early nineteenth century, in a current of the modern world where religion did not count and was not worth taking into consideration when the sense of words was being determined. These points should be borne in mind as we proceed.

I have mentioned the distinction between theology and ideology, and the fact that theologians would, in a vast majority of cases, consider 'theology' as a positive term but 'ideology' as a negative one. It may be useful as a next step to consider this distinction.

---

[17] Barstad, *The Myth of the Empty Land* (Oslo: Scandinavian University Press, 1996), 35–6 n. 18.

How and when, exactly, did people begin to use ideology as a central concept in theological and biblical discussion?[18] I have not attempted serious research into the question, but it is easy to surmise two or three paths by which the usage became common. First, I imagine it may have been connected with the major theological changes of the twentieth century. If some older theologies, including that roughly named as 'liberalism', but also some conservative trends, saw some kind of common basis and tendency between theology on the one hand and major environing world-views on the other, the dialectical theology of Barth, Brunner, and Bultmann emphasized the separateness of theology; but, in so doing, it tended to represent these world-views as systems comparable with theology yet radically different from it. On the one hand, the term 'theology' itself was revived as a fully central and positive reality (unlike 'religion', which tended to lose status), and 'ideology' was readily available as an antonym. There was a sense of opposition as against powerful national and political world-views, and along with these perhaps a certain degree of influence from Marxism and sympathy for it, on the part of Barth and some others. Theology came clear and pure from divine revelation: ideology was a human construction of the world, based on human experience and human reason. Moreover, it was stressed that religion was not in essence a set of ideas that had to be accepted or assented to: rather, it was in essence a personal relation with a personal being. If one follows this line of thought, ideologies come close to the sets of ideas which do *not* represent religion, or at least not true religion. I do not have clear evidence to quote, but my feeling is that it was after the Second World War when many of these influences began to become familiar in theological speech.

In any case, it became an obvious enough terminological procedure for all sorts of argument: for example, the numerous arguments between historians and theologians. Some historians might classify theology as a prime example of ideology; theology was not an 'objective' study such as history was. Theologians in reply

---

[18] For the earlier history of the subject, I have found the Swiss philosopher Hans Barth's *Truth and Ideology* (Zurich: Rentsch, 1945), excellent. It was basically completed, however, in 1945, and gives little idea of the more modern developments. And it makes little contact with biblical or theological matters, except for a passage on 'Feuerbach's Reduction of Theology to Anthropology', pp. 55–8.

could argue that every historian himself has some kind of national, political, or economic allegiance, some 'agenda' as people now say; history was not an impartial science, but was, if not simply ideology, at least ideologically influenced. Some went on to argue that theology by contrast is a science, with its base well set upon reality, while other world-views were ideologies—and so on. One way or another, it became a common argument within theology that the critics of religion themselves had some kind of ideological commitment which was just as lacking in scientific proof as theology itself was.[19] And thus, rightly or wrongly, it became common coin within theology to classify anti-religious or non-religious arguments as 'ideological'. This is one path that was taken.

Another path led in the opposite direction: it started from the doubts of biblical scholars about biblical theology, or about the presence of theology within the Bible. The systematic character of traditional theology made it difficult to fit it within the Bible. A theology, it seemed, had to have a character of cohesiveness, comprehensiveness, and coherence which simply could not be applied to biblical texts in their particularity and their historical situation. Decisions about the theology implied by biblical texts seemed to many biblical scholars to be difficult to take, on the basis on which they normally worked. Those who felt this way were unhappy about 'theology' within the Bible but, if it was necessary to use a term for systems or patterns of biblical thinking, 'ideology' might be a better candidate; and it had the advantage, that unlike 'theology', it did not belong to the tradition of theology itself and did not have the authoritarian aspects which had commonly belonged to theology.

A third influence has been, undoubtedly, the increasing influence of sociological thought and methods upon biblical scholarship. Social perspectives promised to provide fresh understandings of biblical texts and biblical religion. But sociologists used the term 'ideology' freely, while the term 'theology' was more unfamiliar or unattractive to many of them. Traditional theology had always taught that the Bible was, in a sense, a community production: it was the voice of ancient Israel, the voice of the apostolic church. But, perhaps even more, it was the voice of great individuals, of Abraham, Moses, Isaiah, Jeremiah, Daniel, Jesus, and St Paul.

---

[19]   We saw a similar argument by Provan in the previous chapter.

Their utterances could, perhaps, be integrated by interpretation with traditional theology. This individual emphasis was deeply affected by biblical criticism, even more again as form criticism developed, and most of all, finally, as more and more attention was devoted to the social aspects of biblical religion. In particular, sociological studies suggested that behind the Bible there were competing groups and strata of society, and that where cohesive expressions of viewpoints appeared they represented the competing interests of these groups or strata: in other words, they were the ideologies of these social entities. What was seen as 'theology' seemed, by the use of that term alone, to demand full acceptance as authority; that which is classed as ideology, or still more as a variety of ideologies, seems to invite criticism and at the best only partial acceptance.

Along these three paths, then, and perhaps others, the use of the term 'ideology', whether used positively or pejoratively, found its way into theology and biblical studies in the later twentieth century.

Moreover, this terminology found much use within the conflicts between theologies and theological interpretations of the Bible. Thus we sometimes find one kind of theology classifying another, if not as being pure ideology, at least as adopting too much from some current ideology. Among biblical scholars this is well exemplified by Brevard Childs. In his language 'theology' is an extremely favourable term: I have said that he 'idealizes' theology. But 'ideology' is at the other end of the spectrum, a term of condemnation. When he is extremely hostile to a direction in biblical theology, he calls it 'ideological'. Thus in describing the work of the Harvard scholar Paul Hanson he writes, 'The ironical feature of this form of biblical theology is that in the name of objective, socio-historical analysis such a highly *ideological* construal of theology could emerge which frequently turns into unabashed propaganda for modern liberal Protestant theology.'[20] In spite of his own general closeness to the work of Hans-Joachim Kraus,

---

[20] B. S. Childs, *Biblical Theology of the Old and New Testaments* (London: SCM, 1992), 18. Cf. ibid. 183, 204, 225, 340, 395, 429, 526, 585, 649, 660. On liberation theology cf. his *Old Testament Theology in its Canonical Context* (Philadelphia: Fortress, 1985), 49: 'the contemporary use of "liberation" is seriously marred by its dominantly political and economic connotations with heavy ideological overtones, which have robbed the word of its rich religious connotations'.

Childs has to warn us against 'the ideological stance of modern liberation theology' in Kraus's work.[21] Moltmann's view of 'panentheism' is 'highly ideologically oriented'.[22] Moltmann is also alleged to have allowed 'his social ideology' to provide 'the actual content of his portrayal of the kingdom [of God] in spite of his efforts to remain biblical'.[23] All these are examples of a usage where one theological position uses the term ideological as a force to discredit another theological position.

And it is indeed possible that one theology may be 'truly theological' while another can be discredited as being 'ideological'. There is, however, an obvious danger in using this argument. For, the more one theology stigmatizes another as ideological in character, the more likely it is that *all* theology will suffer the same fate. People will say: here are theologies A, B, and C. Each says that the other two are actually only ideologies: obviously, all three of them are equally ideologies. The polemical use of 'ideological' as between theologies can only serve to discredit *all* theology. This is the danger in the course adopted by Childs (and quite a number of others).

Childs has also another side to this argument. He not only categorizes wrong theologies as ideological: he also wants to make it very sure that the Bible itself does not contain ideology. As he sees it, one of the great disasters of modern interpretation, from the Enlightenment on, is that it has interpreted the Bible on the basis of the supposed ideologies of its writers. From the Enlightenment on, he tells us, 'The biblical text was no longer considered to be a direct channel of divine revelation, but rather and foremost a product of human culture whose human author reflected his own historically conditioned perspectives and personal ideology.' This Enlightenment position, he thinks, is basically assumed by critical scholarship.[24] Similarly, he writes, 'Although it is certainly wrong to read the New Testament as a manual of dogmatic theology, it is equally a disaster for theology to interpret it as a collection of human ideology.'[25] In other words, Childs appears to imply that there is *no* human ideology in the Bible. He does not say this

---

[21] Childs, *Biblical Theology of the Old and New Testaments*, 649.   [22] Ibid. 395.
[23] Ibid. 655.
[24] Childs, 'Critical Reflections', *JSOT* 46 (1990), 3–9, on my own essay of *JSOT* 44 (1989), 3–17; cf. my rejoinder 'Allegory and Historicism' in *JSOT* 69 (1996), 105–20.
[25] Childs, *Biblical Theology*, 526.

explicitly, but I do not find in his work any admission of any presence of ideology, or any perception of a need to distinguish between ideological and non-ideological elements within the Bible.[26] 'Childs' ideal "community of faith and practice" is oblivious to the function of the canonical text as a site of ideological conflict.'[27] To sum up, therefore, Childs uses 'ideology' in a completely negative way in relation to both Bible and theology, and in relation to biblical theology also. This seems to imply that everything in the Bible is directly related to theology, and none of it to ideology.[28]

Incidentally—for this is not part of our main subject, but may be significant all the same—this may help in understanding the evaluation of historical criticism by Childs in his canonical method. In principle, and when talking in theory, Childs makes many very negative remarks about historical criticism. Yet he always maintains that he is not in principle against it, and this is confirmed when one turns to his commentary on Exodus, where we find that he provides a detailed source criticism, assigning verses, half-verses, and quarter-verses to J or P or whatever source it may be.[29] On the other hand, as everyone knows, he places high emphasis upon the history of reception and the final text. I suggest that the question of ideology is central in this. He does not object to the differentiation of J and P in Exodus because he sees both as handing on and interpreting what is basically the same story and

---

[26] Characteristically, we find on p. 429 a mention of 'the conflict of ideologies within the [Jewish] community'—in the Maccabean period, which for him lies outside the biblical canon and can therefore safely contain ideology.

[27] F. Watson, *Text, Church and World* (Grand Rapids: Eerdmans, 1994), 44.

[28] Contrast W. Brueggemann, who in his *Theology of the Old Testament* (Minneapolis: Fortress, 1997) readily admits the presence of ideology within the Bible, though applying it primarily to certain areas, notably the 'royal ideology' of monarchy and temple. See Barr, *The Concept of Biblical Theology*, 549. Cf. likewise R. Davidson's article 'Covenant Ideology in Ancient Israel', which uses the same phrase repeatedly but mixes it in with 'covenant concept', 'covenant tradition', and 'covenant theology', apparently without any sense of need to distinguish between these.

[29] Thus Provan, 'The Historical Books of the Old Testament', in J. Barton (ed.), *The Cambridge Companion to Biblical Interpretation* (Cambridge: Cambridge University Press, 1998), 209, blames Childs at length for 'presupposing the historical-critical method'. Even if he criticizes it heavily, as he does, he 'takes it as a fairly obvious and self-evident starting point for his interpretative work'. I think this exaggerated, however. Childs certainly took departure in individual cases and passages from historical-critical positions, but long before this he had made it plain that his basic and general starting-point, or 'presupposition', to use Provan's own term, was distinctly canonical and negative towards historical criticism.

the same faith. But where historical criticism implies that there was a stage or an influence that did not derive from that same faith, then he sees it as ideology and illegitimate. Thus take his reaction to Barton's *Oracles of God*; as he interprets Barton,

> it is virtually impossible to recover the original form and function of the pre-exilic prophets because their role has been severely obscured and distorted by the reception within the later Jewish and Christian communities. In fact, the post-exilic tradents construed the material with such heavy-handed, *culturally conditioned* categories that little was left which was not seriously contaminated by *ideological* bias.[30]

For Childs, then, 'ideology' seems to be a symbol invariably negative. This is, however, only one of the ways in which biblical material and ideology may be related. There are several other possibilities.

For a further example of a strongly negative use of 'ideology', yet differing entirely from that of Childs, we may turn to another biblical theologian, also working in the United States but of Dutch origin, Christiaan Beker. Beker, though working, like Childs, in the field of biblical theology, and, in fact, holder of a professorial chair so entitled, has, at least at times, been much more critical of his own subject than is Childs, and his way of expressing this is to say that biblical theology itself can easily relapse into ideology. It formulates itself in such terms as 'kerygma', 'eschatology', 'the Word', and so on, which 'concepts are abstract and remote from experience'. Biblical theology therefore, according to Beker, tends to remove the student from any live contact with the Bible and make him or her into a manipulator of concepts. Thus Beker, while, like Childs, using 'ideology' in a negative manner, aims it in a quite different direction: by Beker's standard some of Childs's own arguments would be a good example of ideology, as when Childs tells us that 'ecclesiology must be derived from christology' and not the reverse—this is exactly the sort of conceptual manipulation that made Beker

---

[30]   Childs, *Biblical Theology*, 173, my italics. Notice, incidentally, the interest in 'recovering the original form and function', which appears to contradict the basic idea of the canonical approach. Why should a canonical theologian *want* to recover these original entities? Cf. also the complaint that Barton 'brings to bear in his analysis only history-of-religion categories which are insensitive to the actual historical process at work' and that he 'posits a radical ideological discontinuity' which causes the loss of 'all sense of continuity' (ibid.).

uncomfortable. Beker co-edited a book called *Commitment without Ideology*. This means, he explains, a commitment that is not a commitment to any *thing*. It is not defined by its object—whether a doctrine, a person (either God or Jesus), or an ethical principle. 'Instead of being committed to some *thing*, the Christian is challenged by Jesus to be committed to growth in a particular direction, outward toward others; and, moreover, to expression of this growth in responsible action.'[31] Thus Beker, like Childs, uses 'ideology' in a negative sense but applies that negativity to a different feature: biblical theology itself is in danger of becoming ideology: 'One inescapably develops a conceptual system which is unresponsive to new experiences . . . Ideology becomes the standard of truth to which experience must conform. One's ideology, one's most deeply held truth and concern, thus becomes one's greatest oppressor.'[32]

Beker's own positive view is directed more towards religion and experience. For him ideology is defined as a control by ideas and concepts; he does not concern himself with the needs and interests of social groups, not to the same extent anyway. His interest is in the domination of ideas, concepts, and systems—*ideology* in a rather literal sense—thus echoing an aspect present in quite a lot of theology, as indicated above. Thus theology itself, and even biblical theology (and, probably, even *correct* biblical theology, though Beker does not specifically say so) can easily assume the oppressive character of ideology. Even where theology is right, a certain escape from it is a necessity for free and genuine religious life. This may be an important insight, of which too little is heard.

A stark opposition between theology and ideology, however, is not the only possibility. A suggestive and potentially creative relationship is stated by our revisionist historian, Lemche,

By 'ideology' I intend that set of opinions which dominated Israelite society and which made up the 'system' of values with which the Israelites' actions corresponded. In an Oriental society like Israel's one should furthermore be aware that *ideology*, *religion*, and *theology* are to a large extent synonyms, since the separation between the sacral and the

---

[31] C. D. Batson, J. C. Beker, and W. M. Clark (eds.), *Commitment without Ideology* (London: SCM, 1973), 12–13.

[32] Slight change in wording by me: in the last sentence I have twice replaced 'his' with 'one's'.

profane realms which characterizes our contemporary European culture was unknown in antiquity.[33]

This approach could reduce a number of difficulties at present felt. For instance, the identification of ideology in biblical passages would not mean the denial of theology in the same; for the two things are the same, or overlap very substantially. Conversely, to say that another theologian's proposals are 'ideological' would not be a serious argument against them. To return to an example used above, if Brevard Childs says that Paul Hanson's ideas are 'ideological', he is only saying that his own ideology is different from Hanson's. Moreover, since for many social scientists all theology, whether good or bad, approved or disapproved of, is an obvious example of ideology, the perception of them as identical, or at least overlapping, would agree with much sociological understanding. Nevertheless it may be wise to observe that Lemche's good suggestion very likely outruns most of what has been written up to now. Theologians, when they say 'ideology', still mostly mean something bad; biblical scholars, when they say 'ideology', often mean something good, particularly because it is not theology, or else, taking another path, they mean something bad, which is how things were in the Bible, even if theologians do not like to know it. Thus when Philip Davies refers to 'the theology (i.e. ideology) of the writer' of a biblical passage as interpreted by a typical commentator, he probably means the equation in a negative sense: i.e. the commentator likes to call it 'theology', but of course that is, in all cases, nothing but ideology. This is the reverse of the implications I have seen in Lemche's statement quoted above.

Before going further we may add another terminological possibility, namely the use of the term 'propaganda'.[34] So wise and central a scholar as Rex Mason published a book called *Propaganda and Subversion in the Old Testament*.[35] He seems to use the word 'ideology' seldom if at all, but 'propaganda' has something of the same effect. There are chapters on 'Royal Propaganda in the Old Testament', similarly 'Priestly Propaganda'; and then we have

---

[33] N. P. Lemche, *Ancient Israel* (Sheffield: JSOT, 1988), 34, n. 1.

[34] On propaganda see also M. Z. Brettler, *The Creation of History in Ancient Israel* (London: Routledge, 1995), 13–14. He likewise suggests that 'ideology will here refer to a specific type of sets of beliefs, while propaganda will refer to the methods used to disseminate and to foster these beliefs.'

[35] (London: SPCK, 1997).

'Propaganda *and* Subversion—the Deuteronomists', and three main chapters on Subversion, by the Prophets, the Visionaries, and the 'Universalists'. Considerable strata of the Old Testament are thus classified as 'propaganda' by, or on behalf of, various parties, and this approach seems to have a similarity to the perception of 'ideology' which we have been discussing. Propaganda seems to refer more to the action of disseminating a world-view, while ideology is more the underlying world-view itself. In a short concluding chapter he discusses the senses in which the terms are used. Mason's balanced presentation shows the partisan interest present in numerous biblical passages. His book as a whole, while noting the propagandist elements in texts, tends, as I read it, to end up with an equable balance: texts may favour the monarchy, but in the long run the monarchy laid a foundation which was necessary for survival after the monarchy had gone, and the same can be said of the priestly community.[36] Not all propaganda is 'bad', nor is it necessarily fictional: indeed, as I have myself written, 'Good propaganda has to have some truth in it'.[37] Germans in the 1930s pointed to the origin of the term 'concentration camp' in British practice in South Africa: it was propaganda, but the historical facts contained in it were more or less true. In general, Mason, though making little use of the term 'ideology', displays some similar features—e.g. the social emphasis—to those of the trend that has emphasized the latter, while on the other hand, if I read him rightly, doing more to leave open a path to historical reality and to theological interpretation and avoiding the creation of an almost impassable gulf between them.

One significant, and also early, recognition of the role of ideology in the Old Testament came from Patrick D. Miller in 1976.[38] A. D. H. Mayes in a recent study has recognized Miller's contribution as opening a new stage in the question.[39] Influenced by Peter Berger's *The Sacred Canopy*,[40] Miller recognized the common pejorative sense of 'ideology' but gave preference to 'a

---

[36] Ibid. 50, 64–5.

[37] J. Barr, *Biblical Faith and Natural Theology*, 116.

[38] Patrick D. Miller, Jr., 'Faith and Ideology in the Old Testament', in F. M. Cross, W. E. Lemke, and Patrick D. Miller, Jr. (eds.), *Magnalia Dei: The Mighty Acts of God*, FS for G. E. Wright (New York: Doubleday, 1976), 464–79.

[39] Mayes, in de Pury, Römer, and Macchi (eds.), 478.

[40] (Garden City, NY: Doubleday, 1969).

more neutral way' of understanding the word 'as a description of the way things are in a society, the values, ideas and conceptions of a society which cause it to do or act as it does'. The use of the term does not necessarily imply a value-judgement.[41] Nevertheless, in Miller's presentation it seems that, though ideology is necessary and is always present, it is something that is inferior in comparison with 'faith': 'Ideology can be thought of as the ego extension of the group whereas faith refers to that process whereby the ego is transcended.'[42] Ideology is certainly present and has its roots in the earliest period: the group, an ethnic and later national group, the notion of a chosen people and the belief in the divine promises—this contains 'almost by definition ideological qualities'. Faith and ideology are closely intertwined, and 'the line between faith and ideology is never drawn completely, but in the early period of Israel's history the two are less clearly differentiated than at later stages'.[43]

There are at least three criteria which 'force Israel's theology out beyond the limits of its own self-interest'. These are: 1. the possibility and presence of self-criticism which means also the possibility of judgement as the end of Israel's history; 2. A positive relationship with the other nations and a sense of responsibility towards them; 3. A moral demand for justice and righteousness as the central characteristics of human conduct.

With this scheme Miller is able to trace in very broad outline a history of the conflict between ideology and faith. Early poetry shows 'an identification of faith and ideology'. With the Yahwist there is a transcending of the 'merely ideological statement'.[44] Later 'Deuteronomic influence is strong and contributes to the formation of ideology.'[45] In general, 'an ideological analysis of the accounts of Israel's origins and early history is possible'. But it is noted that 'there were factors at work keeping the ideology somewhat in check . . . Imperatives of obedience, righteousness, and justice kept the faith of Israel from becoming purely ideological or worked to redeem it when it did so.' The prophets perceived that 'the popular or national theology was simply an ideology without controls, without checks or balances'. The later prophets, notably Deutero-Isaiah, did not bring about the end of ideology; rather, it

---

[41] Miller, 'Faith and Ideology', 465.   [42] Ibid. 467.   [43] Ibid.
[44] Ibid. 469.   [45] Ibid. 470.

is reinterpreted. 'Thus in a sense with Deutero-Isaiah the history of the religion of Israel in its ideological content comes around full circle. The earlier intermingling of faith and ideology takes place once again, only now with the experience of divine chastisement and divine comfort the ideology is redirected, and the theocratic structure of Israel's existence is universalized to a high degree.'[46]

More recently Miller's proposal (and a related one by Brueggemann) has been marked with distinction by Mayes but has also been the object of criticism.[47] It remains, in any case, a pilot investigation into the possibilities of integrating the concept of ideology into the history of Hebrew religion and theology. It does, in principle, support the 'neutral' or non-pejorative use of 'ideology' and therefore supports the necessity of it; yet on the other hand it tends always to imply that ideology is a second-best in comparison with faith.

Another approach, less comprehensive perhaps than Miller's, is to suppose that ideology, though originally a foreign body in the Bible, did in the course of time find its way into it, and that there is as a result something of a contest between ideology and theology within it. A major representative of this direction is Otto Kaiser, who in the 1980s published a small book called *Ideologie und Glaube*.[48] In some ways Kaiser's position is similar to Beker's. His main purpose is to make it clear that Christian faith is not an ideology, not a set of ideas, but a form of personal commitment—a view which in essentials is very familiar and has been so throughout most of this century at least. On the other hand Kaiser does not share the doubts which Beker holds—or then held—about biblical theology, or indeed, so far as one can see, about theology of any kind. A correct theology will make it clear that faith is a commitment and not a belief in a set of ideas—a view that very many theologians will share.

But Kaiser develops this theme in an unusual way. He thinks that there is a danger that faith may come to be 'ideologized', converted into ideology, and he sees this as having happened—or at least as threatened—in the later stages of the Old Testament, and in particular where there were ideas of a simple, rigoristic morality and a simple consequent divine punishment. Thus Job's three

[46] Ibid. 476.   [47] Mayes, 487 n. 25, 499–502.
[48] (Stuttgart: Radius, 1984).

friends, seen this way, were ideologists, and so no doubt was Elihu. But—and this is the central theme of Kaiser's little book—later Hebrew Wisdom produced an antidote to ideology, and this was the meaning of the book of Job and also of Ecclesiastes, and it is a theme which he saw as carried on into the New Testament. Thus for Kaiser ideology was a danger, and one that at least in part effected an entry into the Bible, but was there met by an anti-ideological counterblast.

A similar argument, with reference to the New Testament, is to be found, more briefly stated, by Eduard Schweizer in his *A Theological Introduction to the New Testament*. Having already talked about the early traditions, the work of Paul, and the non-Pauline letters, he comes to the writing of an actual gospel, beginning with Mark: 'It is a crucial theological act that Mark wrote a gospel at all and thus took seriously the idea that narrative represents a form of proclamation of God's action that is just as necessary as the formulation of confessions and the call to a decision to believe and to live out of faith.'[49] He then points out that 'This act is preconditioned by the Old Testament', where 'the history of God with Israel is handed down in narrative fashion'. So he goes on:

> Mark's undertaking was essential; it resolutely recorded the beginnings of the narrative tradition, above all against the danger of a pure ideology, that is, a faith that lives from statements like those of justification of the godless, forgiveness of sins, and the necessity of holding the right truths, without basing all of that on God's historical action in Jesus of Nazareth . . . It was precisely the decision to take it up in narrative form, in which its significance was not simply fixed 'ideologically' but always had to be newly perceived and believed, that preserved the church in the following centuries from becoming simply one more religiously tinted ideology among others. That . . . is still the foremost contribution of Mark . . . to the overall message of the New Testament.[50]

Two pages later Schweizer comes back to this theme, with reference to Matthew's gospel: 'For him it is no longer enough simply to announce like Mark . . . that the authority of God has been revealed in the teachings of the earthly Jesus.' Matthew therefore, if I understand Schweizer rightly, *expands* the gospel with fuller presentation of Jesus' teaching, the effect of which is to

[49] Eduard Schweizer, *A Theological Introduction to the New Testament* (London: SPCK, 1992), 127.   [50] Ibid. 128, cf. also 130.

furnish a much larger amount of prophetic evidence from the Old Testament.

Essential for Matthew is *what* the earthly Jesus taught with such authority . . . The reader is supposed to judge for herself or himself. Only the prophetic word of scripture, which Jesus himself announces as fulfilled, is for him an aid in interpreting these deeds of Jesus as what they really are (11.5). Thus one is not supposed to 'believe' on the basis of the evangelist's message that in Jesus God himself has definitely encountered the world, and that this is true already for the earthly as well as for the resurrected and exalted Jesus, without inquiring into such faith. *For this would again be a regression into ideology.* [my italics]

Now Schweizer does not develop this theme any further, not within this book anyway, but we see enough to understand the general point. Ideology is a bad thing and even some essential New Testament books, if left to themselves, could well have led the church into an ideological form of life and faith; but corrections to these dangerous tendencies were in fact provided by other books. And his reference back to the Old Testament is characteristic: he is here following a line which many others have probably used: it is the historical element in the Bible, the large historical section of the Old Testament, along with the gospels in the New, it is that historical element which provides the antidote to ideology. A religion which contained a base of ideas, however true in themselves, would be more an ideology; the historical elements prevent this from happening. Thus many biblical scholars would be quite willing to think of Gnosticism as an ideology for this reason: its historical content is too slight.

It would be wrong to omit mention here of Robert Carroll of Glasgow. His works on the book of Jeremiah use the term 'ideology' very frequently.[51] There are two sides to his thinking. On the one hand he considers that comparatively little of the book consists of actual words of the prophet Jeremiah. True historical data about him are hard to find. What then are the contents of the main part of the book? To a large extent, Carroll's answer is: 'Deuteronomistic ideology'. John Barton writes:

Jeremiah is not a biography of the prophet, incorporating his recorded utterances in prose and verse, but an anthology of material, only a small

[51] *From Chaos to Covenant: Prophecy in the Book of Jeremiah* (New York: Crossroad, 1981); *Jeremiah* (London: SCM, 1986).

amount of which consists of the genuine (poetic) utterances of the prophet himself. The editors, who belong to 'Deuteronomic' circles of the exilic and post-exilic period, have used Jeremiah's poems together with a great many later narratives and sermons to create a work which conformed to the idea of a 'prophetic' book current in their day.[52]

Now at some points one's impression of Carroll's thinking is that he uses 'ideology' not in the seriously negative sense, but rather in the sense of that which is regular, predictable, customary: if you know the Deuteronomic tradition, he is saying, you can see that most of this material ascribed to Jeremiah does not come from him at all but is a rehash of that 'ideology'. Perhaps it would be better if we had Jeremiah's own words, but in fact it is not that kind of book. To some extent, also, there is the feeling that the Deuteronomic editors made it this way because it was in their own interests to do so. But, the message seems to be, at least as far as concerns this particular book, one had better be satisfied with ideology because that is all one is going to obtain from it. If you want the historic Jeremiah, you will be disappointed; on the other hand 'Deuteronomic ideology', even if disappointing, is at least something in agreement with another major part of the Bible. Thus he writes elsewhere: 'The pejorative view of ideology treats it as the equivalent of "original sin" in literature and politics, but a more dialectical view of the matter is available. Ideas play a necessary part in the human enterprise . . . but they always have the potential for becoming "ideology" in the bad sense of generating distortion and false consciousness.'[53]

In many places, however, Carroll clearly intends a strongly pejorative sense. Thus in *From Chaos to Covenant* he writes: 'Biblical scholars might prefer to use the word theology to describe the deuteronomistic outlook, but that naively overlooks the political organization and control intended by the deuteronomists . . . The deuteronomists produced an edition of Jeremiah *to serve their own purposes* in the exilic and post-exilic political struggles for power in the community'.[54] Again, 'The destruction of the city with its cult was a godsend for these ideologues, because it allowed them to blame previous administrations for the disastrous state of

---

[52] SOTS Book List (1987), 45.   [53] 'Ideology', *DBI* 311.
[54] Carroll, *Chaos to Covenant*, 17–18 (my italics).

affairs prevailing after 587'.[55] *Ideology* is chosen expressly in order to convey a sinister impression. So he writes: 'This is the language of ideological conflict, which substitutes abuse for argument and insult for understanding . . . it is a closed system of thought.'[56] Sometimes we hear of something more like a conflict of ideologies: 'A polemic against religious behaviour . . . reveals a dominant concern with religious ideology. Such a polemic dismisses the religion of the Jewish and Egyptian communities in favour of a different ideology of religion.'[57] The trouble about this, within a commentary on Jeremiah, is that the villainous Deuteronomists are always rather 'off the scene': it would need a commentary on the Deuteronomic writings, rather than on Jeremiah, to demonstrate the depth of this evildoing, which within Jeremiah itself is only reflected!

In any case more can be added that represents other aspects of Carroll's position. His book *Wolf in the Sheepfold: The Bible as a Problem for Christianity*, does not discuss the term 'ideology' and scarcely uses it.[58] But the book, written in a slapdash and uneven manner, works with an almost unbelievable concentration on the collection of features that make the Bible unusable for later religion. The context is one of 'demonstrating the unsuitability of the Bible for the creation of theological dogmas'.[59] Can we, then, as an alternative, form theological concepts and apply them to the Bible? No:

Dogmatic systems which attempt to colonize the Bible are treating the book with contempt and forcing it into a Procrustean bed . . . It is not possible to make any equation between the Yahweh of the biblical narratives and the God of the creeds and confessions of the churches, even though clever theologians may be able to adjust the gap between the two so that it is narrower under certain conditions. The Bible will remain problematic for theology.[60]

Nothing explicit in this, but certainly the general tone gives the impression that the widespread use of 'ideology' in his works on Jeremiah and elsewhere implies a strong negativity towards theology. If this is right, 'ideology' is used not only to indicate the

---

[55] Carroll, *Jeremiah*, 136.   [56] Carroll, *Chaos to Covenant*, 178.
[57] Carroll, *Jeremiah*, 117.
[58] (London: SPCK, 1991); there are slight mentions of 'ideology' at pp. 17, 142.
[59] Ibid. 42.   [60] Ibid.

thoughts of a group much later than Jeremiah himself, but also
something that is also likely to be inferior and theologically value-
less. There thus also is a tone of distinct contempt in 'ideology' as
he uses it of material in Jeremiah.

And this leads to another reflection: supposing that the whole
book was, after all, the words and thought of Jeremiah himself,
what difference would that make? It would only be Jeremiah's
ideology, different no doubt from Deuteronomic ideology but not
qualitatively different, not different in that it was any the less ideology. Since it is all ideology, as is, presumably, everything in the
Bible, it becomes pointless to distinguish the late material in
Jeremiah as ideology.

Or, reversing the argument: consider again the relation to
theology. Carroll, as we have seen, deplores any attempt to bring
'dogmatic systems' into contact with the Bible. He scarcely speaks
of theology and seems to have no idea of any biblical theology.
One of the things against theology is its system character—and
here Carroll is only repeating what countless Old Testament
scholars have said: indeed, it is the commonest single objection
against the idea of biblical theology.[61] Leaving aside later dogmatic
systems, might there be theology, of a different kind no doubt,
within the Bible itself? Carroll may well be nervous of admitting
this possibility, but he seems not to see that his own repeated insistence on the ideology in the biblical text naturally brings it closer
to being theology. For ideology is the main factor that brings
system into the Bible. As we have seen (above, pp. 115–6), Lemche
thinks it a matter of indifference whether we call the material
ideology, or religion, or theology. Quite so. 'Deuteronomic ideology' is very close to being a prime example of theology within the
Bible, and is so called and treated by numerous scholars, notably
including the specialist in history of Israelite religion, R. Albertz.
For, as we saw, Carroll dislikes dogmatic systems, and probably
systems in general, which would contrast with the 'wild' and
'untamed' aspect he emphasizes in the Old Testament. But system
is precisely the character that we have seen to belong to ideology,
as seen by many experts and quoted above. And certainly the
Deuteronomic material is one of the most obviously systematic
areas of the Old Testament. Thus, to sum up this argument,

<hr />

[61]   On this cf. J. Barr, *The Concept of Biblical Theology*, 331–7.

Carroll, by pushing biblical material closer and closer to the character of ideology, has also, perhaps unconsciously but certainly inevitably, been pushing it closer to the character of theology, only the words being different.

Now the scholars I have discussed so far have mostly thought of ideology in a negative manner, but we can now pass to those who probably use the same term in a more neutral way. First of all I think of the work of Meir Sternberg, whose large and interesting book *The Poetics of Biblical Narrative* has the telling subtitle *Ideological Literature and the Drama of Reading*. 'That biblical scholars entertain an extreme "art for art's sake" view of literature, as if it were a machine for pure amusement', he tells us, 'only indicates the need for wider horizons of reading'—it is interesting to ask who are the biblical scholars whom he has in mind at this point. Anyway, he goes on, 'The question is how rather than whether the literary coexists with the social, the doctrinal, the philosophical. In ancient times, the two were so closely related as to become indistinguishable.'[62]

If I understand him rightly, Sternberg wants to affirm that biblical narrative *is* ideological. As against those who, pleased to take the Bible as literature, have gone on to say that it is essentially fiction, or 'historicized fiction' or 'fictional historiography', he places its narratives firmly in the historiographical genre. 'The biblical narrator also appeals to the privilege of omniscience . . . Omniscience in modern narrative attends and signals fictionality, while in the ancient tradition it not only accommodates but also guarantees authenticity.'[63] Moreover, the Bible represents a world-view that is 'singular'—a thought a little bit like that of the older biblical theology: 'All narratives imply and many advocate some ideology-bound model of reality—sacred or secular . . . it remains a universal of writing that representation is never dissociated from evaluation. If the Bible is ideologically singular—and I believe so—then its singularity lies in the world view projected.'[64] But biblical narrative is, in Sternberg's mind, ideological rather than didactic: this, I suspect, is why he does not much use the term 'theological', because to him a 'theological' book would be a didactic book, and it would be going too far to speak of biblical narrative as didactic:

---

[62] (Bloomington, Ind.: Indiana University Press, 1987), 35–6.
[63] Ibid. 34.   [64] Ibid. 37.

the claim may assume a stronger form, namely, that the Bible belongs to that extreme variety of ideological writing known as didactic . . . the didactic genre . . . not only advances a doctrine but also ruthlessly subordinates the whole discourse . . . to the exigencies of indoctrination . . . the whole idea of didacticism is alien, if not antipathetic, to the spirit of Israelite storytelling.[65]

I may be mistaken in this, but it seems to me that ideology in Sternberg's thinking comes closer to the theology of Christian biblical theology than to the use of 'ideology' which we have been discussing so far. The idea is not so much that of a system of ideas that express and formulate the interests and needs of the group: it is more like a traditional doctrine of verbal inspiration, with an omniscient narrator who has a plan and world-view which he inculcates. Here is another final quotation: in his concluding chapter Sternberg claims of the biblical storyteller that 'unlike most speakers . . . his persuasion is not only geared to an ideology but also designed to vindicate and inculcate it'.

I will mention only briefly one other Israeli work, Sara Japhet's book entitled (in its English form) *The Ideology of the Book of Chronicles and its Place in Biblical Thought*.[66] I earlier wrote[67] that we could not press this title too far, because in its original Hebrew form it does not use the word 'ideology', nor 'theology', but rather says 'beliefs and ideas'. Since then I have seen that she, writing in French, does use the term 'ideology' and does so freely.[68] Thus she speaks of the 'eschatological ideology' of Haggai and Zechariah and tells us that 'these various characteristics of historical narration interpenetrate one another and form themselves into a coherent ideology, which is in fact the spiritual response to a historical reality'. She calls 1 Esdras a 'corrective history', and this fact 'manifests itself in two different realms, namely history and ideology'.[69] I do not see any indication that she intends 'ideology' in a pejorative sense: her usage seems, if anything, to be a favourable one, rather like the Christian use of 'theology' (when used by those Christian writers who are favourable towards theology). All I want to say is that, whatever one uses as title, the actual

---

[65] Indiana University Press, 37–8.   [66] (Frankfurt am Main: Peter Lang, 1989).
[67] Barr, *The Concept of Biblical Theology*, 306.
[68] See her 'L'Historiographie post-exilique: comment et pourquoi?' in de Pury, Römer, & Macchi, *Israël construit son histoire*, 123–52.
[69] Ibid. 136, 134, 138.

content is not very different from what one might find in a work that in Christian terms would be called 'Old Testament theology'. There are chapters on 'God's Presence in the World' or 'God's Involvement in the History of Israel', plus attitudes to kingship, people, and the hope of redemption, and we find her in amicable conversation with the Christian Old Testament theologians such as Eichrodt and von Rad. The only real difference is that she confines her study to the ideology or theology of one book or group of books, while Chronicles (or, likewise, 'post-exilic historiography') is only one part of the material which these Christian authors have undertaken to handle. 'Ideology' seems to be used in a sense either neutral or favourable.

Another, and a potentially creative, approach to ideology is found in Christopher Rowland's *Christian Origins*.[70] One of the great books on ideology is Mannheim's *Ideology and Utopia*. Rowland cites this work[71] and maintains that the contrast it offers between ideology and utopia 'is relevant for a discussion of the early Christian outlook'. The matter arises at a point where Rowland is writing that 'Paul was actively engaged in the subversion of much contemporary practice . . . His career is an example of that outlook which, when translated into reality, tends to shatter, either partially or wholly, the order of things prevailing at the time.' But, he goes on,

What we find in I Corinthians is the beginning of Paul's retreat from the first flush of eschatological enthusiasm to an outlook that admits that in Christ there is a new creation but without this having a disturbing effect on the present order. There is evidence of an attitude, which gradually replaces utopian views . . . Clearly utopianism can be immature. Nevertheless in I Corinthians Paul is in danger of undermining that central utopian element in the Christian experience and outlook, which gave the movement such an initial impetus.[72]

On the next page Rowland makes a distinction between three types of ideology:

There is an ideology, which starts life as a reflection of the socioeconomic circumstances; yet this ideology begins to have a retroactive force and an influence on the nature of the very circumstances from which it had its origin. There is another, which offers a contrast with the

---

[70] (London: SPCK, 1975).   [71] Ibid. 370 n. 40.
[72] Ibid. 282–3.

present order but whose fulfilment is transposed into the future, so that an individual can have an idealism, which acts as a spur to gain a future goal. Thirdly, there is the ideology which functions as a legitimation of the present order, by offering a justification for its continued presence within the divine purposes. All these ideological types may be found in early Christian literature. Probably the origin of early Christian utopianism is to be understood under the first head. Secondly, we have the ideological type which predominates in the New Testament: looking forward to a new order but doing little to bring about change in the present . . . Finally, there was the outlook which comes closest of all to a complete legitimation of the present order . . . In a passage like Romans 13 the apocalyptic framework enables Paul to legitimate the powers that be as part of the divinely ordained nature of things.[73]

It seems to me that this differentiation between different ideologies, possible or actual, makes a great advance as against opinions which label thought barely as 'ideology' or which—as is very common—suppose that its only and universal function is to provide legitimation for the existing order. If a principle like Rowland's had been generally used in biblical studies, more might have been achieved with ideology than has been the case. It is interesting to ask what difference it makes, in Rowland's language, that he uses 'ideology' rather than 'theology' in these cases. He is distinguishing three early Christian mental attitudes. Perhaps, we may suppose, he avoids 'theology' here because that would suggest attitudes that had been carefully stated, formalized, made into doctrine. 'Ideology' by contrast suits these examples because it refers to attitudes that are widespread but still hardly defined, perhaps still largely unconscious, neither formalized nor made into doctrine. There is no indication of a pejorative sense, no suggestion of a seeking of power for the group.

Another striking example is to be found in William P. Brown's *Structure, Role and Ideology in the Hebrew and Greek Texts of Genesis 1: 1–2: 3*.[74] Brown compares the two text forms as wholes (suggesting that the *Vorlage* of the Septuagint is the earlier than the Masoretic Text) and shows that a complete ideology is presented by each of them. His usage owes much to the principles enunciated by M. Bakhtin. The term 'ideology' is here used without any pejorative suggestion, nor is it contrasted with 'theology' or any

---

[73] (London: SPCK), 284–5.   [74] (Atlanta: Scholars Press, 1993).

other term. The same biblical text in its two different forms presents two different ideologies; the later represents an attempt to correct the earlier. This helps with historical questions; on the other hand, no attempt is made to argue that one form is 'for use' necessarily better or worse than the other.

'Ideology', used alone as a general term, has little value, especially when intended in its negative sense. Its effect is usually to create a great rubbish heap upon which texts are tossed, one after the other, without their being given proper value or examination. Where texts are labelled as 'ideology', we should insist that this leads on only to the other question: which ideology exactly? They need to be examined for their content as carefully as any other text. To make a distinction, as Rowland and Brown do, between several different ideologies, or ideological stages, within the Bible itself is to make a positive step forward, such as many have failed to do.

With this we pass, at least for the moment, from those who regard ideology as a bad thing. At the other end of the spectrum stand those who think that ideology is a good thing, or at least an unavoidable thing, and that the Bible is full of it. Thus Elizabeth Schüssler Fiorenza cites and discusses at length the 'hermeneutical model of Juan Luis Segundo', according to whom 'Faith is identical with the total process of learning through ideologies, whereas the responses of faith to certain historical situations are ideologies . . . "Faith then is a liberative process. It is converted into freedom for history, which means freedom *for ideologies*" '. She comments: 'It is obvious that Segundo does not understand ideology as "false" consciousness, but as historical–societal expression.'[75]

Segundo, just mentioned, is the most avid enthusiast for ideology that I have come across in my studies. Liberation theology arose, he writes, in reaction against a 'developmentalist' economic model, in which 'the point was often stressed that the modernization process meant that people would have to accept the "death of ideologies" brought about by a scientific and *neutral*

---

[75] *Bread not Stone* (Boston: Beacon, 1984), 49–52, 51 (author's italics). The sentence she quotes is from J. L. Segundo, *The Liberation of Theology* (Maryknoll, NY: Orbis, 1985), 110. The words 'freedom for history, which means' are, however, omitted by Schüssler Fiorenza in the quotation.

technology common to any and every social model'.[76] Later he maintains that:

Faith, when properly understood, can never dissociate itself from the ideologies in which it is embodied—both in the Bible and in subsequent history. It certainly can, and should, dissociate itself as much as possible from the 'ideological' tendencies that wrongfully subordinate it to a specific brand of historical oppression. But it makes no sense at all to ask what faith is when any and all ideology has been stripped from it. Faith without works is dead. Faith without ideologies is equally dead. Faith incarnated in successive ideologies constitutes an ongoing educational process in which man learns how to learn under God's guidance.[77]

Thus in the Bible, through numerous 'different faith-inspired encounters', all of them historical and relative, between human beings and the objective font of absolute truth, 'what came to be known or recognized . . . was an ideology, but that was not what was learned. Through the process people *learned how to learn* with the help of ideologies . . . While faith certainly is not an ideology, it has sense and meaning only in so far as it serves as the foundation stone for ideologies'.[78] These quotations are only fragments from a complicated and many-sided argument presented by Segundo.

In an earlier chapter I have already quoted David M. Gunn and Danna Nolan Fewell, who in the concluding paragraphs of their attractively written *Narrative in the Hebrew Bible* tell us that the Bible has the many voices of many contradictory ideologies. It 'shows us not merely patriarchy, élitism, and nationalism; it shows us the fragility of these ideologies through irony and counter-voices'. Thus these texts 'may be uncovering a world in need of redemption and healing and a world-view much in need of change. This is the kind of reading that can transform us. If we realize that the world of the Bible is a broken world, that its people are human and therefore limited, that its social system is flawed, then we might start to see more clearly our own broken world, our own human limitations, our own defective social systems. And who knows? Maybe we shall find ourselves called to be the agents of change.'[79] The essence of the Bible is the *variety* of ideologies

[76] Segundo, *Liberation of Theology*, 37 n. 37.   [77] Ibid. 181.
[78] Ibid. 108–9.
[79] D. M. Gunn and D. N. Fewell, *Narrative in the Hebrew Bible* (London: Oxford University Press, 1993), 204–5.

that it contains. This is, as already remarked, linked with a strong rejection of any objective or absolute truth: it seems that there is nothing behind any ideology other than the glance it affords us of something that might be different, that could show us how things are wrong and could conceivably suggest something better. The cleverness of the hints and ironies in the biblical narratives delight us, and here we come close to what Sternberg meant when he talked of 'a machine for pure amusement'.[80]

We should notice at this point that our assessment of the place of ideology is related to the kinds of questions of biblical criticism and the history of Israel which were discussed in previous chapters. For it is hardly useful to declare that a passage 'is ideology' unless we can also say *what* ideology it is. But this depends on how it is related to other comparable passages, and also to the historical situations to which it refers and in which it was composed. Thus Römer and de Pury, under the subheading 'Ideology and Theology', point out that 'To characterize the theology or ideology of the Deuteronomic work depends at least partially on diachronic options'.[81] Thus: if one admits the existence of a first edition at the time of Josiah, then the work is witness to a 'triumphalist' vision borne by a promising international conjuncture of events, along with the political energy of this monarch. If, on the contrary, one supposes that the first edition of the Deuteronomic History dates from the time of the exile, then it requires to be considered more as a theodicy (meaning, presumably, an attempt to give a theological explanation for the national

---

[80] A somewhat similar picture is offered by the conclusion of R. P. Carroll's *Wolf in the Sheepfold*, 147: 'The book is too untidy, too sprawling and far too boisterous to be tamed by neat systems of thought. If you want neatness, close the book and turn to theology. But if you can tolerate contradiction and contrariety and can handle hyperbolic drive and chaotic manipulation of metaphor, then the Bible will burn your mind. We humans have produced few things like it.' Carroll, however, quite unlike Gunn and Fewell, ends up with a quite firm approval of (historical) *critical* scholarship, upon which he has commonly relied in his survey of the problematic nature of the Bible. Without 'the arrow of time' religion would be made 'ahistorical and the Bible a filing-cabinet of abstract ideas'. Thus 'The critical reading of the Bible has often been seen as hostile to theology. On the contrary, it is perhaps the first stage in the development of a seriously critical theology' (p. 145). Here, unusually, he uses 'theology' in a favourable sense, as something that could be desirable. And when he advises us that if we want neatness to close the Bible and turn to theology—is it really true that theology is 'neat'? If one penetrates into it, perhaps one finds it just as untidy and untamed as the Bible is.

[81] Römer and de Pury, 'L'Historiographie Deutéronomiste: Histoire de la recherche et enjeux du débat', in de Pury, Römer, and Macchi (eds.), *Israël construit son histoire*, 115.

catastrophe of Judah). But, they ask, can it really be supposed that this great historiographical work was edited and published with the sole purpose of explaining the disaster?

Thus far we have talked mainly about the presence or absence of ideology within the Bible itself. In conclusion, however, we have to say something about the ideology question as it affects the world of scholarship in modern times. And we have to think of ideology not as a matter of scholarship alone but as a reality affecting both society and church (or synagogue).

And here we may usefully introduce the concept of *ideological criticism*, often referred to with its German term *Ideologiekritik*. A useful statement of one view of this is given by Clines. He writes:

Arising perhaps from the questions of a materialist (Marxist) criticism in the first place, but without subscribing necessarily to any particular political or philosophical position, ideological criticism, as I see it, systematically asks about the ideological interests inscribed in the texts. That is to say, it does not view the texts primarily as historical documents . . . nor as theological documents . . . nor as purely literary texts with the status of works of art, but as ideological documents that serve some particular or group interest. Such a criticism is of course not entirely new . . . What is new is the emphasis on the partisanship of every text, on the role of conflict among various groups as a model of ancient society, on a foregrounding of the ideological issue, and especially, on the demand to press beyond mere *description* of the ideology of the texts to a *critique* of it.[82]

This orientation to the texts, Clines continues, has both a historical and an ahistorical dimension. In the former it seeks to identify the groups whose interests brought the text into being and preserved it. In the latter, it aims 'at detecting the impact the texts have upon groups who are currently using them'. Thus 'the net effect of an ideological approach is to *relativize the biblical text and make it less malleable to theological reconstruction*' (my italics). It thus goes much further than historical criticism did in relativizing the authority of the Bible. Thus:

We become even more aware of the relativity of the Bible's authority to the power of the groups that promote it and profess to be governed by it. I do not mean that we necessarily encounter anything illicit, but we do set the Bible and its effect within a framework that is given by our pluralist society.[83]

    [82] 'Biblical Interpretation in an International Perspective', *Biblical Interpretation*, 1 (1993), 67–87, esp. 84–6.   [83] Ibid. 84.

Thus he goes on to give the illustration of the Ten Commandments:

Since societies are not homogeneous, I ask, In which *group*'s interest are these commandments? And since groups are usually in some kind of conflict with other groups, I ask, What kind of *social conflict* is alluded to, or repressed, by this text? And, since it is usually the victors in any social conflict whose texts get preserved, I look carefully at *elites and powerholders* in Israelite society for the matrix of these laws.

He thinks, in conclusion, that 'even the most sophisticated of historical scholars and redaction critics entertain the most appallingly uncritical views about the ideological and ethical status of the ten commandments'.[84] Who, then, are the groups whose social interests were *really* behind the commandments? He does not tell us; this is significant, in view of a further point which will be made below.

It is interesting, considering the distinctly non-theological, if not anti-theological, trend of Clines's argument, to observe how closely parallel it is to a common *theological* argument. As against what is supposed to be a 'historical-critical' approach which only *describes* the past, theologians have often maintained that it is necessary both to follow the texts into the present day and to expound their meaning and authority for the present day. Ideology criticism, according to Clines, agrees with this requirement. Its effect, however, is the opposite of what theologians have intended: it is to dismantle most or all of the theological realities referred to in the text (he cites, just above, a list including: ideas of retribution, covenant, sin, the maleness of God, metaphors of the king and warrior for the divine).[85]

Developed in this way, however, it is difficult to accept Clines's assurance that this form of ideology criticism does not 'subscribe' to a particular political or philosophical position. It is based, as he puts it, on 'the framework that is given by our pluralist society' or, to be more correct, on a world-view that *supposes* itself to be given by this society, *supposed* by that world-view to be pluralist. What the 'pluralist' society definitely affirms is, so far as I can see from Clines's exposition, not pluralist at all: what it affirms is a sort of

---

[84] Ibid. 86.

[85] Most theologians would want to make considerable discrimination between various items on this list.

Hobbesian, Nietzschean, world-view, according to which no one does or says or writes anything except for the sake of *power* for themselves and their own group. But, this being so, Clines falls under the type of critique which, as we saw earlier, Provan levelled against the revisionist historians (there taken as 'positivists'), namely that, if this kind of argument were applied consistently to everything, there could be no knowledge of anything. For it is obvious, under this world-view, that Clines has no reason behind his own arguments other than his desire for the greater power of his own group (whatever group that may be). If he told us his real motive—something we are often bidden to do— namely, that he was writing purely for the sake of that greater power, he would, of course, suffer a loss in credibility. If, on the other hand, he is unconscious of any such motivation—well, that is just normal with ideology.

A somewhat similar, but perhaps more hesitant, position is taken by Robert Carroll, whose mention of *Ideologiekritik* will be noted in the next chapter. In his article, 'Ideology',[86] the term is first described as 'the scrutiny of the Bible for ideology', which makes good sense and agrees with what we will see Carroll himself do in his work on Jeremiah. But then, somewhat surprisingly to me, *Ideologiekritik* is said to 'uncover another layer of textual reading but one which focuses on the exegete more than on the text'. Ideologies of the text, of the communities, and of the later teaching 'guilds' 'all become necessary subjects of the *Ideologiekritik* enterprise'. This in itself may be quite right, but it turns the main attention away from the ideologies contained within the text, which are so heavily emphasized in Carroll's own work on Jeremiah.

We should go back, however, to an even more important point raised by Clines's position discussed above. He pins the identification of ideology resolutely to the discovery of *social conflict*. For this his example of the Ten Commandments is not a good example. Take the command, 'Thou shalt not steal.' Are we to believe that there was a Pro-Stealing class or party whose interests were oppressed or silenced by the Anti-Stealing party, which latter

---

[86] *DBI* 309–11. This is the fullest account of this concept I have seen in Carroll's writings. (I have not been able to see his series of articles on 'The Bible and Ideology', in *JNWSL* (1993–6); nor have I seen the work of Ferdinand Deist on which he relies considerably.)

group were victors in this conflict? Who were the Pro-Stealing people? Thieves? Hardly, because thieves are distinctly anti-stealers, considering it absolutely wrong for other thieves to steal the property that they have themselves stolen. So thieves and non-thieves are united in their opposition to stealing. Who then had an interest in the continuance of stealing? We need to know, because these people are the 'silenced', the 'marginalized', from whom the real message of the text is to come.

The idea that ideology is to be traced back to social conflict seems to me to be mistaken. All that has been said in our discussion of the definition of ideology seems to point in the opposite direction: ideology points towards a consensus, not a consensus with no exceptions at all, but a substantial general consensus. People who say 'Australians like a man to have a fair go'—meaning a fair chance in some matter of disagreement (a phrase I have often heard,[87] and one which clearly belongs to ideology)—mean that this is the general consensus. Or take that impressive work by F. X. Sutton, S. E. Harris, C. Kaysen, and J. Tobin, *The American Business Creed.* This describes an ideology which is, roughly speaking, a consensus among business men. There may be exceptions but it is generally the case. It is not a matter of 'conflict' between them. Those anxious to discover conflict somewhere may say that it nevertheless represents the underlying conflict with the class of non-business men, and this might seem so to academics looking at the matter. But in the society as a whole, as it seems to me, the reverse is the case: the silenced or marginalized class of non-business men, at least in America, quite admire the business ideology and think it is appropriate for business men and good for society as a whole. It is a matter of consensus. And this fits in with most of what we said at the beginning of this chapter.

And it fits in, very obviously, with the Ten Commandments, nowhere better. For it was a consensus in the society that stealing was wrong and must be forbidden. There is no evidence that anyone thought the contrary. And it is a consensus that is not in any way attached to one group or another, and one that is not confined to Israel in the slightest, for stealing was condemned in

[87] See ample evidence in G. A. Wilkes (ed.), *A Dictionary of Australian Colloquialisms*, 2nd edn. (Sydney: Sydney University Press, 1985), 169–70.

the law-codes of many nations.[88] The commandment was there because of consensus.

I pointed out earlier that the tendencies I am discussing could not be simply aligned with the older categories of conservative and liberal, and this continues to be true of the use of ideology as a key concept in scholarship. Or one can rephrase this by saying that the meanings of terms such as 'liberal' are themselves changing once again. What is now the political ideology of 'conservative' Christianity in the United States is largely a new re-formation of the *laissez-faire* ideology of an older liberalism. That liberalism (as I see it, roughly speaking) split in the earlier twentieth century, one portion sticking more to *laissez-faire* and becoming what is now 'conservative' (though still sometimes called 'new liberalism'), and the other turning to something like greater governmental intervention, a New Deal, social security, and so on. The latter side, though still often called 'liberal', is now splitting again or has already done so: we hear more and more of a split between 'liberal' and 'liberationist', which is said to be tearing the mainstream churches apart.

In this the question of ideology has a central part. The reality of ideology, in some sense, as a part of the human make-up seems to be undeniable. If this is so, the recognition of it as a reality, within religion as elsewhere, should be salutary. But some modern tendencies have so emphasized ideology as to make it a destructive force once again. I think it regrettable that, in the process in which women have become much more prominent in both religion and education, so many women scholars—certainly not all, but a substantial proportion—have so totally and consciously embraced ideology as their key instrument for the understanding of the world—an action which is likely to have negative effects upon the position of women in the long run.[89] It is even more regrettable

---

[88]   In Rome, for example, 'by the XII Tables a thief who came by night, and any thief who used a weapon, might be killed out of hand' (*Oxford Classical Dictionary* (1970), 451, s.v. Furtum). This is similar to the biblical law of Exod. 22: 2.

[89]   Interestingly, Robert Carroll, who has so strongly emphasized ideology, as we have seen, remains critical of the feminism which often accompanies that emphasis. Thus in his *Jeremiah* he writes: 'Contrary to modern feminist rhetoric, biblical condemnation of sexual activity, whether real or metaphorical, is a balanced matter of condemning male as well as female behaviour' (p. 180), and: 'Recent feminist theological writing has complained about the misogynistic character of this biblical element . . . Without knowing the psychological nature of the language used (masculine as well as feminine) it is not possible to evaluate the degree to which their writings may be characterized as misogynistic or otherwise . . . caution is warranted before jumping to the wrong conclusions' (p. 134).

that, in the well-meant attempts to overcome racial tension and racial prejudice, here once again the primacy of ideology has been so widely accepted. Ideology here can lead to the conception of a racial truth, a truth that is true only for the experience of a racial or ethnic group. The role of ideology can be properly assessed and understood only when it is balanced by a concept of truth that is not defined by racial, ethnic, or other identity. And, within religion, the role of ideology within the Bible and within its interpretation can be properly assessed only by a theology that has truth as its primary canon and standard.

Finally we may perhaps go back to historical criticism. As we saw earlier, it has been alleged against historical criticism that it, though pretending to an objective status, is also ideological. A good example comes from Walter Brueggemann, who writes:

In my field of Scripture study, *historical criticism* has become a mode of silencing the text by eliminating its artistic, dramatic, subversive power. I do not wish to overstate my critique of historical criticism.[90] It is, nonetheless, increasingly clear that historical criticism is no objective, disinterested tool of interpretation, but it has become a way to trim texts down to *the ideology of Enlightenment reason and autonomy* and to explain away from the text all the hurts and hopes that do not conform to *the ideology of objectivity*. In the end, the text is thereby rendered voiceless. It becomes only an echo of the passionless containment of knowledge by the teaching, interpreting monopoly. The voiced text is the natural partner and practice of the marginal who depend on such texts. If the texts can be silenced by their disuse or reinterpretation, then the marginal lose their chance of speech and of power. In an odd interpretive maneuver long established among us, we tend not to notice that the voiceless text has been made into a silent support for the status quo, holding all memory in a contained present, numbed to protest, resistant to alternative, and all in the interest of objectivity.[91]

Brueggemann here plunges deeply into the waters of postmodernity. He ignores the old anti-critical arguments about the stupidity of J and P and the critical dating of parts of Isaiah; these seem no longer to matter. He ignores the traditional anti-critical

---

[90] Here Brueggemann (ibid. 64 n. 25) inserts a note as follows: 'The most frontal attack on historical criticism is that of Walter Wink, *The Bible in Human Transformation* (Philadelphia: Fortress, 1973). Since his publication, a great deal has happened to sustain his argument. Perhaps his extreme language was essential to advancing the conversation.'

[91] *Old Testament Theology* (Minneapolis: Fortress, 1992), 64–5. In the second sentence the italics are mine.

argument that critical views are only the subjective judgements of individuals. What matters now is that the Enlightenment is an ideology, and historical criticism was not only a support for precisely this ideology, but enforced it upon everyone and deprived them of every possibility they might have had of escaping from it. These are in part old-time arguments which could have been uttered a century ago; but Brueggemann now adds to them the sociopolitical concerns of postmodernism. Historical criticism not only enforced this ideology on people, but in doing so it marginalized them and silenced them (the marginal who lose their chance of speech and of power are the normal figures of liberationist rhetoric). All the beaten wives, exploited labourers, and political prisoners of these centuries could have been free from their miseries if only they could have used the Bible without the bonds of historical criticism! Yet can Brueggemann really have meant what he said? Is it really credible that historical criticism made Hosea into a Voltaire, Amos into a Rousseau, the Emmanuel 'God with Us' into an Emmanuel Kant? I do not believe that the churches of the Enlightenment period, or the churches that were accustomed to historical criticism, ever thought or did anything of what Brueggemann here says. Even the most ardent foes of the Enlightenment inheritance never produced such an argument.

In any case Brueggemann's argument certainly misfired. For he in his well-meaning way was trying to assist Childs, seeking—vainly, as it turned out—to accept much of the latter's canonical approach and yet to modify it for the better. This remarkable anti-Enlightenment statement was intended, perhaps, to prepare the ground for some compromise in this respect. Childs, however, was not impressed and brusquely pushed away the overtures. According to him, every point in Brueggemann's argument is wrong:

The result is fully predictable. The theological appeal to an authoritative canonical text which has been shaped by Israel's witness to a history of divine, redemptive intervention has been replaced by a radically different construal. The saddest part of the proposal is that Walter Brueggemann is sincerely striving to be a confessing theologian of the Christian church, and would be horrified at being classified as a most eloquent defender of the Enlightenment, which his proposal respecting the biblical canon actually represents.[92]

---

[92]   Childs, *Biblical Theology*, 72–3.

The moral is: when it comes to ideology, it is difficult to be sure that you are on the right track.

To sum up, with some exceptions, the entry of the concept of ideology into biblical scholarship cannot be said to have been a happy event. That there is such a thing as ideology and that the term may well be useful for biblical exegesis may be freely granted. But the way in which it has actually worked, so far at least, has been little short of chaotic. Widely various definitions of it have been in use.[93] Although the rather better definitions describe it in a neutral fashion, as neither necessarily good nor bad, the majority of users have followed the popular pejorative understanding. Writers who are opposed to theology call things 'ideology' in order to discredit them as theological sources. Writers who like theology use 'ideology' as the term for what they consider to be *bad* theology. Others again use 'ideology' for systems of *ideas*, which they place in strong contrast with stories or narratives. Others again seem to think that there is no truth or reality, so that every intellectual perception or comprehension is ideology, with the result that there is nothing left to contrast it with. Many writers, as we have seen, move back and forwards between one usage and another, according as they wish to express favour or disfavour.

The most serious fault is the undoubtable fact, illustrated in several examples above, that some of the introduction of ideology into biblical studies is the obvious and sometimes deliberate intrusion of the modern scholar's own mentality. Postmodernism, being an ideology (for what could be higher praise for it?), needs everything possible to be seen as ideology too. As Brettler notes, 'the understanding of ideology . . . has become highly ideological'.[94] In this sense some of the use of ideology in interpretation of the Bible has exactly the same status as the parallel use of theology in the same activity.

The curious thing, in view of this latter phenomenon, is that the postmodernist has no defence to offer. He cannot appeal to truth or rationality. He cannot say that he is not swayed by unconscious

---

[93] One of the best discussions, though brief, within biblical scholarship is that of M. Z. Brettler in his *Creation of History*, 12–14. He wishes to avoid the pejorative usage. Excellent discussions are furnished also by M. Rose and A. D. H. Mayes in de Pury, Römer, and Macchi (eds.), *Israël construit son histoire.*

[94] Brettler, *Creation of History*, 13, citing Clifford Geertz, *The Interpretation of Cultures*, 193.

ideological drives, because his whole case is that everyone is so swayed, all the time. All he can say is that his ideology is as good as anyone else's, or better; or, perhaps, that he, unlike others, is fully conscious of his own ideological being. But there is no reason to accept this latter claim: those who press the use of ideology, far from being fully conscious of their position, seem to have only a very poor, vague, and confused idea of what they are trying to say. Often they end up with moral blame: 'You others have an unconscious ideology which has a record of oppressing classes A, B, and C in the past.' The high point of this is when we hear: 'Your system has been oppressive in the past, and we are better in that we intend to be oppressive, openly, consciously, and deliberately, in the future.' An example will appear in the next chapter.

If texts are to be classified as 'ideology', then it should be made clear that that is not to be a convenient way of consigning them to the rubbish bin: they should be analysed and interpreted just as carefully and fully as if they were historically accurate, or theologically authoritative, or otherwise intellectually powerful. And the same applies if we consider 'ideological criticism' to extend not only over the ideologies of the text but also to the ideologies of interpreters, older or more modern. Such work of this kind as I have seen does not impress me: for the most part it is only the sermonic repetition of postmodern attitudes, and comes nowhere near the quality of studies in the history of scholarship that were published before *Ideologiekritik* was ever thought of.

In general, then, there is no reason at all why the concept of ideology should not be used; but if it is used, it should be properly analysed and clearly explained, and the advantages expected to come from it should also be explained.

6

Postmodernism

IN his article 'Poststructuralist Approaches: New Historicism and Postmodernism', Robert Carroll offers a good characterization of postmodern thinking. He begins with the following explanation of the difficult term 'poststructuralism': 'Rejecting structuralism's obsession with discovering binary oppositions everywhere in the text, poststructuralism emphasized the instability of the signifier, especially in its deconstructive mode.'[1] In itself this will not be very clear to many readers, and the best one can do is to read on, in the hope that what follows will elucidate these enigmatic words, which hope is at least in part justified by the exposition that follows. Those who find the need for still further explanation should try J. Barton, *Reading the Old Testament*, where on 'binary oppositions' they should see especially:

Structuralists tend to argue that all structures within which meaning can be generated, whether they be linguistic, social or aesthetic, can be analysed in terms of pairs of opposites. Although it may be going too far to make so much of the *binary* character of the contrasts through which meaning is produced (since, as we have seen, it is often a matter of multiple contrast), it is surely right to see contrast as such as of the essence of meaning.[2]

To this we add: 'The contention of literary structuralists is that literature is a cultural system exactly analogous to a language, a society or a game'.[3] It seems to me, incidentally, that this structuralist contention was simply wrong. Literature is *not* exactly analogous to language, nor is society. The 'poststructuralist' move to 'the instability of the signifier' mistakenly took this structuralist position as a basis from which to construct a move to a new position, instead of perceiving that the position in itself was erroneous.

---

[1] In J. Barton (ed.), *The Cambridge Companion to Biblical Interpretation* (Cambridge: Cambridge University Press, 1998), 50.

[2] J. Barton, *Reading the Old Testament* (London: Darton, Longman & Todd, 1984), 111.   [3] Ibid. 113.

Anyway, proceeding on our way towards poststructuralism, we continue with a further quotation from Barton:

'Every signified is also a signifier', or, in other words, texts refer to objects but the objects the texts refer to themselves refer to further objects, and so on ad infinitum. It makes as much sense to say that a text reads me as that I read a text . . . The difference between text and reader dissolves, to be replaced by the institution of textuality, in which the difference between reading and writing no longer exists, but the social reality of the interplay between writers and readers becomes 'yet more shimmering webs of undecidability stretching to the horizon' [Eagleton].[4]

But first, since this has brought us to the equally awful term 'deconstruction', we cannot do better than to refer, for an elucidation of it, to Barton once again:

The term is more often used than understood . . . An uninformed use of the word to signal one's disapproval of the modern world is not surprising. In such popular usage, 'deconstruction' is taken to be more or less equivalent to 'destruction'. None of this has much connection with the meaning of 'deconstruction' in literary studies.[5] For one thing, in literary theory critics do not deconstruct texts: texts deconstruct themselves . . . Deconstruction is a theory about the character of all texts, which claims that every text always and necessarily undermines or contradicts the philosophy on which its own plausibility relies.[6]

And so:

The fact that we can deconstruct a text, or show that it deconstructs itself, does not imply hostility to that text, for it is not just bad texts that can be deconstructed, but all texts. Learning systematically to distrust texts is a necessary part of reading.[7]

---

4 Barton, *Reading the Old Testament* (2nd edn. 1996), 220–1.
5 A similar, and relevant, misunderstanding is often found with the term 'hermeneutic of suspicion'. Conservative religious people often think this refers to a suspicion or *distrust* of the Bible and its historicity or authority, and that it is a term referring to such phenomena as biblical criticism; on the contrary, more properly it is used to refer to a suspicion or distrust of the self or of the interpreter, and in this sense it can be fully compatible with biblical criticism but suspicious of the 'conservative' interpreter. For a brief account see Thiselton in Barton (ed.), *Companion*, 105–6, who writes: 'The axis of suspicion encourages *Ideologiekritik* of the text and suspicion concerning the interests of the interpreter and the interpreter's community-tradition.' Thiselton appears to *support* this hermeneutic of suspicion, though associating with it, after Ricœur, another motif: 'willingness to suspect, willingness to listen'.
6 Barton, *Reading the Old Testament*, 2nd edn., 224.   7 Ibid. 226.

Armed with this information, we can return to Carroll's presentation. His article is short, well constructed and well written, ironic and paradoxical, and (within the limits of possibility, given the subject-matter) clear. There are four sections, one on post-structuralist approaches in general, one on 'New Historicism', one on postmodernism, and a conclusion.

Introducing the theme in general, Carroll tells us how, under the 'new generation of theory-driven scholars', texts have tended to become 'mirror images of the readers, who assume into their textual readings their own values as explicit modes and strategies for their reading processes'.[8] Such readings, he goes on, seek to transform biblical study from 'being in the (concealed) service of traditional western cultural hegemonic values into serving newer values reflecting the theopolitical demands of various post-sixties social movements and political lobbies'. The correctness of at least the latter part of this description will be evident to those familiar with the 'liberal' side of modern Christianity. We may note also the implication: traditional values were bad because they were 'hegemonic', but it is good that the newer values should become 'hegemonic' in their place. That is the whole purpose.[9]

Following this he introduces a point of importance, on which we have only touched so far but which will concern us further. The new approaches just mentioned, themselves entirely a recent creation, actually assisted 'older and more reactionary theological values' to reassert themselves, so that a certain alliance between the new poststructuralism and a renascent 'neo-fundamentalism' became possible. These links are usefully described as follows:

Poststructural approaches to the Bible not only permitted new avenues of theoretical readings to be explored, they also greatly assisted older and more reactionary theological values and practices to revamp themselves and to regroup for a concerted attack on the common enemy identified as the Enlightenment and historical-critical biblical scholarship. This

---

[8] Carroll, in Barton (ed.), *Companion*, 50. Contrast an opposing view from F. Watson, *Text and Truth* (Edinburgh: T. & T. Clark, 1997), 97: 'A Christian faith concerned to retain its own coherence cannot *for a moment* accept that the biblical texts (individually and as a whole) lack a single, determinate, meaning, that their meanings are created by their readers' (my italics: note the emphasis in 'cannot for a moment'). But what if there is *some* truth in the reader-response approach, even if not much: are believers required to deny what is true?   [9] Cf. the remarks of Gary Phillips quoted below, p. 147.

principle of 'my enemy's enemy is my friend' allowed poststructuralism and biblical structuralism to bracket out the Enlightenment, to ward off the critical reading of the Bible . . .[10]

Thus 'much of what passes for postmodernist practice looks like a kind of neo-fundamentalism'.[11] We shall return to this theme. Carroll goes on to consider the New Historicism. The newer approaches within biblical studies (he seems to have in mind the 'revisionist' work on the history of Israel, discussed above), which might in one sense be understood as a completion of the older Enlightenment-based project,[12] may also be considered analogous to the movement of New Historicism. What is this? The reader may well ask. It is a movement, well represented by L. Montrose as 'a reciprocal concern with the historicity of texts and the textuality of history'.[13] The revisionist historians mentioned above are classed by Carroll along with the work of John Van Seters, whose thoughts are considered to be 'a formidable body of work contributing to laying the foundations of a New Historicist approach to reading the Hebrew Bible'. Carroll goes on in the same style to accept that 'the Hebrew Bible begins to look more like a product from the Persian or, more especially, the Greek period'.[14] This allows (why?[15]) for a serious *Ideologiekritik* (a term he does not really explain in this article, but says that it is 'another formidable poststructuralist approach to reading the Bible').[16] All

---

[10] Carroll, in Barton (ed.), *Companion*, 51.   [11] Ibid.

[12] To cite one of the most serious thinkers on the subject, J. Habermas, among others, insists that 'the postmodern turn is a phase within the Enlightenment paradigm'; in other words, postmodernism is not a completely different entity, but is itself a part or phase within the entity of 'modernity' which preceded it: 'Modernity—an Incomplete Project', repr. in Hal Foster (ed.), *The Anti-Aesthetic: Essays on Postmodern Culture* (Port Townsend, Wash.: Bay, 1983), 3–15; wording quoted from P. C. Hodgson, *God in History* (Nashville: Abingdon, 1989), 254 n. 47 (ref. to p. 29).

[13] Carroll, in Barton (ed.), *Companion*, 52. Quotation from Louis A. Montrose, 'Professing the Renaissance: the Poetics and Politics of Culture', in H. Aram Veeser, ed., *The New Historicism* (London: Routledge, 1989), 20.   [14] Carroll, ibid. 54.

[15] I fail to see the connection. There is on the one hand the question about the period of the texts, and on the other hand the question of what can be achieved by *Ideologiekritik*. But it is impossible to see why a temporal location in the Greek period should make a criticism of ideology any easier or harder. On the subject as a whole, refer back to Ch. 5, pp. 132–4.

[16] If *Ideologiekritik* is thought by Carroll (cf. Ch. 5, p. 134) to 'uncover another layer of textual reading but one which focuses on the exegete more than on the text', so that ideologies of the text, of the communities, and of the teaching 'guilds' 'all become necessary subjects of the *Ideologiekritik* enterprise', one cannot see, as mentioned in the previous note, why the temporal location of the text in the Persian or Greek period should have anything to do with it.

this leads 'to a retuning of the historical dimensions detected in the text and to a rethinking of the literature as a reflection of the time in which it was written rather than as evidence for what is supposed to be represented within the text itself'.[17] This means, still, an essentially historical study, but one aiming at 'the time in which it was written' and not the time ostensibly referred to.[18] The 'overall production of the literature is now postdated by perhaps a millennium from what used to be thought'.

New Historicism is well named, because in contrast with some other elements of poststructuralist theory it continues to be interested in history: in contrast with views that deny all relevance to any reference outside the text, New Historicism 'would not deny the possibility of such referentiality'[19]—hardly a ringingly positive affirmation, but at least something. It thus 'retains the older focus on history characteristic of the Enlightenment'; it is also 'very resistant to the wilder forms of postmodern theory with their rejection of the possibility or desirability of the critical retrieval of the past'.[20]

But there is a difference from the older historical approach. According to Carroll, the New Historicism, thus seen, challenges the monopoly of the Bible's presentation of history: it wants to redress the balance by reintroducing what was left unspoken by the biblical text. The Bible is a collection of writings:

which isolate, exclude, repress and misrepresent as much as they may be deemed to advocate. New Historicism has as one of its aims the reinscription of the repressed and excluded, the inclusion of the excluded and the breaking of the silences which have lasted since the documents in the Bible were written . . .[21]

The 'repressed and excluded' might well, of course, include the Canaanites, though Carroll does not say this expressly. One of the

---

[17] This, however, is nothing new at all; on the contrary, it has been widespread in critical scholarship for over a century: the story of Abraham, as told by J, still more as told by P, told the scholar what J or P thought about Abraham, not what Abraham actually said or did. Perhaps not everyone took this approach, but it was certainly extremely common in traditional criticism.

[18] Here Carroll seems again to depart from his description of ideological criticism as a process that leaves the time of the text behind and moves on to include modern interpretations of the text. [19] Carroll, in Barton (ed.), *Companion*, 54.

[20] Ibid. 57.

[21] Ibid. 55. Note the similarity to the quotations from F. Schüssler Fiorenza as cited above, pp. 48 n., 50–2.

historians in question, Lemche, wrote a book about them,[22] and Whitelam's emphasis on 'the Palestinians' belongs to the same interest. Ahlström's main book, similarly, is not a history of Israel but a history of Palestine.[23] Carroll rightly admits that the new 'very different writers on biblical historiography . . . do not form a school or even a united approach'.[24] This qualification could be made more strongly than has been done by Carroll himself, for only one or two of the 'revisionist' historians as listed by him[25] seem to me to belong to New Historicism as it has been defined by him. Thus I would much doubt whether John Van Seters is really to be classed with it;[26] he seems to me to be more a rather idiosyncratic deviation within traditional historical criticism.[27] Ahlström and Garbini also, I would say, belong to a different approach and have little contact with the more 'theory-driven' modern revisionists: Ahlström, for instance, cared nothing for theory and such airy imaginings, just as he cared nothing for biblical theology. As a matter of fact, I am doubtful if *any* of the historians of Israel whom Carroll lists have much contact with the New Historicism movement as explained by people such as Montrose, at least in the passages quoted.

Carroll gives more substantial discussion to the work of Whitelam and Thompson. With Whitelam we see a much more distinct attachment to the postmodern approach. In his work we should note the questioning of the whole idea of Ancient Israel, which is said to be a construct not corresponding to any historical reality.[28] It is 'an imagined community', represented by the writers 'as having lived in an imagined past'; the function of such a construction would be the 'legitimation and justification of the present'. Of Thompson, Carroll admits that his concerns 'reflect

---

[22] N. P. Lemche, *The Canaanites and their Land* (Sheffield: JSOT, 1991).

[23] G. W. Ahlström, *The History of Ancient Palestine* (Sheffield: JSOT, 1993).

[24] Carroll, in Barton (ed.), *Companion*, 55.

[25] Ibid. 53.   [26] Cf. ibid. and pp. 92–3 above.

[27] For a recent criticism of Van Seters's approach, see E. W. Nicholson, *The Pentateuch in the Twentieth Century* (Oxford: Clarendon, 1998), esp. 134–43, 146–53, 233–7. An idiosyncratic feature of Van Seters's argumentation is his reliance on similarities between Greek historians, especially Herodotus, and the 'Yahwist' of the biblical narrative: for the main criticism of this see Nicholson, ibid. 149–53. In any case, I do not see in Van Seters's work, however we assess it, any of the characteristics that Carroll identifies as belonging to the New Historicism. Where, for instance, do we find him worrying about the 'reinscription of the repressed and excluded' and other such features mentioned above?

[28] See also Philip R. Davies, *In Search of 'Ancient Israel'* (Sheffield: JSOT, 1992).

rather different interests, approaches and methods'—and indeed, while he also likes to see the Hebrew Bible as 'constituted by a cumulative, collected tradition coming from the Persian period which is essentially folkloristic and which reflects a constructed entity called Israel',[29] Carroll does not really place Thompson firmly within the postmodern context.

Turning in his next section towards real postmodernism as distinct from the New Historicism, Carroll is much more ironic and critical. He perceives postmodernism, for a while at least, as authoritarian and dictatorial. He writes: 'Something of the authoritarian attitude of postmodernist writers may be detected in the prescriptions laid down by Gary Phillips in his article "Exegesis as Critical Praxis" '.[30] I quote a passage from the latter's Introduction:

Biblical criticism in the wake of poststructuralism concerns itself centrally with questions of *institutional control* and *power*—over reading methods, over hirings, firings and promotions; over production and dissemination of knowledge to guild members, etc. . . . Criticism and the critics are repositioned squarely, self-consciously, within the institutional power grids of Church, Synagogue and Academy; to talk of theory (or not) *is* to engage in the praxis of institutional power and control . . .[31]

There is no question that this is right, because:

Poststructural criticism, in particular criticism owing to deconstructive thought, seeks to amplify the unvoiced and unthought by demystifying the 'natural', the 'intuitive' and the 'abstract' of criticism for what they are—institutionalized, cultural constructs which articulate very specific arrangements of power and control.

There can be no use, therefore, in offering any contrary arguments: for Phillips has already explained that they cannot be anything but false.[32]

Again, the composite volume called *The Postmodern Bible*, authored by a group calling itself The Bible and Culture Collective, receives from Carroll (very rightly, in my opinion) a distinctly negative review. It has 'a highly authoritarian and totalizing ideology of its own (made up of so many parts race and

[29] See fuller quotation, Carroll, in Barton (ed.), *Companion*, 56.
[30] Ibid. 64 n. 16. Carroll refers esp. to the final section of the article, pp. 33–6.
[31] G. Phillips, 'Introduction', *Semeia*, 51 (Atlanta: Scholars Press, 1990), 2.
[32] Cf. also the remarkable aggressiveness and bellicosity of pp. 33–6 of Phillips' article, cited by Carroll, in Barton (ed.), *Companion*, 64 n. 16.

gender and so many parts egalitarianism)'[33] and its writers are 'making a serious bid for intellectual hegemony'.[34] Carroll gives a witty listing of the 'gods' by whom they swear: Louis Althusser, Roland Barthes, Jonathan Culler, Jacques Derrida, Terry Eagleton, Michel Foucault, Gerard Genette, Mieke Bal, Fredric Jameson, and Julia Kristeva. 'Little criticism of these gods', he tells us, will be found in the work. Playfulness and irony are conspicuously lacking in it.[35] The writers have succeeded only 'in being didactic as well as deadly dull'. The book 'easily deconstructs itself': it will provide good material for criticism by 'modernist' (i.e. old-fashioned) scholars looking for means to hit back at postmodernism. Its advocacy of 'popular readings' of the Bible is undermined by the complex, non-popular composition of the Collective;[36] while 'insisting on the open acknowledgement of individual personal political and ideological commitments the writers themselves are able to hide their own personal and political baggage behind the anonymity afforded by being part of a collective'.[37] *The Postmodern Bible* actually lacks any 'sustained readings of biblical texts'. Carroll goes on, however, to give some examples of what he considers really good works using postmodern theory.[38]

In the end, anyway, Carroll sums up by remarking on the 'great power of the newer ways of reading the Bible according to the

[33] 'Totalizing' is a fashionable term of postmodernism; the reader will find plenty of examples in W. Brueggemann's *Theology of the Old Testament*. Seen from this point of view, postmodernism seems like a new language full of new words which one *must* use, and full also of strings of exotic names of persons with whom one must be familiar, or at least pretend to be familiar: e.g., the throw-away phrase in Carroll, in Barton (ed.), *Companion*, 60, writing about White, *Narration and Discourse* (Cambridge: Cambridge University Press, 1991): 'using the work of Edmund Ortiguez on semiotics and in conjunction with the writings of Eugenio Coseriu, Émile Benveniste, Julia Kristeva, Lubomir Dolezel and Michael Bakhtin'—naturally, one knows all these people, does one not, but isn't there a slight risk, with the deafening clatter of so much name-dropping, that one will appear to be seeking to make an impression?

[34] Carroll, in Barton (ed.), *Companion*, 58.

[35] By contrast, these are the aspects of postmodernism appreciated by Barton, *Reading the Old Testament*, 235; quoted below, p. 161.

[36] This is not an unfamiliar phenomenon. Both Brueggemann and I recently made a similar criticism of Carl E. Braaten and R. W. Jenson (eds.), *Reclaiming the Bible for the Church* (Grand Rapids: Eerdmans, 1995): though professing to 'reclaim' the Bible for the church and its 'ordinary' members as distinct from academic specialists, this book is written almost entirely by persons with academic posts and makes no attempt to gain any expression of what the 'ordinary' church member thinks.

[37] Carroll, in Barton (ed.), *Companion*, 59.   [38] Ibid. 60–1.

developing canons of contemporary literary criticism'. They 'effect a marriage between modernity and postmodernity which gives birth to the reader as active subject in the construction of meaning'. This is a significant sentence: if there is really a 'marriage between modernity and postmodernity', that could be very important. But we need some guidance about how such a marriage could take place (or could have already taken place).[39] They avoid the old-fashioned search for 'objective meanings' which may then be imposed on all readers in 'authoritarian modes'. This means 'the rescue of the Bible from its ecclesiastical and academic captivities in hermeneutic forms which have grown sclerotic over the centuries'. Central, then, to this summary are two points: the dominance of 'the developing canons of contemporary literary criticism' and the avoidance of objective meanings which, he implies, are the source by which the Bible has been led captive over the centuries.

Carroll himself, however, has all the irony needed for successful deconstruction of his own argument. His summary at the end depicts 'a paradise of different readings with none privileged and all equally valid': the old hierarchies and hegemonies of historical-critical biblical studies will have gone for ever. But no!—this utopia may find itself deconstructed by advancing fundamentalistic revivalisms. 'Modernistic' (i.e. out-of-date) values such as reason and truth (cf. Provan's thoughts, quoted above, p. 79) may reassert themselves. But, in the last phrase, we look for a 'brave new world of kaleidoscopic biblical readings'. Carroll probably adds to himself: 'Maybe!'

Two or three points can now be added as additions and/or qualifications to Carroll's exposition. What I have said above would indicate an approval of the New Historicism in its interest in history and its affirmation of a critical approach to it, thus rightly overturning 'the wilder forms of postmodernism'. That this naturally leads on to the Persian period, and still more to the Greek, seems to me a quite unwarranted conclusion, as already argued above. The will to include whatever has been omitted is entirely right, but anything that has been omitted should be included only

---

[39] This question seems to be one of the main issues between Habermas and the postmodernists: according to him, postmodernism belongs within the movement of that which has gone before; cf. n. 12, above.

on the basis of actual evidence and not on the basis of theories founded on modern sociopolitical drives. The prejudice against leadership and the élite—coming, as Carroll rightly notes, almost always from persons enjoying modern élite positions—is to be absolutely repudiated.

The connections between postmodernism and 'neo-fundamentalism' deserve further remark.[40] Relations here are, as usual, paradoxical. We have heard much in recent years of the connection between biblical criticism and the Enlightenment, and conservative and fundamentalist opinion, mainly evangelical, has learned to put the Enlightenment in the forefront of its (extensive) heresy list. But I suspect that the anti-Enlightenment argument is fairly recent in origin among evangelicals, and has been promoted especially by neo-orthodox, mainly Barthian, influences: fundamentalists of earlier times had mostly never heard of the Enlightenment. Anyway, as Carroll says, there is a distinct convergence in recent times: the anti-Enlightenment sense of fundamentalists, focused mainly on biblical criticism, finds some support in the anti-Enlightenment hatred of postmodernists, focused rather on ideas of truth and rationality. Postmodern readings of the Bible, some of them totally ignoring historical aspects, might therefore seem welcome: the Bible can be read without all that critical stuff! And undoubtedly some important elements in postmodern biblical interpretation have come out of the soil of fundamentalism. But there must also be some unease about this alliance on the fundamentalist side.[41] First, fundamentalists

---

[40] Carroll, in Barton (ed.), *Companion*, 63 n. 1, has a note 'on fundamentalism as a postmodernist phenomenon', with citation of literature; cf. also his 65 n. 20. His actual text, p. 51, uses the term 'neo-fundamentalism', while p. 62 speaks of 'advancing fundamentalistic revivalisms'. It is not clear just how precisely he intends these terms to be used. I suspect he would intend them to be understood in a rather wide sense, which would include modern trends such as canonical approaches and, generally speaking, any other attempts to reinstate traditional church doctrine as an interpretative guide. This is probably supported by his approval of the rescue of the Bible from an 'ecclesiastical captivity', p. 61.

[41] For one example among hundreds: L. C. Barrett, reviewing Henry H. Knight III, *A Future for Truth: Evangelical Theology in a Postmodern Age* (Nashville: Abingdon, 1996), in *Interpretation* 52/4 (1998), 442, writes that Knight 'helpfully distinguishes an ultra-critical variety of postmodernism' from a 'post-critical type'. Then: 'According to Knight, post-critical postmodernity is good news for evangelicalism in that its critique of universal rationality liberates Christianity from the temptation to accommodate itself to extrinsic cultural values, as both liberal and fundamentalist apologetics have done. Ultra-critical postmodernity is potentially bad news for evangelicalism, raising the spectre of relativism and the indeterminacy of the meaning of scripture.' This is a typical example of the sort of questioning that is likely to continue in the relevant circles.

should not be too confident in allying themselves with a totally non-Christian and non-religious philosophy and practice of very modern times: do they want to do just the same as they blamed liberal Christianity for doing earlier on? Second, fundamentalists are not so sure that they want to abandon history as an important ground: it is exactly because the Bible is *historically* true that they have confidence in it, and exactly when its historical reliability is questioned that they become most upset. They may not want critical history, but they do need historical fact. Third, truth and rationality are rather essential for the traditional fundamentalist position: to have truth and rationality disappear out of the window is uncomfortable. Fourth, reader-response theories are highly ambiguous. They may work in one way, suggesting that, as all meaning is created by the reader, so it is entirely proper that evangelical readers may create evangelical meanings. But this is slippery ground. A more secure foothold is offered if one goes the other way and thinks that the Bible has its own, clear, meaning, which anyone can perceive. Fifth, if we consider the ultimate philosophical grounds, the dominant intellectual basis of most Anglo-Saxon fundamentalism came from the Princeton theology of the nineteenth century, and it took as its explicit foundation the Scottish Common Sense realism, roughly of the previous century. But the Common Sense philosophy was itself *an Enlightenment phenomenon*, one central to the Scottish Enlightenment and widely accepted from there into American culture. It worked, as a cultural phenomenon and a basis for general education, precisely because it was *not* a narrowly biblically based or religiously determined philosophy. It admired Francis Bacon's 'inductive method'. The contemptuous dismissal of 'fact' by modern neo-orthodox theologians (and postmodernists) was entirely foreign to it. Harriet Harris sums it up: 'biblical conservatives took from Common Sense philosophy an empirical-rationalist framework for their biblical apologetics, and this has been a significant factor in the formation of the fundamentalist understanding of scripture'.[42]

For all these reasons the connections between neo-fundamentalism and postmodernism are likely to remain distant, unless the neo- of neo-fundamentalism is to become more emphasized and a really different fundamentalism, with only limited points of contact with the older fundamentalism, should emerge. This is, of

---

[42] Harriet Harris, *Fundamentalism and Evangelicals* (Oxford: Clarendon, 1998), 130.

course, quite possible. The only question then will be how far the adherents of this new movement realize the distance that separates them from the old.

There is, however, another side to this whole matter, which Carroll does not touch on at all and, so far as I know, has had little attention in spite of the swelling literature on fundamentalism. That is the tendency of liberal/liberationist Christianity, commonly under the influence of postmodernism, to assume some of the characteristics that have in the past been thought to belong to fundamentalism.

Carroll referred to 'the theopolitical demands of various post-sixties social movements and political lobbies'.[43] Nothing could better express an important characteristic of certain currents of Christianity, as seen in mainstream Protestantism and notably in academic institutions. In essence, these theopolitical convictions have come to be the essential dogmas of the modern liberal churches and institutions.[44] They have replaced the older ecclesiastical dogmas but assumed a similar function of control. The older dogmas are not necessarily repudiated or forgotten, but they are more marginal and optional. 'Commitments' to the theopolitical demands are serious, and where possible are enforced. They apply, for instance, to the making of appointments, which are in many cases heavily influenced by matters of race, sex, and ideology;[45] this may be denied officially, but everyone knows that it is so. Generally speaking, it is inconceivable that anyone who did not support the ordination of women would be appointed, no matter how great a genius in Bible or theology he or she might be. One could continue with examples, but it is not necessary: this is the way things are. In respect of these theopolitical demands, a sort of liberal fundamentalism can come into existence. It is as strict, narrow-minded, and intolerant in respect of these drives as it is open-minded and tolerant in other respects. Fundamentalists often say in despair about liberal Christianity that in it 'anything goes'. They are much mistaken. Anything very definitely does not go. There can be found in it a Pharisaic, inquisitional watching over words and deeds that runs parallel to the same phenomenon in

---

[43] Carroll, in Barton (ed.), *Companion*, 51.

[44] I use the word 'liberal' as it is widely used, both by conservative Christians and in general speech, as in the media. Whether this form of church life is really liberal is another matter.   [45] Cf. the demands of Gary Phillips, quoted above, p. 147.

conservative fundamentalism. Its most serious manifestation, however, is not in the matter of appointments but in the control of speech. You have to use certain words and not others. Certain ideas cannot be expressed. 'Political correctness', as it is called (I do not know who invented the expression) is an important ingredient in the liberal-fundamentalist gospel.

How then does this fit in with Carroll's fine analysis from which we started? It means that there is not only a possible old-fundamentalist alliance with postmodernism; there is also a possible liberal fundamentalism equally associating itself with postmodernism. Though postmodernism can be seen as a phenomenon quite separate from religion, it can equally be perceived as a vehicle for religious realization of more or less the same values. If postmodernism can help old fundamentalism to ignore the challenges posed by biblical criticism and thus to remain within older religious patterns, it can also help a new fundamentalism to discover vast fields of new meanings, highly acceptable to the modern theopolitical drives, which would hitherto have been hindered by constraints of both biblical criticism and biblical theology, as well as of traditional dogma. They will seem interesting, stimulating, and satisfying; and truth and rationality are out-of-date concepts which can be disregarded.[46] And some at least of such meanings will come close to being canonical or authoritative, at least in the sense that it will be dangerous to dispute them. In all these regards postmodernism seems to be a surrender to the pressures of modern culture, spreading over more and more of the world from its centre in the United States. But with this the United States, which more than any other country has its constitution firmly fixed in the Enlightenment, must suffer severe strains. One such strain has just been mentioned, because highly relevant to our subject: the strain between the traditional (Enlightenment-based!) insistence on freedom of speech and the newer insistence on political correctness, reaching in extreme cases toward criminalization of the incorrect expression. Another such strain lies in the overwhelming power of *money* as a means by which democratic procedures can be circumvented: 'Since the dominance of money in capitalist democracies threatens the autonomy of the other spheres of justice . . . its influence must be

---

[46] Carroll, in Barton (ed.), *Companion*, 62.

curtailed or confined more thoroughly to the sphere of commodity exchange than it presently is . . .'[47]

One is aware of a culture where there is much radicalism, populism, and egalitarianism (all of them, however, often working to the advantage of those already well placed), but where there is practically no remanent awareness of socialism, even as a mere possibility, except for limited pockets.[48] Postmodernism as a whole, with some exceptions, seems to me to belong to this trend.[49] Its apparent radicalism is not to be taken too seriously. Fredric Jameson's book title, *Postmodernism, or, the Logic of Late Capitalism*, is not lacking in insight. Postmodernism, we should remember, according to some interpreters is not only a set of ideas or interpretative modes, but a state of society as a whole. The *world* has become postmodern, and so our thinking must conform.

We return, however, to Carroll's presentation. One aspect that is missing from his exposé is a discussion of the place of his subject in relation to theology. What we hear about is mostly readings: one can read a passage in this way or in that. But is there a place for theology in this, whether a 'biblical' theology or the theology of a church or a religious organization? Or is theology altogether one of the 'ecclesiastical captivities . . . which have grown sclerotic over the centuries'[50] and from which the Bible has to be rescued?

Two things worry me about these 'readings'. The first is that they sound incredibly individualistic: anyone can read anything in any way he likes—the hypothetical utopia that Carroll describes so well: where 'the modernistic lion will lie down with the post-modernist lamb, the Marxist bear will eat straw with the capitalist goat'.[51] Carroll is quick to make this utopia sound truly utopian, and in that respect something that will never come to pass. But what will there be instead? Some controls will be insisted on:

[47] So David Ingram, 'The Subject of Justice', in M. Passerin D'Entrèves and S. Benhabib, *Habermas and the Unfinished Project of Modernity* (Cambridge Mass.: MIT, 1997), 294.

[48] I do not take seriously the supposed Marxism that inspires various biblical and other scholars. For them Marxism is cheap, because they know that it is not going to be put into practice. 'The last refuge of neo-Marxism', said Prof. P. Higonnet, is 'well-endowed universities in America' (*New York Times*, 8 March 1999).

[49] For the sort of socialistic thinking I have in mind, see Brian Barry, 'The Continuing Relevance of Socialism', in B. Barry, *Democracy, Power, and Justice* (Oxford: Clarendon, 1989), 526–42.   [50] Carroll, in Barton (ed.), *Companion*, 61.

[51] Ibid. 62.

'New Historicist readings will insist on certain values accompany-ing all readings—slavery is wrong, oppression is to be resisted, etc.' Yes, indeed. But will there be some sort of organized discussion of these and other possible values: in other words, will there be a rational discussion, or will it be decided by power and influence?[52] And, again, why should the Bible, once detached from its church connections and academic captivities, be so important for us to read at all?[53] Perhaps some such connections, even if not captivi-ties, are necessary: otherwise the Bible might be only one among many texts upon which one might amuse oneself with the obser-vation of its self-deconstruction? Perhaps therefore a *theological* assessment is necessary?

I do not consider readings of the Bible, just as readings, even when conducted in a religious context, to be theology, or to be able to take the place of theology. Only when they are related to a network of conceptions of God and his relations with the world are they meaningful in a religious sense. Otherwise they look to me as if they were either a subset of general individual readings of literature, or else a means of expression for political and social ideologies.

In summary, while recognizing what Carroll wrote about the

---

[52] Some sentences from the concluding paragraph of Hans Barth, *Truth and Ideology* (Zurich: Rentsch, 1945; ET Berkeley: University of California Press, 1976), 192–4, read: 'If the nature of intellectual achievements is ideological, in that their appearance conceals their "real" meaning which is to manifest the will to power or a set of social conditions, the prac-tical consequence will be that critical intellectual discussion is replaced by political decision . . . The reduction of intellectual content to social power is self-defeating . . . Human asso-ciation is dependent on agreement, and the essence of agreement, be it concerned with common behavior, rational action, or scientific investigation, is the idea of truth. If this idea is denounced as ideological, we are left, in Nietzsche's language, with individual quanta of will which, according to the measure of their power, arbitrarily determine what truth and justice are to be.' Note the similarity of this thinking to Provan's thinking as cited above, p. 79.

[53] Carroll's *Wolf in the Sheepfold* (London: SPCK, 1991) does contain various sections on the 'challenge' of the Bible and its 'life-changing' quality; but in the book as a whole they are overwhelmed by his amassing of negative, contradictory aspects, both within the Bible and between the Bible and theology. 'The thing written need not be profound but because it is always *other* than oneself its alterity can penetrate consciousness and radically alter how one thinks, behaves or lives' (p. 124). But this would be true not only of the Bible, but of any book written from, or portraying, a very different world. Carroll's final recourse (in that book) seems to be to the *wildness* of the Bible and the importance of not 'taming' it (pp. 136–43)—ironically, the same concept that, expressed as 'domestication', is favoured in the work of biblical theologians such as Childs and Brueggemann. On this see J. Barr, *The Concept of Biblical Theology* (London: SCM, 1999), 409 and 683 n. 17.

'great power' of postmodern readings, something on the negative
side must be added. Reader-response theories have to be qualified
and limited by controls. For modern people just to read their own
ideas and ideologies into the Bible is an invitation to folly and
chaos. A suitable qualification would be a historical one: that is to
say, the response of readers within the biblical times and cultures.
It is sometimes said that traditional historical reading was itself
merely a reading-in of modern ideologies—for instance, we are
sometimes told that German scholars were interested in David and
Solomon because of the reunification of Germany under the
Empire—but such suggestions are usually no more than a fancy,
not to be taken seriously.

Similarly, the recognition of 'great power' in postmodernist
readings has to be qualified by the recognition of the rubbishy
character of much that is now being written about the Bible. One
may criticize the older scholarship for its dullness and pedestrian
character, but one cannot deny its *solidity*. The same cannot be said
of much that is now being produced. The pursuit of rapidly
changing fashions, the dominance of theory over serious knowledge, the absence of connection with religious traditions, and the
readiness at any time to overturn that upon which one stood in
one's own learning only a few years before—all these produce a
fevered atmosphere which is likely to do considerable damage.

Postmodernism, as will already have become evident, is somewhat like learning a new language. One *has to say* 'totalizing',
'marginalized', 'closure', 'metanarrative', 'reinscription', and, of
course, 'deconstruction'. In French it is worse, for one has to use
différance, which is quite different from *différence*, plus many other
such. This is the fashion. It is manifest in the titles of books, articles, chapters, and academic papers. Consider the title of Stephen
D. Moore's *Poststructuralism and the New Testament: Derrida and
Foucault at the Foot of the Cross*, regarded by Carroll as a 'sophisticated' work,[54] with such section titles as 'The Hydraulics of a
Liquid Metaphor' (concerning the woman at the well in Samaria):
bad taste? black humour? self-advertisement? One way or the
other, there is nothing *special* about it: go to the annual meeting of
the American Academy of Religion/ Society of Biblical
Literature, and you will see on the programme literally hundreds

---

[54] Carroll, in Barton (ed.), *Companion*, 57, 64 n. 14.

of papers with this sort of title. It is part of the fashion, but in such a way as to suggest that postmodernism cannot express itself except in such a language.

Of the serious thinkers, basically philosophers, continually quoted in postmodernist work, we may name two Frenchmen, Foucault and Derrida, and in the English-speaking world a tradition of American pragmatism, in which Richard Rorty is most often named. And I have no intention here of expounding these persons or offering a critique of their thoughts. I will make only two points: first, to distinguish, among the biblical scholars discussed here, the degree to which they show dependence on the philosophies of postmodernism, and second, to indicate that there is such a thing as a philosophical opposition to the postmodernist ideas.

What I noticed here is that the work on the history of Israel, which in a way has formed the centre of our presentation, referred very little to this philosophical underpinning. It is much more in the 'literary' production of 'readings' that such a dependence appears. Did Ahlström, or Van Seters, or Thompson, or Lemche appeal much to any of the relevant philosophers, or 'critical theorists' as most of them are better termed?[55] Even Davies, who in his claims about method might come closest to a philosophical position, seems to mention none of these leading figures in his *JBL* article,[56] or, so far as I see, in his other works that I have mentioned here. Dever, as we have seen, dismissed deconstruction as a 'fad' which had already been abandoned by those who had tried it. In this respect not only the earlier historians mentioned, such as Ahlström and Van Seters, but also the more fully revisionist historians may not be as much postmodernist as might at first appear. Indeed, as we may have already suggested, a good deal of their thinking may be more easily understood as a continuation and radicalization of the older modernist position, i.e. of the approach commonly known as historical-critical as applied to historiography (rather than to the analysis of texts). The question

---

55 Thompson does mention Habermas, but in a sentence that, significantly, says that 'No one is disagreeing (or agreeing) with J. Habermas or M. Hesse. They have nothing to do with the discussion' ('A Neo-Albrightean School in History and Biblical Scholarship?', *JBL* 114 (1995), 690).

56 P. R. Davies, 'Method and Madness: Some Remarks on Doing History with the Bible', *JBL* 114 (1995), 699–705.

I ask myself is: among the biblical scholars concerned (unlike the theologians who have concerned themselves with the same questions), how many of them have really worked through the philosophers and critical theorists whom they quote from time to time? Have they really read Derrida or Foucault and considered whether their arguments are valid or not? Or, by contrast, are their convictions simply expressions of popular trends of present-day fashion, which are then confirmed by occasional quotations from the great names?

And, in particular, do they ever face the possibility that postmodernist practices and convictions may be simply *wrong*? Seldom in the literature concerning the Bible have I seen serious discussion of any views critical of postmodernism. It seems to be often *assumed* as the right thing, so much so that critical analysis of it is not necessary. It becomes a dogma, enforced not by church authority but by social and educational pressure. There follow some considerations which point in the other direction.

The idea that some, or much, of postmodernism is really after all not a breakaway from modernism but a continuation, deepening, and completion of it has been touched on at one or two points and was hinted at by Carroll in one or two of his remarks as quoted above. This is significant because it leads us on to one of the main intellectual critics of postmodernism, Jürgen Habermas, who maintains something of just this kind: that postmodernism is not, as it tends to claim, a 'turn' (another of the modern—sorry, postmodern!—code-words) to something quite different, but is a completion of the older (Enlightenment) modernist trend. The title of the major volume of essays, *Habermas and the Unfinished Project of Modernity*,[57] indicates this central point clearly. I quote from the essay of Christopher Norris: '[Habermas's book] makes out a very strong case . . . for seeing postmodernism not on its own professed terms as a radical challenge to the outworn enlightenment paradigm, but rather as the upshot of a widespread failure to think through the problems bequeathed by that tradition.'[58]

This might suggest that we do not have a clear distinction, which would lead to a quite different new situation, but rather an untidy mixture of factors belonging to one or another. In biblical studies, we can be sure that it is the latter.

57   Passerin d'Entrèves and Benhabib (eds.).   58   Ibid. 97.

We may add some words from Richard Rorty, certainly one of the leading figures quoted. In a short article in the *New York Times*, under the title of 'Lofty Ideas that may be Losing Altitude', he wrote under the heading 'Post-Modernism':

The first thing that comes to mind is post-modernism. It's one of these terms that has been used so much that nobody has the foggiest idea what it means. It means one thing in philosophy, another thing in architecture and nothing in literature. It would be nice to get rid of it. It isn't exactly an idea; it's a word that pretends to stand for an idea. Or maybe the idea that one ought to get rid of is that there is any need to get beyond modernity.[59]

Moreover, Terry Eagleton, certainly one of the 'gods' (in Carroll's terms) of postmodernism, published his *The Illusions of Postmodernism*.[60] Far from being directed *against* postmodernism, it sympathizes with it but sadly identifies all sorts of weaknesses and failures that exist within it. Look, for one example, at its criticism of the emphasis on 'the body' which is characteristic of many postmodernist biblical scholars[61] (I once heard a lecture in which the speaker clearly thought that the way to succeed was to repeat the phrase 'the body' infinitely, two or three times in every sentence if possible). And look at his concluding paragraph, which touches on the possibility of fascism:

Postmodern end-of-history thinking does not envisage a future for us much different from the present, a prospect it oddly views as a cause for celebration . . . Its rich body of work on racism and ethnicity, on the paranoia of identity-thinking, on the perils of totality and the fear of otherness: all this, along with its deepened insights into the cunning of power, would no doubt be of considerable value. But its cultural relativism and moral conventionalism, its scepticism, pragmatism and localism, its distaste for ideas of solidarity and disciplined organization, its lack of any adequate theory of political agency: all these would tell heavily against it.

I do not say Eagleton is always right: but he is better to read by a long way than most biblical postmodernists are. The qualifications he expresses, to value them no higher, ought to be known and faced by all postmodernists.[62]

---

[59] 1 November 1997.   [60] (Oxford: Blackwell, 1996).

[61] Ibid. 69–75.

[62] Cf. also John O'Neill, *The Poverty of Postmodernism* (London: Routledge, 1995).

Zygmunt Bauman, again an attractive and persuasive writer, is more positive. He thinks that postmodernity is not only here, but here to stay:

Postmodernity is not a transitory departure from the 'normal state' of modernity; neither is it a diseased state of modernity, an ailment likely to be rectified, a case of 'modernity in crisis'. It is, instead, a self-reproducing, pragmatically self-sustainable and logically self-contained social condition defined by *distinctive features of its own*.[63]

Similarly, again:

The phenomena described collectively as 'postmodernity' are not symptoms of systemic deficiency or disease; neither are they a temporary aberration with a life-span limited by the time required to rebuild the structures of cultural authority. I suggest instead that postmodernity . . . is an aspect of a fully-fledged, viable social system which has come to replace the 'classical' modern, capitalist society and thus needs to be theorized according to its own logic.[64]

In other words, a utopia, as Carroll said, or a kingdom of God; and, like the latter, it is going to go on for ever! I beg to doubt this. I see too many contradictions and tensions, too many possibilities of looming disaster, too many likelihoods of a relapse to something worse than 'modernity' was. Certainly, if one is to take biblical study as an example, one could hardly say that its level now is higher than it was a century ago; and the work that is solid and likely to be lasting is mostly, though not exclusively, carried on by those who pay no attention to postmodernism.

Moreover, there are other philosophical lines that are critical of the whole postmodern project. Notable among these is that taken by Ernest Gellner in his *Postmodernism, Reason and Religion*; it is obviously relevant to our theme, as can be seen from this passage:

The postmodernists have gone one step further . . . It isn't *superficial* objectivity which is repudiated, but objectivity as such . . . Objective truth is to be replaced by hermeneutic truth. Hermeneutic truth respects the subjectivity both of the object of the inquiry and of the inquirer, and even of the reader or listener. In fact the practitioners of the method are so deeply, so longingly, imbued both by the difficulty and the undesirability of transcending the meanings—of their objects, of themselves, of

---

[63] Bauman, *Intimations of Postmodernity* (London: Routledge, 1992), 188.
[64] Ibid. 52.

their readers, of anyone—that in the end one tends to be given poems and homilies on the locked circles of meaning in which everyone is imprisoned, excruciatingly *and* pleasurably.[65]

Anyone who has listened to the papers at a congress on biblical studies will find these remarks to resonate. Incidentally, these remarks may suggest a thought that goes much further: the thought that the centrality accorded to *hermeneutic* thinking in modern biblical studies and theology, a centrality strongly asserted and vigorously enforced, may have been the source of much of our present difficulty.

Gellner is important from another angle, because he concerns himself directly with religion, and, within that, with fundamentalism, and especially with Islamic fundamentalism.

To conclude, therefore, I wish to cite (once again!) the thoughts of John Barton about postmodernism as a whole:

As 'a theory' (sometimes, with staggering imperialism, just 'theory' with no article!) claiming to explain or expose culture, art, meaning, and truth, I find postmodernism absurd, rather despicable in its delight in debunking all serious beliefs, decadent and corrupt in its indifference to questions of truth; I do not believe in it for a moment. But as a game, a set of *jeux d'esprit*, a way of having fun with words, I find it diverting and entertaining. I enjoy the absurd and the surreal, and postmodernism supplies this in ample measure.[66]

I fully agree with this (especially, perhaps, with the first part of it). The decadence and corruption, we may remember, fit well with the end-of-millennium situation. I remain thoroughly grateful to Carroll for his account of the matter, on which I have so much depended, and for his wit and irony, which leave me feeling that more will come out of this than I at present see.

I remarked earlier that the term 'ideology', so important for our discussions, had come into use largely in a milieu where religion and theology did not matter much; only late in the twentieth century was it taken over and became prominent in Bible and religion. I want to widen out this insight somewhat, in the following sense. So much of the modern discussion is focused on the relations between the modernity of the Enlightenment and the postmodernity of today. All this talk is as if these were the only two

---

[65] (London: Routledge, 1992), 35.   [66] Barton, *Reading the Old Testament*, 235.

possible states, as recognized primarily by sociology. But religion is a different state and a different tradition. It is interesting to recollect that religion is today the only sphere where *texts from the ancient world* are read, studied, and interpreted within a wide and popular set of communities of widely various educational, cultural, racial, and ethnic identities. There was religion in the time of past 'modernity', but, though influenced by that modernity, it was not identified with it or swallowed up in it. It should not let itself be identified with postmodernity either, or be swallowed up in it.

7
Postmodernism and Theology

THE title of this chapter suggests, perhaps, something more ambitious than I wish to attempt. My subject is not postmodernism as a whole and theology as a whole, which would be well beyond my reach, but, more modestly, the connections with theology of things said in this book, plus some limited additional exemplification. For the reader may have noticed that, in many of the discussions of such topics as biblical criticism, the history of Israel, and postmodernism in general, theology as such has not often come to the fore, or, where it has been noticed, has often been referred to negatively. And this is not surprising, for whole chapters and indeed whole books about biblical interpretation in the modern discussion have been written which contain practically not a word about theology, or which see it as an entity lying outside the sphere of biblical interpretation.

Thus for the most part I have concentrated on the discussions and conflicts between different currents in biblical scholarship. But opinions that have been advanced within these discussions have often come close to, or even been identical with, opinions that theologians, doctrinal theologians in the full sense, have also advanced. For they also obviously have an interest in the ways in which the Bible is to be interpreted, and they have often offered criticisms of the prevailing currents in biblical scholarship. Moreover, just as biblical scholarship is affected by trends in philosophy, sociology, and general cultural theory, so theology is affected by these same trends: thus, to take our obvious example, postmodernism is affecting both alike. We should consider therefore how it relates to both.

Postmodernism is not something completely new, that had no background in the earlier history of thought. Its major thinkers have, and acknowledge, their background in Heidegger, in Nietzsche, in Marx, in Hegel, in Kant. But these (Nietzsche perhaps not so much) are exactly the same thinkers who exercised a profound influence on the theology of the last two centuries. It is not surprising therefore if thoughts that appear, as if new, in postmodernism have some kind of consonance with ideas that, whether positively or negatively, have had an effect in theology. It is interesting, incidentally, that, while the five thinkers mentioned above were all Germans, the dominant leaders in postmodernism have been French. David Clines wrote: 'It was very instructive, if also shocking, to observe at the recent meeting of the International Organization for the Study of the Old Testament in Paris, July, 1992, [that] not one of the invited speakers ever referred to Roland Barthes, Jacques Derrida, Michel Foucault, or Jacques Lacan—four Parisians who have radically changed the agenda, I thought, for the ways we think about texts'.[1] Equally interesting is the fact that, at a time of very considerable friction between French and American culture in general, exactly these names are commonly accepted as guides by large numbers of American students, the idea that they might be subject to criticism being almost unheard-of.

Moreover, and perhaps still more important, it can happen that trends of opinion in postmodernism which affect biblical studies come also very close to similar tendencies in which theology itself has impinged upon the work of biblical exegesis. In these matters there can be a temporal overlap. There is not a clear point at which postmodernism begins and before which all lay in the darkness of 'modernity'. Just as at present much theology is rather untouched by postmodernism, so in older times much or most theology was by no means at home with the 'modernity' that then existed in the rest of the intellectual world. Theological criticism of biblical scholarship has been frequent and sometimes drastic; and in some cases, with the arrival of new viewpoints through postmodernism, theologians have been tempted to utter the ever-unwelcome phrase, 'We told you so!'

This is all the more so because 'theology' is not a united force that supports one unified opinion (an impression that is given by a number of the comments by biblical scholars that have been quoted in this book). This is clear when we look at some of the subjects we have been discussing. One that has repeatedly arisen

---

[1] D. Clines, 'Possibilities and Priorities of Biblical Interpretation in an International Perspective', *Biblical Interpretation*, 1 (1993), 75.

is the conflict between objectivity and subjectivism. While some trends in theology have upheld the 'objective truth' of the Bible in its historical aspect, others have advised that no such objectivity can be relied on. The hostility to objectivity which is so manifest in postmodernism is nothing new in theology; subjectivism has had a long-standing place in it, and still more in general religious practice. Again, our revisionist historians have been accused of excessive scepticism towards history, but such scepticism also has an illustrious tradition within theology: John McIntyre, addressing the problem of 'Historical Criticism in a "History-Centred Value-System" ', points to 'the historical scepticism so potent in writers of such different periods and standpoints as Kierkegaard, Kähler, Brunner, Barth, Tillich and Bultmann'.[2] Such historical scepticism now has a clear manifestation, at one end of the spectrum in revisionist historiography and at the other in some forms of canonical criticism. Philip Davies, in the final sentence of his *In Search of 'Ancient Israel'*,[3] calls upon biblical scholarship 'to cease to practise a theologically-dictated form of historical criticism', but it is doubtful whether the aspects against which he protests so vehemently were 'theologically dictated' at all. Many currents within theology have strongly argued the opposite position, namely that it is wrong for theology to base its judgements on historical certainties, whether within the Bible or outside it. Again, in spite of the historical zeal of Davies and others, which some see, in any case, to end up as a nihilistic destruction of history, an indifference to history is agreed to be a manifest characteristic of postmodernism in many forms—for example in its literary interpretation; but here also there is a parallel in the ideas of an 'end' or 'death' or 'collapse' of history within theology. As for the characteristic postmodern hostility to the heritage of the Enlightenment, such a hostility has been endemic in many theological traditions, as has been exemplified in these pages, so much so that it would be easier to speak of a 'convergence' of postmodernism with long-established currents of theology. Postmodernism has thus had a certain *praeparatio evangelica* within traditions of theology, which in turn makes it unsurprising

---

[2] J. McIntyre, in 'Historical Criticism in a History-Centred Value-System', in S. E. Balentine and John Barton (eds.), *Language, Theology and the Bible* (Oxford: Clarendon, 1994), 370–84, 372.

[3] (Sheffield: JSOT, 1992).

that its influence in theology and in biblical interpretation is so considerable.

An obvious first example would be Karl Barth, who on the one hand incorporated large amounts of biblical exegesis within his theology and on the other hand maintained a distance from most of the biblical scholarship of his time. He had ideas about text and context, about the place of history, about intention and referentiality. As we shall see, some scholars have identified postmodern ideas of language and literature as having an earlier representation in his thinking. As the new wave of interest in 'holistic' interpretation, stimulated largely by trends in literary criticism, became more influential, it was natural that some would perceive parallels in Barth's thinking to the latest trends.

The very term 'postmodern' highlighted the desire and longing for something that would come *after* the accepted and traditional approaches. In 1966 the central Old Testament scholar Rudolf Smend contributed an essay entitled 'Postcritical Exegesis of Scripture' to a Festschrift honouring Barth.[4] In Barth's thinking as Smend expounded it, the New Testament was to be understood as the historically given body of material, and thus not a hypothetical entity: every 'historical-critical construction or reconstruction' was excluded—a step that was to lead towards canonical criticism and the emphasis on final-form exegesis. The post-critical attitude thus not only relativized contemporary work on the history of Israel, of Jesus and of early Christianity; it also relativized the work of biblical 'Introduction', not only of 'literary-*historical*' but also of '*literary*-historical' analysis.[5] All this refers to thoughts of Barth going back to the 1920s and 1930s.

If there was an interest in the 'postcritical', there was likewise something of a longing for the 'postliberal'. To move *beyond* the critical and, still more, the liberal stages was an end very profoundly desired by many. Postmodernism as it now exists hardly existed then, but a certain trend in the same direction may be perceived. Postmodernism may realize certain impulses which were already present in theological movements existing earlier in the twentieth century.

[4] R. Smend, 'Nachkritische Schriftauslegung', most accessible in R. Smend, *Die Mitte des Alten Testaments* (Munich: Kaiser, 1986), 212–32.
[5] Ibid. 231.

Among more recent works, from a time when postmodernism was very definitely established as a major cultural force, we may mention, in order of publication, four in particular: Stephen H. Webb, *Re-Figuring Theology: the Rhetoric of Karl Barth*;[6] Graham Ward's two books, *Barth, Derrida, and the Language of Theology*[7] and *Theology and Contemporary Critical Theory*;[8] and W. Stacy Johnson, *The Mystery of God: Karl Barth and the Postmodern Foundations of Theology*.[9] Here are two sentences from Johnson's concluding chapter:

With increasing frequency, one hears the suggestion that Karl Barth was the first 'postmodern' or 'postliberal' theologian. I have taken the risk, then, of applying the term 'postmodern' to Barth out of the dual conviction that theology in a postmodern age is worth doing and that the theology of Karl Barth has much to contribute to that venture.[10]

Or again, to quote Webb, 'Barth and Derrida share a similar theory of language'.[11] But is this really credible; and, if it is, will it actually work to the favour of Barth's reputation in the long run?

One or two questions can hardly be left unasked about this approach. Notable, from our point of view, is the lack of reference in these works either to the Bible itself or to the problems of biblical studies. The impression left with the reader is that the relation between Barth and the postmodern trends in cultural theory, whether in agreement or in disagreement, is basically a philosophical or a rhetorical matter. The effect would surely be to relativize the commonly held impression that Barth was a 'biblical' theologian and that his 'biblical' approach outflanked the various philosophies and provided a basis substantially independent of them. Or, to put it in another way, it would relativize the thought that any philosophical views implied in Barth's thought would be specific and integral to his theology as a whole: for how could such views be shared with positions markedly distinct from Christian doctrines of revelation, Trinity, and the like? And how can the whole subject be discussed without entering into the various developments and (alleged) crises in biblical studies which we are considering in the present volume?

---

[6] (Albany, NY: State University of New York Press, 1991).
[7] (Cambridge: Cambridge University Press, 1995).
[8] (London: Macmillan, 1996).
[9] (Louisville, Ky.: Westminster Knox, 1997). For ample further references see the useful note in Johnson, ibid. 210 n. 2.   [10] Ibid.
[11] *Re-Figuring Theology*, 147.

Moreover, I find striking in these books the very slight element of critique towards the postmodern movements. The general impression they create is one of complete acceptance, with perhaps only some degree of differentiation where leading postmodernists differ from one another. The possibility of serious challenge to the postmodern viewpoints is very muted in them. Yet, without serious critique and discussion, one cannot help being left with the impression that postmodernism must be accepted because it is avant-garde and the present fashion.

It is not my purpose, however, to discuss these works in detail; nor do I wish to present a conspectus of the thinking of the major postmodernist thinkers or to attempt a comparison of it with the thinking of Barth or other modern theologians. All I can do is to indicate the existence of a possible set of analogies or conflicts in which theology and postmodernism have come into contact, biblical studies being one of the major points of contact. I can only present a series of what seem to me to be relevant examples, illustrating the way in which the contacts may lead us.

I begin with another quotation from Johnson:

Some are justifiably suspicious of postmodernity, believing that it signals, at best, a sort of perpetual adolescence that refuses to take responsibility for its ideas and actions, or at worst, a radical form of nihilism that questions the meaning of all inherited verities. For example, according to Jean-François Lyotard, the dominant feature of the 'postmodern' is what he calls an 'incredulity toward metanarratives (*grands récits*)'. On this view, postmodernity represents a protest against every abstract, comprehensive, universally-applicable, and legitimating 'story'—whether Christian, Marxist or otherwise—by which people have sought to understand life in its 'totality'.[12]

And, after the first sentence he adds a note which reads: 'An example of the type of postmodern theology that we should not follow is the brilliant but unacceptable proposal of Mark C. Taylor, *Erring: A Postmodern A/theology.*'[13]

Some remarks about this work may be useful. Taylor stands in the tradition of the 'death of God' theology: hence the odd term 'A/theology' in the title. I remarked above that postmodernism is like a new, almost entirely strange, language which one has to learn: decentring, logocentric, ontotheology, metanarrative, totalizing.

---

[12]   *The Mystery of God*, 4–5.   [13]   Ibid. 193 n. 12.

You have to know this language, otherwise you might as well not exist. Nowhere is this feeling more easily to be experienced than in reading Taylor's book, as demonstrated in this passage:

> Let me pause to recapitulate the tangled course I have been pursuing. From the point of view of deconstructive a/theology, the death of God is realized in the radically incarnate word. The disappearance of the transcendental signified creates the possibility of writing. No longer completely bound to, or by, the traditional (theological) structure of representation and signification, writing articulates word(s) by inscribing an errant margin that simultaneously joins and separates opposites. As a play of differences that establishes the relationships that constitute all that is and is not, writing is no thing and yet is not nothing. Within this script, there are no discrete things or separate entities. Things, which are always already signs, 'are because of interrelations or interactions'.[14]

It goes on like this for most of 200 pages. I said above that this language is 'almost' entirely strange: 'almost' is correct, because the elements are mostly familiar: one knows the prefix 'de-' and the term 'construction'; but 'deconstruction' is part of a new language—especially when, as is common in postmodern discourse, absolutely no attempt is made to explain the terms in language that the uninitiated can understand.

One other remark that follows out this theme of the language 'almost entirely strange'. One of my main achievements in life has been to question, and very largely to overcome (for my arguments were largely accepted) the use of etymology to prove meanings of words in theological exegesis and biblical theology.[15] This message, however, did not penetrate into the world of postmodernism, for spurious etymological explanations have proliferated in it. This is not entirely surprising when one considers the influence of Heidegger, whose work contained far more examples than all biblical theology ten times over. This is one place where, it seems, doctrinal theology has learned nothing from what happened in biblical theology—and at a point which has nothing to do with historical criticism and is also an insight very important for the move towards postmodernism! (Heidegger, I imagine, did not think that these etymological connections were really valid or

---

[14] Mark C. Taylor, *Erring: A Postmodern A/theology* (Chicago: University of Chicago Press, 1984), 108.
[15] In *The Semantics of Biblical Language* (London: Oxford University Press, 1961). For a retrospect on the matter, see my *The Concept of Biblical Theology*, 232–6.

proved anything: they were more like a sort of linguistic illustration which happily captured some philosophical relationship.)
Anyway, such central postmodern figures as Derrida produced
some choice examples. Taylor follows and multiplies these:

'Hieroglyphic' derives from the Latin *hieroglyphicus*, which was in turn
borrowed from the Greek *hierogluphikos* (*hieros*, sacred, plus *gluphē*, carv-
ing). The hieroglyphic is thus sacred inscription, holy writ. The hiero-
phantic character of scripture must not be allowed to obscure the
'materiality' of the word. Writing, which is necessarily bound to the
death of the father, is bodily or incarnate.[16]

All this comes out of Derrida, and a whole section of the book
is devoted to the theme.[17] The peculiar title *Erring* is elucidated by
almost a page of cognates from Provençal through Gothic to Old
French, which proves that '*Erring*, then, is "wandering, roaming"';
deviating from the right course; missing the mark'[18]—which, of
course, everyone knew already. Whatever the status of this work
as theology, and I shall not try to analyse that, it undoubtedly
exemplifies a deep linguistic fault which may not apply to all postmodernism but is certainly characteristic of much of what has
come out of it so far.[19] We shall not entirely depart from Mark
Taylor's work, however, for it will be mentioned again in another
context below.

The reference to biblical theology in the title makes it natural
to say something about B. D. Ingraffia's *Postmodern Theory and
Biblical Theology*.[20] Attractively produced by Cambridge University
Press, it seems to be well informed about postmodernism, its
philosophical basis and its language. Though not necessarily against
postmodernism in its entirety, however, it is strongly against the
view of Christianity that postmodernism constructs, a view encap-
sulated in the term 'ontotheology', a term that means roughly the
same as 'the god of metaphysics' or Pascal's 'the god of the
philosophers'. In the postmodern view, as Ingraffia sees it,

[16] Taylor, *Erring*, 106.   [17] Ibid. 97–112.   [18] Ibid. 11–12.
[19] Thus Peter Hodgson, whose work will be discussed below, thinks he can prove
something by pointing out that 'our words *friend* and *freedom* are etymologically associated'
(*God in History*, 218) and that *liberty* is related to Latin *liberi* 'children'. He also argues that
'spirit is not a masculine figure', for 'the word is grammatically feminine in Hebrew and
neuter in Greek and English': hence 'the personifying translations of it as "he" are
completely unjustified' (ibid. 111).
[20] (Cambridge: Cambridge University Press, 1995).

Christianity can be dismantled and demystified through an uncovering of its strict dualisms between body and soul, the temporal and the transcendental.

Ingraffia's answer to this is a new version of the well-known claim that the god of the philosophers (here, of ontotheology) is quite different from the God of Abraham, Isaac, and Jacob. The ontotheology that postmodernists have constructed is a quite false version of Christianity, one quite contrary to the Bible and the great central tradition of Luther, Pascal, Kierkegaard, Barth, Bonhoeffer, and Moltmann. This central tradition he calls 'biblical theology' in order to distinguish it clearly from ontotheology. The latter is built not upon the Bible but upon the traditions of Greek metaphysical philosophy. Biblical theology in his sense has thus to be strictly distinguished from the ontotheology conceived by the postmodernist leaders to be Christianity. The programme is thus quite close to that of the Biblical Theology Movement as described by Childs—of which and its history, unfortunately, Ingraffia seems to be largely ignorant.

Biblical theology, in the sense in which the term is now generally used, scarcely comes into the book. Bultmann is the only major figure mentioned, Cullmann also but rather briefly. Eichrodt and von Rad are not mentioned, nor is Childs. Old Testament theology is scarcely considered. Although he follows the well-established tradition of pitting Christianity against Greek philosophical culture, he does not really deploy the other side of the same coin, namely the emphasis on the Old Testament and the Jewishness of Christianity. In spite of this he does battle over *anthropos* and *sarx* and *soma*, but all in a very elementary way—he even assures the reader that he has verified all biblical quotations against the Hebrew and the Greek through the use of *The Interlinear Hebrew-Greek-English Bible*.[21] (A. K. M. Adam in a good review comments: 'Nietzsche could at least read his New Testament in Greek'!)[22] He assumes too readily that all the central Christian tradition (*his* 'biblical theology') is substantially agreed and that all the theology of the Bible agrees with it. In a very general sense, however, as an argument that postmodernism and Christianity are quite contrary to one another, its thesis deserves to be noted. Some will feel that, in spite of its failures in articulation,

[21] Ibid. p. xvi.   [22] *Theology Today*, 53 (1996–7), 560–2.

it reaches the core of the matter.[23] It points out that the freedom
of modern philosophy, according to Heidegger, is defined,
whether expressly or not, as against Christianity.[24] Negatively,
Adam, in his review, complains that Ingraffia

will not allow the postmodern critics *any* valid complaint against
Christian theology . . . he attributes all such problems to the malign influence of Hellenistic Greek philosophy . . . He treats biblical theology as
unproblematically univocal, without even articulating just what this
single biblical theology entails . . . He presents a poorly argued case on
behalf of a biblical theology that is at best insufficiently articulated and at
worst clearly wrongheaded.[25]

In spite of these criticisms Ingraffia sounds a note that is likely to
be heard more widely as time goes on: 'Most work on postmodernism and theology to date seeks a reconciliation between these
two discourses, a postmodern theology of some sort (even if this
be an "a/theology") . . . I seek to deny the possibility of such a
synthesis, to set up an either/or between postmodern thought and
biblical theology.'[26]

   I would like to end this chapter with a reference to the work of
my Vanderbilt colleague, Peter Hodgson.[27] The first sentence of
the Preface indicates its relevance to our subject: 'This book is an
attempt to reconstruct a theology of history in light of the challenges of postmodernism.'[28] And note the centrality of the word
'history'—the subject with which we began.

   The basic starting-point of Hodgson's work is the 'widespread
collapse of the classic framework of Christian faith known as
"salvation history" '. We thus have a theme similar in its shape to
that of Leo Perdue's *The Collapse of History*.[29] But Perdue is essentially a *biblical* theologian, while Hodgson, though taking his starting-point within biblical material, is much more a general
doctrinal and philosophical theologian. He begins from 'Scriptural

---

   [23] Cf. a very warm welcome by Amy Mandelker, *Christianity and Literature*, 47
(1997–8), 79–81. She writes: 'The book is a major and significant contribution that strikes
at the very core of contemporary critical thought . . . The "ontotheology" targeted by the
three major thinkers of Ingraffia's study—Friedrich Nietzsche, Martin Heidegger, and
Jacques Derrida—proves to be a fallacious and distorted construct, a shadow of philosophy's
own nightmares.'   [24] Ingraffia, *Postmodern Theory*, 3.
   [25] *Theology Today*, 562.   [26] Ingraffia, *Postmodern Theory*, 14.
   [27] *God in History: Shapes of Freedom* (Nashville: Abingdon, 1989).
   [28] Ibid. 7.   [29] (Minneapolis: Fortress, 1994).

Foundations' but the main argument of the book is an essay in trinitarian theology, deeply related to the two figures of Hegel and Troeltsch.

The 'Scriptural Foundations'[30] begin with the 'Classic Model', a story 'with which we are all familiar':

the story of God's creation of the world, the fall of humanity into sin, the infectious spread of evil, and God's providential guidance of the affairs of history toward the end of salvation, an end already accomplished (for Christians) in the earthly appearance of the Messiah but to be consummated by the victorious return of Christ and the final destruction of evil powers at the close of world history. It is a story with a plot that unfolds along a line . . . our inner life histories are in many respects microcosms of this outer history . . . God is believed to exercise world governance on the political model of the rule of a monarch over a realm . . . An important corollary . . . is the belief that God is able to accomplish what God wills to accomplish in earthly affairs, either indirectly through the contingencies of nature and human purposes or, when necessary, by exercising a direct causality—the logic of divine sovereignty or triumph, as it has been called.[31]

Or, putting this in more specific terms: the various complexes of tradition, as identified by von Rad, were organized 'into a sequential story of salvation with decisive moments of transition marked by specific events: creation, fall, punishment, wanderings, bondage in Egypt, exodus, Sinai, and possession of the land'. The assumptions underlying this were 'radically altered' by the destruction of Jerusalem and the temple. Prophetic insight interpreted this not as 'proving the impotence of God but as the result of God's judgement on the chosen people'. Eventually God would restore the people to land and prosperity with the coming of the messianic king. This belief, it is briefly stated, was adopted and modified by the early Christians: the life, death, and resurrection of Jesus, believed to be the Messiah, marked 'the beginning of a final intervention in human affairs by the same God who had acted in Israel's past'. Thus, Hodgson concludes, 'a revised salvation history was fashioned by the author of Luke–Acts'.[32]

Now Hodgson, having presented this sketch of the biblical material, does not go on to discuss the matters of biblical historiography

---

[30]   Hodgson, *God in History*, 12–14.   [31]   Ibid. 11–12.
[32]   Ibid. 13–14.

that have occupied us hitherto in this volume. Rather, he goes on to trace the development of the biblical 'salvation history' into later and modern times. Very strikingly, and in marked contrast with most traditions of biblical theology, he maintains that 'the construction of a fully elaborated salvation history was primarily the accomplishment of Latin Christianity during the period following the recognition of the church as the official religion of the Roman Empire', foreshadowed by the adaptation of classical Roman *historia* to a Christian framework by Tertullian.[33] The survey that follows gives special attention to Augustine, to Thomas Aquinas, to Calvin, to the rise of modern consciousness with a stress on Hegel and Schleiermacher, and to Barth.[34]

Hodgson then passes on to 'The Challenge of Postmodernism'. Here, though there is a section on the New Historicism,[35] we find little or nothing of the questions about the history of Israel that have exercised us above, but more a survey of general modern thinking about history, especially American 'neopragmatist' philosophers such as Richard Rorty,[36] and continuing with Foucault and postmodernist 'a/theology', as represented by Mark C. Taylor.[37]

The next section goes on to consider a possible constructive response.[38] It is marked by its positive interest in Troeltsch and Hegel.[39] There is an emphasis on the centrality of freedom. Earlier Hodgson had criticized the work of both Calvin and Barth for excessive emphasis on terms derived from 'sovereignty' and 'domination':[40] to him terms of shaping, transforming, configurating, luring, even the typically postmodernist 'empowering', of which we hear plenty in the modern world, are more appropriate.

This is where Hegel particularly comes in: 'Hegel understood world history to be precisely "the progress of the consciousness of freedom" . . . My proposed theology of history is at heart an

---

[33] Ibid. 14.

[34] Ibid. 16–28. Note that in presenting Barth he speaks of 'Barth's Two Histories', which reminds us a little of the 'two histories' that constituted a dilemma for von Rad (above, pp. 93–4). Barth's two histories, however, are differently conceived, being the history of creation (or of the world) and the history of the covenant (or of salvation): see Hodgson, ibid. 26.

[35] Ibid. 31–6. The New Historicism, as judged by Hodgson, 'when taken to extremes, ends in the destruction of history' (p. 35).   [36] Ibid. 32–3.

[37] Ibid. 36–9.   [38] Ibid. 39–50.

[39] Ibid. 41–2, 47–9; 45, 47–50.   [40] Ibid. 23, 28.

adaptation of this brilliant Hegelian vision to a postmodernist context.'[41] And thus, beginning the final page of his first chapter, Hodgson writes:

> Might we be so bold as to suggest that the end of salvation history offers the possibility of the beginning of the history of freedom? The mythos of salvation history, with its logic of triumph, its linear teleology, and its suprahistorical eschatology must be allowed to die out in order to salvage its enduring conviction that God acts redemptively in history, a conviction from which might be fashioned a new theology of the history of freedom. Precisely this is the task of a postmodernist revisionist theology.
>
> One might argue, with Hegel, that the ancient, medieval and modern worlds slowly achieved a consciousness of freedom. The task of the postmodern world is to put this consciousness to practice.[42]

Now we shall not attempt to follow out the rich and important argument of the chapters that follow in Hodgson's book. Only several points that are particularly relevant to biblical interpretation and biblical theology will be noted. First of all, Hodgson's central theme is not the Bible but rather the Trinity, and here we note that the Trinity is expounded in terms of the two sets of relations, those within God and those between God and the world outside himself; here it is worth while to compare the thought of the 'Biblical Dogmatician' (his own term) Friedrich Mildenberger, whose work I have discussed at length in my *The Concept of Biblical Theology*.[43]

Secondly, we should note the prominence of both Hegel and Troeltsch. Both of these are thinkers who have, in general, been neglected by biblical scholars: indeed, the name of either of them has tended to count as a 'bad word'.[44] Mere association with Hegel has often been thought enough to discredit a scholar: Wellhausen, in particular, was frequently condemned on the grounds that he had followed ideas from Hegel. As for Troeltsch, although he is considered in a way to be the great theologian of history and historical criticism, it is probable that, during the period when historical criticism was flourishing, very few of the critics had a high opinion of him: he was commonly regarded as

---

[41] Ibid. 47.   [42] Ibid. 49–50.

[43] Barr, *The Concept of Biblical Theology*, ch. 29.

[44] Gordon Kaufman, reviewing Hodgson's book as 'brilliant' in *Theology Today*, 46 (1989–90), 442–4, writes that 'for many years, Hegel has received a bad press on the American scene . . . Hegel radicalized Christian teaching about God's "mighty acts in history" '.

too 'relativistic', while biblical studies, even in the most 'critical' days, tended to look for, and depend on, the 'absolutes' which he declared to be unavailable.[45]

Thirdly, Barth, whose influence upon modern biblical theology has been much greater, is indeed introduced here, and highly esteemed and praised, but also seriously criticized,[46] in particular for his attachment to metaphors of sovereignty and authority,[47] for misplacing freedom which he himself had 'brilliantly' emphasized,[48] and for 'his conviction that the actual relationship between creator and creature must not be imported into the being of God',[49] so that world-relatedness has no place in the inner life of God. And so, in general, though the contribution of Barth is very highly valued, the impression of the book is that he, though notable, falls into place in a line of major theologians among whom he is only one: the really great contributions come from Hegel and Troeltsch.

It is not to be supposed that Hodgson's carefully thought-out theology will answer the questions that have occupied us in this book, questions that concern the Hebrew Bible specifically. But at least it provides us with an account of a *history*, the theme with which we started, and a history in which the biblical story forms a beginning, is later transformed into formal theology, and then as formal theology passes through processes that bring us down to modern times. This is surely significant, at least for Christianity; for Judaism, perhaps something analogous could be thought out.

Perhaps the most difficult point, for biblical scholars, will be to understand what the 'history of freedom' can be or can be like. The scholar may be *interested* in Hegel's analysis of four cultural worlds, the Oriental, the Greek, the Roman, and the Christian-European,[50] but will tend to see in this the triumph of purely philosophical theory-spinning over serious knowledge of the cultures concerned. This is exactly the sort of idealistic schematism

[45] For a typical and influential older depiction of Troeltsch, see H. R. Mackintosh, *Types of Modern Theology* (London: Nisbet, 1937), ch. 6, pp. 181–217. The writer refers to Troeltsch's 'uncompromising relativism in history' and attributed to him the view that 'Jesus is a great religious personality, and to contemplate Him is uplifting'. For an expert response to these assessments, see Sarah Coakley, *Christ without Absolutes* (Oxford: Clarendon, 1988), esp. 188–97.

[46] Hodgson, *God in History*, 25–8, 97–8, 108–10.

[47] Ibid. 28. This criticism is one very typical of postmodernism.

[48] Ibid. 97–8.   [49] Ibid. 26.   [50] Ibid. 124–5.

that may have made sense in Hegel's own time but is remote from what scholars know today. Nevertheless scholars must be aware that they use the term 'history' every day, without themselves having any absolutely clear idea of the limits and contours of this reality.

Perhaps the main point that is to be learned for our purposes in this book is that 'there is no triumphal march of God in history, no special history of salvation, but only a plurality of partial, fragmentary, ambiguous histories of freedom',[51] and for me the emphasis lies on the second part of the sentence. Whatever be the case about history of salvation, which I do not want to debate here, the idea of the partial, fragmentary, ambiguous histories has a powerful appeal. On the one hand it allows room for something of the postmodern criticism of grandiose schemes and principles. On the other hand it allows for criticism of the aggressive cultural imperialism which all too plainly underlies the apparent multiculturalism and pluralism of much postmodern thought and action. This may be what people *want* it to be; I am not so sure that 'ours is an age of thoroughgoing pluralism and relativism' in practice. If I have any criticism of Peter Hodgson's argument, it is on this last point: I fear he may be too optimistic that the 'freedoms' being achieved in the postmodernist world are really such. To me freedoms such as equality of status and opportunity do not count for so very much in a world where inequalities of wealth are increasing on a vast scale and where these inequalities are steadily eroding the reality of the democratic processes on which freedoms depend. But in any case his book is a fine example of a creative and imaginative theological approach through which some of the questions considered in this book might be rethought.

The importance of our discussion of Hodgson's book is that it has offered a theological interpretation of 'history', of a kind that is intended to meet the difficulties raised by postmodern thinking. Not only does it end up by affirming a history, the 'history of freedom', but it does so through an impressive account of the history of theological thought, related to the social setting. The Bible itself, however, appears almost only as the *starting-point* in this history: 'Scriptural Foundations' occupy only two pages at the

---

[51] Ibid. 233.

beginning[52] and other biblical material appears in only a few places. We come back in the end therefore to the question: even if the postmodernist challenge is answered, as it may well be, where does it leave us with the Bible and with the Old Testament in particular? That it is the starting-point of all this process can be readily granted. But when so much of the discussion has gone through Augustine, Hegel, Barth, and various modern American theologians, and not specifically returned to the Bible, in what way does the Bible continue to help us with these problems? Or may there be something in the Old Testament itself that may alter the shape of the problems as they have appeared in the discussion hitherto?

Hodgson gives no indication as to how, starting from his theology, one could come back to the Old Testament texts and interpret them. Naturally, it is not his duty to do that, but we from our standpoint must consider it. In his scheme these texts form the starting-point which is eventually gathered together into a scheme of salvation history. But salvation history, as seen in that scheme, has to die, and has died (One reviewer, however, wrote that the book 'is suffused with a not-altogether-justified certitude that the classical salvation-history model has not only lost its hold but is unredeemable in principle').[53] But why and how do we interpret these texts from the early stages, rather than reading Hegel and Troeltsch in church? (Another reviewer, perhaps with this question in mind, wrote 'It is doubtful if this theology could ever be preached').[54]

Perhaps one would have to supplement what Hodgson says with the idea that the spiral or helix of the total process[55] carries within it at all stages shapes that form analogies to the shapes of the original stages; and perhaps this is what he had in mind. Such a theology would form a possible matrix for the interpretation of the Old Testament (and of the New). It is certainly a proposal that brings together—even without mentioning them!—many of the questions that have occupied us in this book.

[52] Hodgson, *God in History*, 12–14.
[53] C. O'Regan, in *Theological Studies*, 51 (1990), 142–3.
[54] R. P. Roth, in *Interpretation*, 44 (1990), 436. Roth also describes the book as 'a revisionist response to postmodern deconstruction and nihilism'.
[55] Hodgson, *God in History*, 185, 243–6.

8

Conclusion

I HAVE not sought to bring to a conclusion most of the questions that have been considered in this book. My purpose was more to inform readers about the state of the questions than to tell them what the answers are. Thus I would not like to be required to state my definite opinion about what the reigns of David and Solomon were like, historically, or about how the 'return' of 'the Jews' from 'exile' was effected. Nor would I wish to say, quite definitely, whether I accept as valid and adequate the theological proposals offered by Peter Hodgson and surveyed in the last chapter. To say the least, such questions would require much more work on them than I have been able to do, before an attempt at an answer could be made. But I hope that I have been able to survey some of the major areas of contemporary discussion, and have not hesitated to make a distinct, if not a final, assessment where I was ready to do so.

The areas taken up for discussion are only loosely connected, and this is intentional on my part. As I have suggested, we do not have a simple opposition between two 'sides', but rather a sliding series of alignments. It is certainly wrong to think of an opposition between the 'old ways' and the ultra-modern, or of one between theological conceptions and academic, scientific, or historical ones. 'Historical criticism', now deemed by many to be old-fashioned, actually converges with aspects of the revisionist historiography, supposed to be the 'new idea'. The use of the key term *ideology* is a confused medley, integrated by different scholars into quite different scholarly visions and approaches. Movements which from one point of view can be seen as working for freedom and equality can from another be seen as excellent opportunities for a neo-fundamentalism of some kind. Finally, the entire question of the sense in which 'history' can be evaluated as a central theological concept remains to be discussed. All these questions come together as aspects of the apologetic task, which, as I have suggested, is now not so much the task of convincing unbelievers of what we believe, but rather the task of facing *for ourselves as believers* the uncertainties which are posed by recent discussion.

The only firm advice that I would give is that tradition and continuity should be prized and preserved as far as is possible. Too much of the recent discussion has involved a fevered grasping at innovation and a willingness to make a quick abandonment of what earlier scholarship had achieved.[1] The wise saying should be heeded: that revolution devours her children.

---

[1] Supporters of canonical approaches have often deprecated the neglect of 'pre-critical' scholarship by critical scholars. This is in itself quite right, but fits badly with the identification of the canonical approaches with the great breakers of tradition—Luther, Calvin, and Barth. Critical scholarship, by contrast, grew up by slow and gradual development out of preceding tradition.

Bibliography

ABRAHAM, WILLIAM J., *Divine Revelation and the Limits of Historical Criticism* (Oxford: Clarendon, 1982).

AHLSTRÖM. G. W., *Who were the Israelites?* (Winona Lake: Eisenbrauns, 1991).

—— *The History of Ancient Palestine from the Palaeolithic Period to Alexander's Conquest* (Sheffield: JSOT, 1993).

ALBERTZ, RAINER, *A History of Israelite Religion* (2 vols.; London: SCM, 1994).

AULD, A. GRAEME, 'Re-Reading Samuel Historically: "Etwas mehr Nichtwissen" ', in V. Fritz and P. R. Davies, *The Origin of the Ancient Israelite States*, 160–9.

—— *Kings Without Privilege* (Edinburgh: T. & T. Clark, 1994).

BARR, JAMES, *Old and New in Interpretation* (London: SCM, 1966).

—— *Comparative Philology and the Text of the Old Testament* (Oxford: Clarendon, 1968; repr., London: SCM, 1983; repr. with additions, Winona Lake: Eisenbrauns, 1987).

—— Introduction to British edn. of P. Stuhlmacher, *Historical Criticism and Theological Interpretation of Scripture* (London: SPCK, 1979), 9–12.

—— 'Historical Reading and the Theological Interpretation of Scripture' in *The Scope and Authority of the Bible*, Explorations in Theology, 7 (London: SCM, 1980).

—— 'Bibelkritik als theologische Aufklärung', in Trutz Rendtorff (ed.), *Glaube und Toleranz: Das theologische Erbe der Aufklärung* (Gütersloh: Gerd Mohn, 1982), 30–42.

—— Review of William J. Abraham, *Divine Revelation and the Limits of Historical Criticism*, in *The Times Literary Supplement*, 24 Dec. 1982, pp. 1422–3.

—— *Holy Scripture: Canon, Authority, Criticism* (Oxford: Clarendon, 1983).

—— Review of W. J. Abraham, *The Inspiration of Scripture*, in *Journal of Theological Studies*, 34 (April 1983), 370–6.

—— Review of W. J. Abraham, *Divine Revelation and the Limits of Historical Criticism*, in *Scottish Journal of Theology*, 36 (1983), 247–50.

—— 'Biblical Language and Exegesis—How Far does Structuralism Help Us?', in *King's Theological Review* (London), 7 (1984), 48–52.

—— Review of M. Brett, *Biblical Criticism in Crisis?*, in *JTS* 43 (1992), 135–41.

—— 'Interpretation, History of: Modern Biblical Criticism', in B. M. Metzger and M. D. Coogan, *Oxford Companion to the Bible* (New York: Oxford, 1993), 318–24.

—— *Biblical Faith and Natural Theology* (Oxford: Clarendon, 1993).

—— Review of Jon Levenson, *The Hebrew Bible, the Old Testament and Historical Criticism*, in *JTS* 47 (1996), 555–60.

—— 'Allegory and Historicism', *JSOT* 69 (1996), 105–20.

—— *The Concept of Biblical Theology* (London: SCM, 1999).

—— 'A Question of Method: the Alleged Leviathan of Historical Criticism in Speiser's Genesis Commentary', in *God Who Creates: Essays in Honor of W. Sibley Towner* (Grand Rapids: Eerdmans, forthcoming).

BARRY, BRIAN, 'The Continuing Relevance of Socialism', in *Democracy, Power, and Justice* (Oxford: Clarendon, 1989), 526–42.

BARSTAD, HANS M., *The Myth of the Empty Land: A Study in the History and Archaeology of Judah during the 'Exilic' Period*, Symbolae Osloenses Fasc. Suppl. xxviii (Oslo: Scandinavian University Press, 1996).

—— 'History and the Hebrew Bible', in L. L. Grabbe (ed.), *Can a 'History of Israel' be Written?*, 37–64.

BARTH, HANS, *Wahrheit und Ideologie* (Zurich: Rentsch, 1945; 2nd edn., 1961); ET, *Truth and Ideology* (Berkeley: University of California Press, 1976), from German 2nd edn.

BARTON, JOHN, *Reading the Old Testament* (London: Darton, Longman & Todd, 1984; 2nd edn. 1996).

—— *Oracles of God* (London: Darton, Longman & Todd, 1986).

—— *The Spirit and the Letter* (London: SPCK, 1997).

—— (ed.), *The Cambridge Companion to Biblical Interpretation* (Cambridge: Cambridge University Press, 1998).

BATSON, C. D., BEKER, J. CHRISTIAAN, and CLARK, W. M., *Commitment without Ideology: The Experience of Christian Growth* (London: SCM, 1973).

BAUMAN, ZYGMUNT, *Culture as Praxis* (London: Routledge, 1973).

—— *Intimations of Postmodernity* (London: Routledge, 1992).

—— *Postmodernity and its Discontents* (Oxford: Polity, 1997).

BEGRICH, J., *Die Chronologie der Könige von Israel und Juda und die Quellen des Rahmens der Königsbücher* (Tübingen: Mohr, 1929).

BERGER, PETER, *The Sacred Canopy* (Garden City, NY: Doubleday, 1969).

BHASKAR, ROY, 'Ideology', in Harré and Lamb, *Encyclopedic Dictionary of Psychology*, 292.

BIBLE AND CULTURE COLLECTIVE, THE, *The Postmodern Bible* (New Haven: Yale, 1995).

BISMARCK, KLAUS VON, and DIRKS, WALTER (eds.), *Christlicher Glaube und Ideologie* (Stuttgart: Kreuz-Verlag, 1964).

BRETT, M., *Biblical Criticism in Crisis?* (Cambridge: Cambridge University Press, 1991).

—— 'Biblical Studies and Theology: Negotiating the Intersections', *Biblical Interpretation*, 6/2 (1998), 131–41.

BRETTLER, MARC ZVI, *The Creation of History in Ancient Israel* (London: Routledge, 1995).

BRIGHT, JOHN, *A History of Israel* (Philadelphia: Westminster, 1959).

BROWN, DAVID, *Tradition and Imagination* (Oxford: Clarendon, 1999).

BROWN, WILLIAM P., *Structure, Role and Ideology in the Hebrew and Greek Texts of Genesis 1:1–2:3*, SBL Dissertation Series, 132 (Atlanta: Scholars Press, 1993).

BRUEGGEMANN, W., *Old Testament Theology* (Minneapolis: Fortress, 1992).

—— *Theology of the Old Testament* (Minneapolis: Fortress, 1997).

BUTLER, CHRISTOPHER, *Interpretation, Deconstruction and Ideology*. (Oxford: Clarendon, 1984).

CARROLL, ROBERT, *When Prophecy Failed: Reactions and Responses to Failure in the Old Testament Prophetic Traditions* (London: SCM, 1979).

—— *From Chaos to Covenant: Prophecy in the Book of Jeremiah* (New York: Crossroad, 1981).

—— 'Ideology', *DBI* 309–11.

—— 'Jeremiah' in *DBI* 331–3.

—— *Jeremiah* (London: SCM, 1986).

—— 'Prophecy and Society', in R. E. Clements (ed.), *The World of Ancient Israel: Sociological, Anthropological and Political Perspectives* (Cambridge: Cambridge University Press, 1989), 203–26.

—— 'Textual Strategies and Ideology in the Second Temple Period', in P. R. Davies (ed.), *Second Temple Studies*, i. *Persian Period* (Sheffield: JSOT, 1991).

—— *Wolf in the Sheepfold: The Bible as a Problem for Christianity* (London: SPCK, 1991).

—— 'The Myth of the Empty Land', in *Ideological Criticism of Biblical Texts*, Semeia, 59 (Atlanta: Scholars, 1992), 79–93.

—— Series on 'The Bible and Ideology', in *Journal of Northwest Semitic Languages:* 'As Seeing the Invisible: Ideologies in Bible Translation', 19 (1993), 79–93; 'On Representation in the Bible: An *Ideologiekritik* Approach' 20/2 (1994), 1–15; 'An Infinity of Traces: On Making an Inventory of our Ideological Holdings: An Introduction to *Ideologiekritik* in Biblical Studies' 21/2 (1995), 25–43; 'Jeremiah, Intertextuality and *Ideologiekritik*' 22/1 (1996), 15–34.

CARROLL, ROBERT, 'Madonna of Silences: Clio and the Bible', in L. L. Grabbe (ed.), *Can a 'History of Israel' be Written?*, 84–103.

—— 'Poststructuralist Approaches: New Historicism and Postmodernism', in J. Barton (ed.), *The Cambridge Companion to Biblical Interpretation* (Cambridge: Cambridge University Press, 1998), 50–66.

CHILDS, B. S., *Old Testament Theology in a Canonical Context* (Philadelphia: Fortress, 1985).

—— 'Critical Reflections on James Barr's Understanding of the Literal and the Allegorical', *JSOT* 46 (1990), 3–9.

—— *Biblical Theology of the Old and New Testaments* (London: SCM, 1992).

CLINES, D. J. A., 'Possibilities and Priorities of Biblical Interpretation in an International Perspective', *Biblical Interpretation*, 1 (1993), 67–87.

—— 'Holistic Interpretation', in *DBI* 292–5.

COAKLEY, SARAH, *Christ without Absolutes: A Study of the Christology of Ernst Troeltsch* (Oxford: Clarendon, 1988).

COGGINS, R. J., 'Israel, History of', *DBI* 328–30.

COOTE, R. B., and WHITELAM, K. W., *The Emergence of Early Israel in Historical Perspective* (Sheffield: JSOT, 1979).

CURTIN, TERENCE, *Historical Criticism and Theological Interpretation of Scripture: The Catholic Discussion of a Biblical Hermeneutic, 1958–1983* (Rome: Gregorian University Press, 1987).

DAVIDSON, R., 'Covenant Ideology in Ancient Israel', in R. E. Clements (ed.), *The World of Ancient Israel: Sociological, Anthropological and Political Perspectives* (Cambridge: Cambridge University Press, 1989), 323–48.

DAVIES, P. R., 'Sociology and the Second Temple', in P. R. Davies (ed.), *Second Temple Studies,* i. *Persian Period* JSOTSup 117 (Sheffield: JSOT Press, 1991).

—— (ed.), *Second Temple Studies,* i. *Persian Period,* JSOTSup 117 (Sheffield: JSOT, 1991).

—— *In Search of 'Ancient Israel'*, (JSOTSup 148 (Sheffield: JSOT, 1992; 2nd edn. 1995).

—— 'Method and Madness: Some Remarks on Doing History with the Bible', in *JBL* 114 (1995), 699–705.

—— 'Introduction', in V. Fritz and P. R. Davies (eds.), *Origins of the Ancient Israelite States*.

—— 'Whose History? Whose Israel? Whose Bible? Biblical Histories, Ancient and Modern', in L. L. Grabbe (ed.), *Can a 'History of Israel' be Written?*, 104–22.

DEVER, WILLIAM G., 'The Contribution of Archaeology to the Study of Canaanite and Early Israelite Religion', in P. D. Miller, Jr., P. D. Hanson, and S. D. McBride (eds.), *Ancient Israelite Religion*, 209–47.

—— 'Will the Real Early Israel Please Stand Up?', in *BASOR* 297 (1995), 61–80; 298 (1995), 37–58.

—— 'What Did the Biblical Writers Know, and When Did they Know It?', in J. Magness and S. Gitin (eds.), *Hesed ve-Emet*, FS for E. S. Frerichs (Atlanta: Scholars Press, 1998), 241–53.

EAGLETON, T., *Ideology* (London: Verso, 1991).

—— *The Illusions of Postmodernism* (Oxford: Blackwell, 1996).

EICHRODT, W., *Theology of the Old Testament* (2 vols.; London: SCM, 1961).

ELLIOTT, JOHN, *Social-Scientific Criticism of the New Testament* (London: SPCK, 1995).

ENGNELL, IVAN, 'The Traditio-Historical Method in Old Testament Research', in I. Engnell, *Critical Essays on the Old Testament* (London: SPCK, 1970), 3–11.

ESKENAZI, TAMARA C., and RICHARDS, KENT H. (eds.), *Second Temple Studies* ii, JSOTSup 175 (Sheffield: JSOT, 1994).

FORD, DAVID F., *The Modern Theologians* (2 vols.; Oxford: Blackwell, 1989).

FOWLER, JEANEANE D., *Theophoric Personal Names in Ancient Hebrew*, JSOTSup 49 (Sheffield: JSOT, 1988).

FREI, HANS, *The Eclipse of Biblical Narrative* (New Haven: Yale, 1974).

—— 'The "Literal Reading" of Biblical Narrative in the Christian Tradition: Does it Stretch or Will it Break?', in F. McConnell (ed.), *The Bible and the Narrative Tradition* (New York: Oxford University Press, 1986), 36–77.

FRITZ, VOLKMAR, and DAVIES, P. R., *The Origins of the Ancient Israelite States*, JSOTSup 228 (Sheffield: JSOT, 1996).

GADAMER, H.-G., *Truth and Method* (London: Sheed & Ward, 1975); German, *Wahrheit und Methode* (Tübingen: Mohr, 1960).

GARBINI, G., *History and Ideology in Ancient Israel*, ET (London: SCM, 1988).

GEERTZ, CLIFFORD, *The Interpretation of Cultures* (New York: Basic Books, 1973).

GELLNER, E., *Postmodernism, Reason and Religion* (London: Routledge, 1992).

GORE, C. (ed.), *Lux Mundi* (London: John Murray, 1889).

GRABBE, LESTER L. (ed.), *Can a 'History of Israel' be Written?*, JSOTSup 245 (Sheffield: JSOT, 1997).

GUNN, DAVID M., *The Fate of King Saul*, JSOTSup 14 (Sheffield: JSOT, 1980).

—— *The Story of King David*, JSOTSup 6 (Sheffield: JSOT, 1978).

GUNN, DAVID M., and FEWELL, DANNA N., *Narrative in the Hebrew Bible* (London: Oxford University Press, 1993).

HAARDT, ALEXANDER, 'Ideologie/Ideologiekritik', in *TRE* 16 (1986), 32–9.

HABERMAS, JÜRGEN, *The Philosophical Discourse of Modernity* (Cambridge, Mass.: MIT, 1987).

HARRÉ, R., and LAMB, R., *Encyclopedic Dictionary of Psychology* (Oxford: Blackwell, 1983).

HARRIS, HARRIET, *Fundamentalism and Evangelicals* (Oxford: Clarendon, 1998).

HARVEY, VAN A., *The Historian and the Believer* (London: SCM 1967).

HEINTEL, P. and BERGER, W., 'Ideologie', *EKL* 2 (1989), cols. 601–6.

HENDEL, R. S., 'The Date of the Siloam Inscription: A Rejoinder to Rogerson and Davies', *BA* 59/4 (1996), 233–7.

HENGEL, MARTIN, 'Historische Methoden und theologische Auslegung des Neuen Testaments', *KuD* 19 (1973), 85–90.

HODGSON, PETER C., *God in History: Shapes of Freedom* (Nashville: Abingdon, 1989).

IGGERS, G. G., 'The Image of Ranke in American and German Historical Thought', *History and Theory*, 2 (1962), 17–40.

INGRAFFIA, BRIAN D., *Postmodern Theory and Biblical Theology* (Cambridge: Cambridge University Press, 1995).

JAMESON, FREDRIC, *Postmodernism, or, the Logic of Late Capitalism* (London: Verso, 1991).

JAPHET, S., *The Ideology of the Book of Chronicles and its Place in Biblical Thought* (Frankfurt: Peter Lang, 1989).

—— 'L'Historiographie post-exilique: Comment et pourquoi?', in A. de Pury, Th. Römer, and J. D. Macchi (eds.), *Israël construit son histoire*, 123–52.

JOBLING, D., and PIPPIN, T. (eds.), *Ideological Criticism of Biblical Texts*, Semeia 59 (Atlanta: Scholars Press, 1992).

JOHNSON, WILLIAM STACY, *The Mystery of God: Karl Barth and the Postmodern Foundations of Theology* (Louisville, Ky.: Westminster John Knox, 1997).

KAISER, OTTO, *Ideologie und Glaube: Eine Gefährdung christlichen Glaubens am alttestamentlichen Beispiel aufgezeigt* (Stuttgart: Radius, 1984).

KERMODE, FRANK, *History and Value* (Oxford: Clarendon, 1988).

KNIGHT, HENRY H. III, *A Future for Truth: Evangelical Theology in a Postmodern Age* (Nashville: Abingdon, 1996).

KNOX, JOHN, *Chapters in a Life of Paul* (Nashville: Abingdon-Cokesbury, 1950).

KOLAKOWSKI, L., *Main Currents of Marxism* (3 vols.; Oxford: Oxford University Press, 1981).

KRENTZ, EDGAR, *The Historical-Critical Method* (Philadelphia: Fortress, 1975).

LARSEN, MOGENS TROLLE, *Power and Propaganda: A Symposium on Ancient Empires*, Mesopotamia, Copenhagen Studies in Assyriology, 7 (Copenhagen: Akademisk Forlag, 1979).

LEMCHE, N. P., *Ancient Israel: A New History of Israelite Society* (Sheffield: JSOT, 1988).

—— *The Canaanites and Their Land* (Sheffield: JSOT, 1991).

—— 'Clio is also among the Muses! Keith W. Whitelam and the History of Palestine: A Review and a Commentary', in L. L. Grabbe (ed.), *Can a 'History of Israel' be Written?*, 123–55.

LONG, BURKE O., 'Ambitions of Dissent: Biblical Theology in a Postmodern Future', *JR* (1996), 276–89.

LOUTH, ANDREW, 'Barth and the Problem of Natural Theology', *Downside Review*, 87 (1969).

—— *Discerning the Mystery* (Oxford: Clarendon, 1983).

LOWE, WALTER, 'Barth as Critic of Dualism: Re-reading the *Römerbrief*', *SJT* 41 (1988), 377–95.

LÜDEMANN, GERD, *The Unholy in Holy Scripture: The Dark Side of the Bible* (London: SCM, 1997).

MCCONNELL, F. (ed.), *The Bible and the Narrative Tradition* (New York: Oxford University Press, 1986).

MCINTYRE, JOHN, 'Historical Criticism in a History-Centred Value-System', in S. E. Balentine and John Barton (eds.), *Language, Theology and the Bible* (Oxford: Clarendon, 1994), 370–84.

MACKINTOSH, H. R., *Types of Modern Theology* (London: Nisbet, 1937).

MAN, P. DE, *The Resistance to Theory* (Minneapolis: Minneapolis University Press, 1986).

MANNHEIM, KARL, *Ideology and Utopia* (New York: Harcourt, Brace, 1936).

MASON, REX, *Propaganda and Subversion in the Old Testament* (London: SPCK, 1997).

MAYES, A. D. H., 'De l'idéologie deutéronomiste à la théologie de l'Ancien Testament', in A. de Pury, Th. Römer, and J.-D. Macchi (eds.), *Israël construit son histoire: L'historiographie deutéronomiste à la lumière des recherches récentes* (Geneva: Labor et Fides, 1996), 477–508.

MILLER, PATRICK D., Jr., 'Faith and Ideology in the Old Testament', in F. M. Cross, W. E. Lemke, and Patrick D. Miller, Jr. (eds.), *Magnalia Dei: The Mighty Acts of God*, FS for G. E. Wright (New York: Doubleday, 1976), 464–79.

—— HANSON, P. D., MCBRIDE, S. D. (eds.), *Ancient Israelite Religion* (Philadelphia: Fortress, 1987).

MILLS, C. WRIGHT, *The Sociological Imagination* (New York: Oxford University Press, 1959).

MITCHELL, BASIL, *Faith and Criticism* (Oxford: Clarendon, 1994).

MONTROSE, LOUIS A., 'Professing the Renaissance: The Poetics and Politics of Culture', in H. Aram Veeser (ed.), *The New Historicism* (London: Routledge, 1989).

MOORE, STEPHEN D., *Literary Criticism and the Gospels: The Theoretical Challenge* (New Haven: Yale University Press, 1989).

—— *Mark and Luke in Poststructural Perspectives* (New Haven: Yale University Press, 1992).

—— *Poststructuralism and the New Testament: Derrida and Foucault at the Foot of the Cross* (Minneapolis: Augsburg Fortress, 1994).

—— (ed.), 'The New Historicism', *Biblical Interpretation* 5/4, 1997.

NICHOLSON, E. W., *The Pentateuch in the Twentieth Century* (Oxford: Clarendon, 1999).

NIELSEN, E., *Oral Tradition* (London: SCM, 1954).

NOORT, E., 'Fundamentalismus in Exegese und Archäologie: Eine Problemanzeige', *JBTh* 6 (1991), 311–31.

NOTH, MARTIN, *History of Israel* (New York: Harper, 1958).

OEING-HANHOFF, L., *Anfang und Ende der Welt* (publisher not known: 1981).

O'NEILL, JOHN, *The Poverty of Postmodernism* (London: Routledge, 1995).

OXENIUS, H. G., 'Anmerkungen zu einer Sendereihe', in K. von Bismarck and W. Dirks (eds.), *Christlicher Glaube und Ideologie*, 9–14.

PASSERIN D'ENTRÈVES, M., and BENHABIB, S., *Habermas and the Unfinished Project of Modernity* (Cambridge, Mass.: MIT, 1997).

PERDUE, LEO G., *The Collapse of History* (Minneapolis: Fortress, 1994).

PERLITT, L., *Vatke und Wellhausen* (Berlin: Töpelmann, 1965).

PHILLIPS, GARY A. (ed.), 'Introduction', in Semeia, 51 (Atlanta: Scholars Press, 1990), 1–5.

—— (ed.), *Poststructural Criticism and the Bible: Text/History/Discourse*, in Semeia, 51 (Atlanta: Scholars Press, 1990), 7–49.

—— 'Exegesis as Critical Praxis: Reclaiming History and Text from a Postmodern Perspective', in Gary A. Phillips (ed.), *Poststructural Criticism and the Bible*, 7–49.

PIPPIN, TINA, 'Ideology, Ideological Criticism, and the Bible', *Currents in Research: Biblical Studies*, 4 (1996), 51–78.

PLAMENATZ, J., *Ideology* (New York: Praeger, 1970).

POLAND, LYNN M., *Literary Criticism and Biblical Hermeneutics: A Critique of Formalist Approaches*, AAR Academy Series, 48 (Chico, California: Scholars Press, 1985).

PROVAN, IAIN W., 'Ideologies, Literary and Critical: Reflections on Recent Writing on the History of Israel,' *JBL* 114 (1995), 585–606.

—— 'Canons to the Left of Him: Brevard Childs, his Critics, and the Future of Old Testament Theology', *SJT* 50 (1997), 1–38.

—— 'The Historical Books of the Old Testament', in J. Barton, *Cambridge Companion*, 198–211.

—— 'The End of (Israel's) History? A Review Article on K. W. Whitelam's *The Invention of Ancient Israel*', *JSS* 42 (1998), 283–300.

—— Review of L. L. Grabbe, *Can a 'History of Israel' be Written?*, in *JTS* 50 (1999), 178–81.

PURY, A. DE, RÖMER, T., and MACCHI, J.-D. (eds.), *Israël construit son histoire: L'Historiographie deutéronomiste à la lumière des recherches récents* (Geneva: Labor et Fides, 1996).

REID, J. K. S., *Christian Apologetics* (London: Hodder & Stoughton, 1969).

RICHARDSON, ALAN, *Christian Apologetics* (London: SCM, 1948).

RICHES, JOHN, 'Text, Church and World: in Search of a Theological Hermeneutic', *Biblical Interpretation* 6/2 (1998), 205–34.

RICŒUR, P., *Lectures on Ideology and Utopia* (1986).

ROBINSON, JAMES M., *The New Hermeneutic* (New York: Harper & Row, 1964).

ROGERSON, J., and DAVIES, P. R., 'Was the Siloam Tunnel built by Hezekiah?', *BA* 59:3, 1996, 138–49.

RÖMER, TH., and DE PURY, A., 'L'Historiographie Deutéronomiste: Histoire de la recherche et enjeux du débat', in A. de Pury, Th. Römer, and J.-D. Macchi (eds.), *Israël construit son histoire*, 9–120.

ROWLAND, CHR., *Christian Origins* (London: SPCK, 1985).

SAID, EDWARD W., *Orientalism: Western Conceptions of the Orient* (London: Routledge, 1978).

—— *Culture and Imperialism* (London: Chatto & Windus, 1993).

SANDERS, E. P., *Paul and Palestinian Judaism* (London: SCM, 1977).

—— *Paul, the Law, and the Jewish People* (Philadelphia: Fortress, 1983).

SANDERS, JAMES A., *Torah and Canon* (Philadelphia: Fortress, 1972).

SCHÜSSLER FIORENZA, ELIZABETH, *Bread not Stone: The Challenge of Feminist Biblical Interpretation* (Boston: Beacon, 1984).

SCHWEIZER, EDUARD, *A Theological Introduction to the New Testament*, ET (Nashville: Abingdon, 1991; London: SPCK, 1992), German edn. 1989.

SEGOVIA, FERNANDO F., and TOLBERT, MARY ANN, *Reading from this Place: Social Location and Biblical Interpretation in the United States* (Minneapolis: Fortress, 1995), i.

SEGUNDO, JUAN LUIS, *The Liberation of Theology* (Maryknoll, NY: Orbis Books, 1985).

SMEND, R., 'Nachkritische Schriftauslegung', first published in E. Busch, J. Fangmeier, and M. Geiger (eds.), *Parrhesia: K. Barth zum 80. Geburtstag* (Zurich: EVZ, 1966), 215–37; repr. in R. Smend, *Die Mitte des Alten Testaments* (Munich: Kaiser, 1986), 212–32.

SMITH, MORTON, *Palestinian Parties and Politics that Shaped the Old Testament* (New York: Columbia University Press, 1971).

SPEISER, E., *Genesis*, Anchor Bible (New York: Doubleday, 1964).

STERNBERG, M., *The Poetics of Biblical Narrative: Ideological Literature and the Drama of Reading* (Bloomington, Ind.: Indiana University Press, 1987).

STUMP, ELEONORE, and FLINT, THOMAS P. (eds.), *Hermes and Athena: Biblical Exegesis and Philosophical Theology* (Notre Dame: University of Notre Dame Press, 1993).

SUTTON, F. X., HARRIS, S. E., KAYSEN, C., and TOBIN, J., *The American Business Creed* (Cambridge, Mass.: Harvard University Press, 1956).

SWEENEY, M., 'The Critique of Solomon in the Josianic Edition of the Deuteronomistic History', *JBL* 114/4 (1995), 607–22.

TAYLOR, MARK C., *Erring: A Postmodern A/theology* (Chicago: University of Chicago Press, 1984).

THOMPSON, THOMAS L., *The Historicity of the Patriarchal Narratives* (Berlin: de Gruyter, 1974).

—— *Early History of the Israelite People* (Leiden: Brill, 1992).

—— 'A Neo-Albrightean School in History and Biblical Scholarship?', in *JBL* 114 (1995), 683–98.

—— 'William Dever and the not so New Biblical Archeology', in V. Fritz and P. R. Davies (eds.), *Origins of the Ancient Israelite States* (Sheffield: JSOT, 1996), 26–43.

—— 'Defining History and Ethnicity in the South Levant', in L. L. Grabbe (ed.), *Can a 'History of Israel' be Written?*, 166–87.

VAN SETERS, JOHN, *Abraham in History and Tradition* (New Haven: Yale, 1975).

—— *In Search of History: Historiography in the Ancient World and the Origins of Biblical History* (New Haven: Yale, 1983).

WARD, GRAHAM, *Barth, Derrida and the Language of Theology* (Cambridge: Cambridge University Press, 1995).

—— *Theology and Contemporary Critical Theory* (London: Macmillan, 1996).

WATSON, F., *Text, Church and World* (Grand Rapids: Eerdmans, 1994).

—— 'Enlightenment', *DBI* 191–4.

—— 'Bible, Theology and the University: A Response to Philip Davies', *JSOT* 71 (1996), 3–16.

—— *Text and Truth* (Edinburgh: T. & T. Clark, 1997).

—— 'A Response to John Riches', *Biblical Interpretation*, 6/2 (1998), 235–42.

WEBB, STEPHEN H., *Re-Figuring Theology: the Rhetoric of Karl Barth* (Albany: State University of New York Press, 1991).

WESTERMANN, C., 'Schöpfung und Evolution', in H. Böhme (ed.), *Evolution und Gottesglaube: Ein Lese- und Arbeitsbuch zum Gespräch zwischen Naturwissenschaft und Theologie* (Göttingen: Vandenhoeck & Ruprecht, 1988), 240–50.

WHITE, HAYDEN, *Tropics of Discourse: Essays in Cultural Criticism* (Baltimore: Johns Hopkins University Press, 1978).

WHITE, HUGH C., *Narration and Discourse in the Book of Genesis* (Cambridge: Cambridge University Press, 1991).

WHITELAM, K. W., 'Israelite Kingship: The Royal Ideology and its Opponents', in R E. Clements (ed.), *The World of Ancient Israel: Sociological, Anthropological and Political Perspectives* (Cambridge: Cambridge University Press, 1989), 119–40.

—— *The Invention of Ancient Israel: The Silencing of Palestinian History* (London: Routledge, 1996).

—— 'The Social World of the Bible', in Barton, *Cambridge Companion*, 35–49.

WILKES, G. A. (ed.), *A Dictionary of Australian Colloquialisms*, 2nd edn. (Sydney: Sydney University Press, 1985).

WINK, W., *The Bible in Human Transformation* (Philadelphia: Fortress, 1973).

WOLTERSTORFF, NICHOLAS, *Divine Discourse: Philosophical Reflections on the Claim that God Speaks* (Cambridge: Cambridge University Press, 1993).

WRIGHT, G. E., *Biblical Archaeology* (Philadelphia: Westminster, 1974).

WÜRTHWEIN, E., 'Zur Komposition von I Reg 22 1–38', in *Das ferne und nahe Wort*, FS für L. Rost (Berlin: Töpelmann, 1967), 245–54.

—— 'Die josianische Reform und das Deuteronomium', *ZTK* 73 (1976), 395–423.

Index